THE

MAN

WHO

WAS

MARK

TWAIN

The Man Who Was Was Mark Twain

IMAGES
AND
IDEOLOGIES

GUY
CARDWELL

▲▲▲▲▲▲▲▲▲▲▲▲▲▲▲▲▲▲▲▲▲▲

Yale University Press

New Haven & London

Published with assistance from the Kingsley
Trust Association Publication Fund established
by the Scroll and Key Society of Yale College.

Designed by Richard Hendel.
Set in Galliard type by Keystone Typesetting,
Orwigsburg PA.
Printed in the United States of America by
Vail-Ballou Press, Binghamton NY.

Cardwell, Guy, 1905–
The man who was Mark Twain :
images and ideologies /
Guy Cardwell.
p. cm.
Includes bibliographical references
and index.
ISBN 0-300-04950-1
1. Twain, Mark, 1835–1910—
Political and social views. 2. Twain,
Mark, 1835–1910—Biography—
Psychology. 3. Authors, American—
19th century—Psychology. 4. Social
problems in literature. I. Title.
PS1342.S58C37   1911   90-48630
818'.409—dc20   CIP
The paper in this book meets the guidelines
for permanence and durability of the
Committee on Production Guidelines for
Book Longevity of the Council on Library
Resources.
10 9 8 7 6 5 4 3 2 1

FOR

MARGARET

RANDOLPH

CARDWELL

▲ ▲ ▲ ▲ ▲ ▲ ▲ ▲ ▲

CONTENTS

ILLUSTRATIONS

▲ ▲ ▲ ▲ ▲ ▲ ▲ ▲ ▲

ACKNOWLEDGMENTS

▲ ▲ ▲ ▲ ▲ ▲ ▲ ▲ ▲

Over the years during which I have worked on Mark Twain, I have been aided by librarians and curators at widely scattered institutions, among them Tulane University, Washington University of St. Louis, the University of Virginia, and the Pierpont Morgan Library. I am grateful to all of the individuals and to all of the institutions.

Ellen Graham, of Yale University Press, has given exceptionally sympathetic and experienced attention to the manuscript for this book during each phase of the publishing process. The editors of *ESQ: A Journal of the American Renaissance* have authorized me to use portions of an essay first published in *ESQ* (First Quarter 1977).

Three editors of the Mark Twain Papers at the Bancroft Library of the University of California, Berkeley, have been generous about answering inquiries. I am pleased to make known here my gratitude to the late Henry Nash Smith, the late Frederick Anderson, and to the present General Editor of the Mark Twain Project, Robert H. Hirst. Daniel Aaron went beyond the call of friendship in giving advice and assistance. Other indebtednesses are mentioned in the notes.

I am most obligated to my daughter Margaret R. Higonnet and to my wife, Margaret R. Cardwell. Margaret Higonnet rescued me from desperate, losing battles with my computer and interrupted her own work to prepare letter-quality copies of each chapter of this book as I finished it. Margaret Cardwell involved herself in every aspect of the work. She searched the Harvard libraries for books and for information, read the chapters more times than I like to remember, and did the major part of preparing the index.

CHRONOLOGY

▲ ▲ ▲ ▲ ▲ ▲ ▲ ▲ ▲

1835   Samuel Langhorne Clemens born November 30 in Florida, Missouri.

1839   Family moves to Hannibal, Missouri, where Sam begins working in printshops at the age of twelve and remains until he is seventeen.

1853–61   Works as a printer in St. Louis, New York, Philadelphia, Keokuk, and Cincinnati; begins writing for newspapers; serves as river pilot on the Mississippi.

1861–65   Spends Civil War years in the West (Nevada Territory, with trips to San Francisco), engaged chiefly in journalism.

1866   Contributes commissioned travel letters to the Sacramento *Union* on a journey of five months to the Sandwich Islands (Hawaii). Begins career as public reader and lecturer by speaking about the Islands.

1867   Voyages to Europe and the Holy Land on board the first cruise ship, the *Quaker City*. Sends travel letters to the San Francisco *Alta California*. Back in New York, he is introduced on December 27 to Olivia Louise Langdon, then twenty-two, a sister of Charles Jervis Langdon (b. 1849), who had sailed with Clemens on the *Quaker City*.

1869   His reworked travel letters published as *The Innocents Abroad*.

1870   Marries Olivia Langdon on February 2. Moves to Buffalo, where he owns one-third interest in the Buffalo *Express*. Son, Langdon, born November 7, 1870.

1871   Moves to Hartford, Connecticut.

1872   Daughter, Susan (Susy), born March 19. Son, Langdon, dies in June. *Roughing It* published.

1873   With family, makes first of several extended stays in Europe. *The Gilded Age* (with co-author Charles Dudley Warner) published.

1874   Daughter, Clara, born June 8. Builds a baronial mansion in Hartford.

1875   Publishes "Old Times on the Mississippi" in the *Atlantic Monthly*.

1876   Publishes *The Adventures of Tom Sawyer* and makes a start on *Adventures of Huckleberry Finn*.

1880   Enters upon costly speculation in the Paige typesetter. Daughter, Jane (Jean), born July 26. *A Tramp Abroad* published; *1601* privately published.

1882   *The Prince and the Pauper* published.

1883   *Life on the Mississippi* published.

1885   *Adventures of Huckleberry Finn* published.

1889   *A Connecticut Yankee in King Arthur's Court* published.

1891   In June goes to Europe and remains there for most of the next decade.

1894   Loses approximately $110,000 of his own money and $60,000 of Olivia's in the bankruptcy of his publishing house. "Pudd'nhead Wilson, A Tale" published in *Century Magazine*.

1895–96   Makes worldwide lecture tour to raise money to repay creditors.

1896   Daughter Susy dies of meningitis. Daughter Jean diagnosed as epileptic. *Personal Recollections of Joan of Arc* published.

1897   *Following the Equator* published.

1900   Returns to New York from England.

1902   Isabel Lyon becomes Clemens's secretary and general functionary. (In 1909, she is dismissed and vilified.)

1903   For benefit of Olivia's health, establishes family in Florence.

1904   Olivia dies in Florence on June 5.

1906   *What Is Man?* published.

1908   Moves to newly built home, Stormfield, near Redding, Connecticut.

1909   Daughter Jean dies in epileptic seizure.

1910   Clemens returns, ill, from a visit to Bermuda; dies at Stormfield on April 21.

THE

MAN

WHO

WAS

MARK

TWAIN

INTRODUCTION

▲ ▲ ▲ ▲ ▲ ▲ ▲ ▲ ▲

This book treats vexed questions of identity. Americans have cherished and magnified versions of an idealized Mark Twain. We admire and are amused by Twain the celebrity, who sold his pseudonym and his carefully composed face to advertise pipe tobacco, cigarettes, whiskey, and postcards. The extent to which the received images are authentic or inauthentic is, however, in doubt. Common images must be modified when we examine the thoughts and emotions important to the mind and heart of Samuel L. Clemens, the private man.

The term *ideologies* in the book's title is intended in its ordinary, unbiased meaning—systems of ideas and ways of thinking—but it inevitably includes a Marxian sense of ahistorical, illusory idealizations. The reader interested in approaches to Mark Twain's writings may also be reminded that ideology has been called a kind of Unconscious of the text: ideologies hint at meanings which the reader attempts to identify as he interprets the author's always occluded writings.

I have not tried to tell everything about the heroizing of Mark Twain or about all of the ideas that contributed to the set of his mind. Although I allude to his writings frequently, I attempt no systematic analyses of even his more important works. As the chapter titles indicate, I have attempted, instead, to gather, order, and interpret information on a few key topics in order to begin to distinguish Samuel Clemens from his personae.

I hope that the study will help to clear away a number of conceptual and biographical encumbrances and so enable us to move toward a reasonably persuasive likeness of Samuel Clemens. Because, as hermeneuticists point out, the past functions in our present temporal horizon, we need to understand mediating persons and processes: writers as different as Van Wyck Brooks and Bernard DeVoto constitute part of our effective history.

Historians, particularly chauvinistic historians, in Europe and in America have occupied themselves—most energetically since the latter years of the eighteenth century—with identifying and describing national archetypes. It follows naturally that selected individuals would be supposed to possess qualities like those alleged to typify their several nations. For nearly a century now, bearing such correspondences in mind, American literary historians have tended to concentrate their attention—usually commendatory—on Mark Twain: no other writer has seemed to be so exactly representative, so Herderian, so Tainean, so certainly a New Adam in the New World.

Approbative students of Twain generally suppose that Clemens's character, his writings, and the American character are of a piece; the writings derive from the soil or from the society and express the virtuous aspects of the national psyche. Censorious critics—today they are rare—accept the model but reverse the medal: Mark Twain's writings express defects in the national character. A corollary analogy: writers often identify with the man they write about; they see a likeness between the humorist's chief traits and their own. To be similarly American is, for good or bad, their fate. Thus Mark Twain, the writings, the national character, and the self-images of critics become intertwined. Critics, biographers, and historians become the unsuspecting prisoners of their images and ideologies.

The images that are projected aggrandize and impose optimistic categories; they promote idealizing social considerations. Since well before Twain's death in 1910, critics have tended to see him as superlatively a man of the people, monumental and monolithic—like an obelisk or a culture hero— without individualizing warts and wrinkles. They force his texts to exemplify a uniquely American ethos, a uniquely American aesthetic; the writings are poetic, epistemic, absolute representations of a folk and a land. Recently a number of qualifying observations have appeared, but these are likely to be put within parentheses and to be dropped from consideration when final judgments are rendered. Heroes are heroically unblemished; canonized texts are canonical, standard.

When Samuel Clemens arrived in New York from California, readers and newspaper critics, if they knew him at all, viewed him as one of the better western writers of comedy. With remarkable rapidity his status improved; he became accepted as preeminent in his field, and it was not long before magnification transformed him into a mirror of western America. This is not to say that what it meant to be western was universally agreed on or, for that matter, what it meant to be American. Attitudes toward the West, even more than toward America, depended on opinions about such concepts as nature, civilization, progress, regress, democracy, and elitism. As a metaphoric figure and as a writer, Mark Twain could be condemned as boisterously comic and crude or, as was the practice of more and more critics, praised as amusingly original, spontaneous, authentic, and admirably representative.

Grant Allen, in the British *Fortnightly Review* in 1888, expressed the pejorative view. Writing in a well-established disparaging tradition, Allen associated Mark Twain with the vulgar and buffoonish: "A large style of cheap and effective humour . . . flourishes everywhere on the borderlands of Western civilisation." As we shall see at some length in the opening chapter, the pejorative view was championed by Van Wyck Brooks, a rising young captain of the avant-garde, in *The Ordeal of Mark Twain* (1920). According to Brooks, Twain, vividly present in the public mind "as a sort of archtype of the national character," was indeed an archetype in that he was a failed artist, the victim of a culturally barren environment, debased Puritanism, American materialism, and Freudian traumas.

In general, however, praise of Twain has far exceeded blame. British, European, and American critics—Twain's good friend William Dean Howells foremost among them—have valued him as a great writer and as the principal literary hero of the matter of America. Kipling praised Clemens extravagantly; and William Ernest Henley presented him in the *Athe-naeum* in 1880 as sharing with Walt Whitman the honor of being "the most strictly American writer of what is called American literature."

Claims of magnitude (like our prairies and forests) and of significance (American democracy, model for the world) became exclamatory in the United States at the time of Clemens's death. Archibald Henderson (math-ematician, regional historian, and early biographer of Clemens) wrote that Twain and Whitman were "the two great interpreters and embodiments of America," the supreme contributions of democracy to universal literature. In 1913 Henry Mencken, rather oddly when one considers his antipathy toward democracy and the booboisie, pressed the adulatory temper to dizzying verbal heights: Twain was not only the noblest literary artist who ever set pen to paper on American soil, he was also "one of the most profound and sagacious philosophers," the one "authentic giant of our national literature."

By the time of Mencken, American historiography was firmly estab-lished; and the professional study of American literature, though young and thought to be somewhat contemptible, was a rapidly growing industry. Eager scholarly efforts were being made to define America, evaluate its past, and give direction to its future. In the 1920s a hiatus of sorts was created: Brooks and a few like-minded, pessimistic men of letters interrupted the flow of patriotic optimism. They were deeply concerned with questions of political and social justice; and they wished to identify America's usable past, separating it from malignant elements. Like the historians, they be-lieved that they could define America, but their America was rank with social pathologies.

Most academic scholars, with a vision different from that of the Brooks-ians, typically turned for their sanguine conceptions of America to Freder-ick Jackson Turner, who had proposed that truly meritorious American qualities arose from the encounter of civilization and savagery at the shift-ing line that marked the frontier: there Americans came into being. The Turner doctrine helped to establish *culture* as meaning something more than high culture: folk art is actually art; the arguably indigenous humor of the Southwest is not necessarily a debasement of the idea of humor. Scholars, like new Dantes, began to welcome the vernacular—the idioms of common American speech—as adding an immediacy, a vigor, an authen-ticity, and even a desirable moral tone to our literature. They believed in America's exemplary majesty, thought its ills to be few and remediable.

Despite their political, social, and literary differences, critics who praised Clemens and those who were skeptical about his virtues agreed at many points. Brooks, chief of the small group that doubted that Clemens was an unequivocal success, did not doubt that he was a genius, a genius who, until corrupted by the culture, had been potentially a great writer. The East as well as the West was a corrupting influence. Many, though in differing degrees, saw the East as effete and complained that American imitation of European literature was a reprehensible practice. For the most part, they believed in a naive geographical-cultural determinism; and their writings were loosely grounded in Romantic organicism and mimeticism; that is, they were late-nineteenth-century literary realists.

Patriots exalted America by elevating Mark Twain. Much as Brooks brought to a small climax the depreciatory view of Twain, so, a dozen years later, did Bernard DeVoto bring the laudatory view to an impassioned crescendo in *Mark Twain's America* (1932). DeVoto called Mark Twain the greatest of all American writers, not just of western American writers. In addition to attacking Brooks, he challenged hostile criticism of the America that he believed in, which turned out to be America as he conceived it to have been during the presumably virile, adventurous years of westward expansion. Brooks's book had been received with applause and prize awards; then the tide turned and DeVoto's volume was greeted with a comparably flattering clapping of hands.

At present—although many small reservations are entered along the way and differences exist over precisely why Twain's writings are illustrious— only a few dissonant voices question the triumphant virtues of his best work. His identity is not nearly so settled a matter: the nature of his "true" personality is, perhaps more than ever, a question for debate. Definitions of Mark Twain, like those of America, have been chaotic.

An obvious step toward ordering the chaos is to attempt to disentangle Samuel Clemens from his metaphoric roles. Up to the present, however, rearranging our ideas about Clemens has not been easy. Legendary fantasies and anecdotal inventions support erroneous conceptions, spurious portrayals. Blunders and fatuities are solidly built into the biographies and permeate our cultural and literary histories.

Legends and dominant images do possess their own kinds of absorbing truth, much as does the Idea of Progress or the notion that Nature illustrates the Great Chain of Being: we do not like to give them up; believers surrender untenable positions a fragment at a time. As a break with an emotionally satisfying tradition is accomplished only with reluctance, so homeostasis may be expected. A Burkean premise holds that all things being equal (or not proved to be totally unequal), whatever has been said or believed should be said again and should continue to be believed. When interpretations fail to fit the facts, a natural tendency is to disregard the facts, to cling to the old, to hew to the orthodox line.

Clemens's imagined traits as a hero of the culture have been asserted and reasserted; thus he could be confirmed as representative. Emerson, James, Melville—even Whitman—were not and are not tenaciously heroes of the people, popular icons. Europeans agree that Twain is the most American among our men of letters. He has been portrayed as perfect for his role: his roots were in the heartland; and his pen name was as American as Whitman's "leaves of grass" were universal. In the shadows of these portraits lurk Frederick Jackson Turner and a dream of the New World as unique and virtuous. Twain allegedly did not subordinate himself to the genteel East. His writings are not elitist; they may be read with pleasure and profit by everyone. He was so unitary that he could, for the more artlessly single-minded, function as pure sign, simply pointing to the West or to America. DeVoto could believe that Twain had no real weaknesses, that the bracing air of Washoe made him; and DeVoto is one among many.

Biography notoriously invents its subjects; criticism invents the writings it explores. These general truths are, a fortiori, true for Clemens, more so, I think, than for any other major American writer. Clemens began the mounting duplicities, of course, by inventing himself as author, and he usually, though not always, accepted with gratification the deepening chasm between man and heroic image. If Clemens was not what he has been represented as being, neither does the American past as conceived by Twain's exploiters and by his more uncritical admirers resemble at all closely the past of America as currently apprehended by historians. A pseudo-America, a factitious construction concordant with paintings of happy boatmen by George Caleb Bingham, regularly appears in publishers' blurbs, motion pictures, and films made for television.

Explanation for the factitiousness lies in such large, vague influences as the myth of the Garden, such governing sociological understandings as ideas of race and gender, and a need for heroes. The nation was eager to define its character; the people were eager for self-definition. Mark Twain was a figure with whom the public at large could identify. He was the unrivaled platform and newspaper comedian of his time, the darling of reporters and photographers, the master of the demotic; but he was also a wise man, a social philosopher. He was another, better self, more extravagantly, vitally American than America. Or so it seemed.

Rousseau's dictum (in *Lettres à Malesherbes*) that the source of all the miseries of man lies in their false opinions is a provocative exaggeration; but it is safe to propose that faulty images are responsible for much errant opinion on Mark Twain and that it is desirable to establish a Samuel Clemens at a remove from the legends and images—which is to say, in as existentially authentic a context as possible. This book does not presume, however, to intend a universal vastation of existing scholarship: the major documents are part of the *Wirkungsgeschichte*. And as will be obvious from the text and from notes, I frequently rely, with gratitude, on scholars with whom I am at points in basic disagreement. Nor do I presume to imagine that my representation of aspects of Twain's personality and thought will seem precisely right forever.

Among the handful of books and articles on Mark Twain that are helpfully, if inconsistently, revisionist, I am particularly indebted to Justin Kaplan's *Mr. Clemens and Mark Twain* and to Hamlin Hill's *Mark Twain: God's Fool*. Kaplan recognizes Freudian traumas, and Hill paints a laceratingly Hogarthian likeness of Clemens during the last decade of his life. Not revisionist in the same sense, not even necessarily revisionist by intention, but of first importance are the volumes now being published from the Mark Twain Papers, at Berkeley. In headnotes and footnotes these volumes correct past errors and incorporate fresh biographical and contextual materials. Their tendency, like that of this book, is to undermine superstitiously devised memorial statues that have been cherished as acceptable likenesses. As Hegel asserted and as Jean-Paul Sartre noted in his *Search for a Method*, truth about man is something that emerges, something that must become a totalization; and "such a totalization is perpetually in process as History and as historical Truth."

THE

CRITICAL

BATTLEGROUND

1

▲ ▲ ▲ ▲ ▲ ▲ ▲ ▲ ▲

When Mark Twain first invaded the East in 1867 and was adver-
tised as the Wild Humorist of the Pacific Slope, he stood in
synecdochic relationship to frontier comedy. Soon it was possible
for the second term of the trope to identify grander objects; Mark
Twain could be equated with the spirit of the West and the spirit of
the West with America. No other writer has been so extensively
identified with the nation, so strikingly a component of its myth.

Those who honored Twain discovered fresh western qualities in
his writings; but not all honored him or frontier humor. Some
viewed him with condescension and distaste, found him to be
gross, strident, discordant, and uncivilized. These opposed fac-

tions reflected evaluations of the West in its two characters, either as natural and benevolent or as savage and chaotic. Opinion did not always divide along geographical lines. Many easterners and Europeans unequivocally approved Twain's spontaneity, hyperbolic humor, and democratic high spirits. Some geographical westerners were as fastidious as the most genteel easterners and condemned his writings as deficient in refinement and moral tone. A single critic might combine the two attitudes, praising Twain as a vital natural man and at the same time regretting his boorishness.

This opposition of the genteel and the vulgar, the eastern and the western, was usually implicit or explicit in reviews of Twain's books. The Concord library committee notoriously found *Huckleberry Finn* to be coarse and irreverent. Chiming in, the Springfield *Republican* declared that Clemens lacked a reliable sense of propriety, and the Boston *Advertiser* alluded to the slimy trail of the vulgar humorist. Conversely, Thomas Sergeant Perry, Boston man of letters and a superior critic, identified American humor as a product of American democracy and, more specifically, saw Mark Twain as a recorder of "the hideous fringe of civilization" along the Mississippi. To Perry, and to a great many others before and after him, the battle lines were drawn: the American spirit was at odds with European culture, including European linguistic and literary conventions.

The enormous popularity that Twain has had as the model western American or as typifying the entire American branch of the human race has held true both for the general public and for critics. In the early part of this century, critics' wide acceptance of Twain as heroically American is due to a considerable extent to the influence of William Dean Howells. Howells wrote largely and generously of Twain's westernness, of his American style, of how purely and wholly American his humor was—though it had universal qualities, too. In a comparison that strongly reinforced Twain's metaphoric possibilities, Howells declared in "My Mark Twain" that Clemens was "sole, incomparable, the Lincoln of our literature."

A little later, Mark Twain's virtues, defects, and representative nature were the topics of two biased, mutually contradictory, loosely theoretical, often wrong, very popular books: *The Ordeal of Mark Twain* (1920), by Van Wyck Brooks, and *Mark Twain's America* (1932), by Bernard DeVoto. Mark Twain and questions of American self-definition captivated the national imagination. So powerful were the themes and topics treated by Brooks and DeVoto that their books pretty much set the agenda for discussions of Mark Twain for half a century. The agenda comprised, among other things, the nation's cultural achievement or lack of achievement.

Nearly all American artists are failures, Brooks thought, because of an environment hostile to art and to free, healthy personalities. Twain is both the representative failed artist and the archetypal American: "Vividly present he is in the public mind as a great historic figure, as a sort of arch-type of the national character during a long epoch. Will he not continue to be so for many generations to come? Undoubtedly." Throughout *The Ordeal*, Brooks shows the American environment stamping its deleterious imprint on Twain. Cultural determinism takes full effect, and at last Twain and a pathological America may hardly be distinguished. In subsequent writings Brooks continued to speak of Twain as representative, though less positively as victim. In *Days of the Phoenix* (1957), for example, he remarks that Twain was the typical American author as we "knew him at the moment."[1]

DeVoto made brutally plain that the frontier in which Brooks set the young Samuel Clemens was a feebly theoretical construction associated in an ideological system with other ill-advisedly theoretical constructions dealing with art, personality, Puritanism, and humor. By no means all of the ideas within Brooks's schematic framework were original: some came from Waldo Frank or Randolph Bourne, and some could have come from a scattering of others, including Santayana (see such essays as "Tradition and Practice" and "The Genteel Tradition in American Philosophy") and Mencken (see "Puritanism as a Literary Force"). When he was a precocious twenty-two, Brooks introduced this system of ideas in *The Wine of the Puritans* (1908).

In that system, the Pilgrim Fathers were primary villains who put their stamp upon all of America. They were materialists, emphasizing negative and narrow virtues, like thrift and industry. They were suspicious of ritual, pleasure, lightheartedness. The more philosophical of their descendants sought in Transcendentalism a better explanation of the world than Puritan rationalism afforded, but they thus begged the whole question of life. Vulgar New Englanders turned to gross commercialism. Highbrow and Lowbrow courses are equally undesirable, but they have divided American life between them, leaving no middle ground between eternal issues and practical issues.

Like Waldo Frank,[2] Brooks identified the pioneer as a degraded Puritan, one who had denied his religious impulses and in whom whole departments of psychic life were repressed. Frontier communities were irredeemably drab, sodden, barren, loveless, and violent. Much like Margaret Fuller and others before him, Brooks thought that adventurers on the fringes of civilization pursued wealth at any cost, sacrificing individuality and creativity.

The unworthiness of all American humor was from the first an item in Brooks's literary taxonomy. He wrote in *The Wine of the Puritans* that American humor does not depend on being true to life; it whiles away the time with puns, conundrums, and conceits, is harsh and dry, and reflects no philosophy of life. Mark Twain's kind of humor is a product of debased Puritanism, and Twain is quintessentially the preposterous, untrue, rootless writer.

Brooks repeats the essence of these opinions on humor in other writings, as in *America's Coming-of-Age* (1915). Catchpenny opportunism originating in the practical shifts of American life (an aspect of Puritanism) becomes a philosophy in Franklin, passes through American humorists, and results in the atmosphere of business life. America sends up to heaven the stench of atrophied personality: Americans lack intimate feeling, intimate contact, "even humor—that rich, warm, robust and all-dissolving geniality which never, I think, quite reached the heart of Mark Twain."[3]

The point about Twain on which Brooks and DeVoto—each given to a naive cultural determinism—agreed wholeheartedly was his typicality. To DeVoto, enamored as he was of a myth of the frontier, Twain was a wonderfully special American, the archetypal westerner. In contrast to Brooks, he saw Twain as emerging from a shining past. Hannibal was an idyll and a cosmos. Florida and Hannibal were delightfully agrarian communities, "umbilical to a great man's mind." In some mysteriously Herderian way, Mark Twain took his creative sustenance from frontier sources: the West *made* him supreme among American writers, generated in him a kind of greatness that American literature has nowhere else attained. Like Frederick Jackson Turner, DeVoto believed that certain frontier qualities were the fundamentally American qualities. In *Mark Twain's America,* DeVoto's final chapter—a kind of summary statement in reply to Brooks— is entitled "The Artist as American." There Twain instead of being a failure is preeminently the American artist, the greatest of them all.

The nature of the frontier is central to discussions of Twain's personal and literary origins, his early image, and the "true" American character. Brooks's pejorative view of the West drew upon an extensive history which will be sketched in the next chapter. We need to note here only that the view of the conservative East was dominantly conservative from before the Revolution.

The popular, contradictory images of Twain invited polemics; they could be supported by the opinions of authorities; and they branched rapidly out into ideas about nature and pastoralism. And whether one stood with Brooks or with DeVoto, Twain's representative nature held moderately firm: for good or for bad, he was archetypal.

Nearly all academic critics of Twain have taken positions similar to those of DeVoto. Dixon Wecter, who succeeded DeVoto as editor of the Mark Twain Papers, wrote, "In the activities of the external man as well as in character and temperament, Mark Twain was a representative American— from idyllic and ante-bellum boyhood in a river town, to maturity enmeshed in the cross-purposes of the Gilded Age which he christened, and thence to the sunset years of mingled hope and disillusion in the Progressive Era."[4] Robert E. Spiller mounted to more poetically obscurantist heights: "This son of the heartland came to symbolize the variety and range and power of the American spirit. The Mississippi was his blood-stream and his hands reached across two oceans."[5] Optimistic paralogisms and the rhetoric of Davy Crockett abound in such tropological characterizations.

On the side of Brooks, Randolph Bourne declared shortly before the publication of *The Ordeal* that he chortled with joy at the way Brooks was going to show up critics like Stuart Sherman who tried to make out Mark Twain as the Great Man, a typical American who proved the virtues of the land and of the society in which he was born and fostered, "thus reassuring every American in his self-complacency."[6]

The writers with whom Brooks is usually associated were active for more than three decades, beginning about 1910. In a period marked by social and aesthetic turbulence, these writers, though there were many differences among them, considered themselves to be intellectual innovators, a consort of national redeemers. The circle included Randolph Bourne, Harold E. Stearns, Lewis Mumford, Matthew Josephson, Waldo Frank, Gilbert Seldes, Herbert Croly, V. F. Calverton, and Granville Hicks.

Some observers have thought that these on the whole amateurish social philosophers and secular idealists were comparable to principal members of the New England Renaissance. A number of their activities, prepossessions, and ambitions were in fact similar. They sought a supporting tradition that would enable them to establish an identity for themselves and for America, a tradition that would give them power to reshape the world.

Their bibles were, to be sure, different from those of the American Tran-
scendentalists. They made little or nothing of *The Bhagavadgita,* Plato,
Jesus, Kant, Goethe, or the higher law but turned to Marx, Freud, sociology, and economics. They favored both sexual and political revolutions.
Instead of preaching from the pulpit and from Lyceum rostrums, they
exhorted in essays and from college lecture platforms. Like the Transcen-
dentalists, they could be radically individualistic or enthusiastically communitarian. They were utopistic and perfectibilitarian, but after a contemporary, vaguely scientific fashion.

Herbert Croly was in the vanguard of the movement with *The Promise of
American Life* (1909); Randolph Bourne was a social thinker of some
originality who exerted a strong personal influence on Brooks; and in *Our
America* (1919) Waldo Frank presented Twain as a great spirit defeated by
an America that was subservient to the machine.

The titles of a few of the numerous books written or edited by members
of this avant-garde will suggest the evangelical zeal of the writers, if not
their full scope. (They worked in several genres, including fiction and
autobiography.) Waldo Frank, who was closely associated with Brooks in
founding and editing the magazine *Seven Arts,* published among his abundant works *Our America* (1919), *The Rediscovery of America* (1929), and
Dawn in Russia (1932). Indicative titles from a lesser writer, Stearns, are
Liberalism in America (1919) and *America and the Young Intellectual*
(1921). Mumford, whose long, prolific career made him the best known of
the circle, in *The Story of Utopias* (1922) suggested much of the bent of his
later thought and in *The Golden Day* (1926) expressed in summary fashion
many of his ideas on "American experience and culture," as his subtitle put
it. Calverton and Hicks wrote and edited copiously, but the most interesting endeavor of each was to try to interpret and judge American writers by
applying Marxist principles: Calverton in *American Literature at the Cross-
roads* (1931) and *The Liberation of American Literature* (1932), Hicks in *The
Great Tradition* (1933).

Brooks's writings may be divided into two contrasting parts. His authority with his admirers derived primarily from his early, astringent books and
articles. In 1927 he suffered a mental breakdown that kept him in hospitals
for most of four years. Perhaps beginning before the breakdown, certainly
following it, his writings showed him as too willing to be pleased, too
happy with all of the American past to satisfy the less sanguine and more
demanding of those who were previously his enthusiasts. F. O. Matthies-

sen, Harvard professor and author of *The American Renaissance* (1941), considered the early Brooks to be the strongest influence on his own work; the editors of the *Partisan Review* damned the later Brooks as "a pilgrim to Philistia"; and Edmund Wilson wrote that, to his surprise, in *The Flowering of New England* (1936) he found Brooks beaming and crooning.[7]

Although Brooks was greatly admired as a stylist, even his style is said to have deteriorated in his later writings. F. W. Dupee places the date for this deterioration quite early, holding that with the closing chapters of *The Pilgrimage of Henry James* (1925), Brooks's nostalgia begins to affect style and structure: "The pointed, argumentative and analytical manner gives way to a prose of anecdote and local color, a blur of sensuous matter, a dreamlike pastiche of remembered quotations."[8] Stanley Edgar Hyman, perhaps taking his cue from Edmund Wilson, finds that everything about Brooks's writing deteriorated with *The Flowering of New England*.[9] It did without question become more pallidly mannered as his thought turned panglossian. He strewed his pages with a superfluity of quotations, small anecdotes, and decorative allusions. He indulged himself in faded elegancies and mandarin nuances; his work lacked purpose and cohesiveness.

DeVoto abhorred aestheticism and cherished an image of himself as a hard-hitting, pragmatic "professional," but his "no-nonsense" nominalism masked very imperfectly a cloudily naturistic faith in frontier America. During one period he paid lip service to Vico; during another he looked on Robert Frost as an intellectual father. In general, his biases were unrealistic: he sought his model society in a fantasy of the frontier. In shaping an overwrought style, he borrowed flamboyance from writers like Twain and Mencken.

Although often seen by his detractors as unattractively noisy, contentious, and dogmatic, DeVoto was an able, industrious journalist with psychological problems not altogether unlike those of Brooks. He was tormented by insecurities, craved a following, and needed his sessions with psychiatrists. He was never the center of a group that could be considered ideologically coherent, but his good qualities—which included a selective generosity of spirit and a keen sense of personal loyalty—won him a number of devoted adherents, particularly among students, secretaries, colleagues at the Bread Loaf Writers' Conference, and fellow teachers at Harvard. Wallace Stegner has referred to these adherents as "the Tribe of Benny."[10]

DeVoto was condescended to by "the Young Intellectuals," as Harold

Stearns proudly named Brooks's circle. They thought of him as lowbrow or, conversely, because of the tenuous connection he had for some years with Harvard, as academic and therefore pedantic. Edmund Wilson, however, paid him grudging respect; and Lewis Mumford (whom DeVoto despised) once referred to him as unlike James Farrell, the Chicago novelist, in that DeVoto was one of those enemies from whom one can occasionally learn.[11]

For his part, DeVoto loathed the Young Intellectuals and pursued them with derisive whoops, assuring them that they were abysmally ignorant, without credentials as prophets and lawgivers. He remarked several times that Brooks, as chief and best of the group, was most deserving of his adverse attention, but he was also unrelenting in his antagonism toward the others. He crowed over Brooks, Mumford, Joseph Freeman, Max Lerner, and Granville Hicks—all of whom had been socially and politically out of the mainstream—when, following the Hitler-Stalin pact of August 23, 1939, they trooped back into the American fold.[12]

Brooks's writings and career speak pointedly of alienation and return. DeVoto is ordinarily considered to have been consistently patriotic and centrist in his attitudes. Certainly the bulk of his work is chauvinistic and antitheoretical, appealing with often choleric good sense to middlebrow readers of middlebrow periodicals such as *Harper's* and the *Saturday Review of Literature*. He did, nevertheless, undergo an unacknowledged reversal of ideas with respect to the personality of Mark Twain, for he came to see Twain as divided of mind and soul, a manic-depressive teetering above psychic abysses. Thus he conceded much to Brooks and to pessimism, just as Brooks came to concede much to him. Because the relationship in DeVoto's mind between Twain and America was imperatively metaphoric, conversion with regard to Twain was associated at the end of DeVoto's life and perhaps earlier with a subterranean unsettling of his ideas about America. Only the letters written over approximately the last half-year of his life (he died on November 12, 1955), a time when he was unwell and discouraged, make clear that his optimism about America had deserted him.[13]

Mark Twain probably became the focus for the conflict between Brooks and DeVoto in 1920 when DeVoto first read *The Ordeal*; but it is possible that DeVoto fixed on Brooks as a chief ideological foe several years earlier, for Brooks had already set out his main lamentations on America in *The Wine of the Puritans* (1908), *America's Coming-of-Age* (1915), and *Letters and Leadership* (1918). DeVoto—he was only twenty-five at the time—

commented on Brooks's misprisions in a letter of October 22, 1920, remarking that he himself burst with *creative* criticisms of America, that he had found a kind of national self-consciousness. It was not until the spring of 1931, however, that DeVoto printed his first published attack on Brooks. This came in a magazine for Harvard alumni that he was then editing, and he seized the opportunity to sweep into his net all of the Young Intellectuals.[14]

In *Mark Twain's America* DeVoto sharply criticized several of the Young Intellectuals, but his criticism of Brooks gave the book its center. Brooks's wholly wrong ideas about Twain, DeVoto said, had dominated all discussions since their appearance. He charged Brooks with absurdity, wild play of assumption, and ignoring what the context says. Brooks was, he maintained, ignorant of the frontier and of American history, ignorant of the writings of Turner, ignorant of Twain's literary predecessors, of his life, and of his works. Furthermore, Brooks simply did not know what Puritanism was about, showed no understanding of humor, and did not in any way appreciate Twain's greatness. He treated emotionally charged words as facts, misrepresented persons, places, and ideas, contradicted himself, assumed that accuracy is not essential to criticism, exhibited a foolish eclecticism in his amateurish judgments, and, most important of all, constructed theories out of faulty abstractions and then used the theories as though they were proved. In the light of historical fact and of judgments based on fact, DeVoto found it necessary, he said, to reverse all of Brooks's theses.

Correcting Brooks's errors about Mark Twain was, nevertheless, a secondary issue. As a topic, the literal Twain advanced and receded: the important thing was to establish his figurative grandeur. DeVoto drove this point home over a period of fourteen years in "Mark Twain: The Ink of History" (1935); "Mark Twain and the Limits of Criticism" (1936); "A Generation beside the Limpopo" (1936); *Mark Twain at Work* (1942); *The Literary Fallacy* (1944); *The Portable Mark Twain* (1946); and in brief pieces in the *Saturday Review of Literature* and *Harper's*. The basic argument was over American society, the American as artist, and the relationship between life and literature. As DeVoto saw himself, he was a lonely champion, looming large on the national scene, standing for sound thought and feeling.

Fully recognizing what the issues were for him, DeVoto asserted that he directed a lifetime of writing against all that the early Brooks and his circle stood for. In a letter of 1934 he claimed that *Mark Twain's America* challenged the most important critical idea about American life that his generation produced, and in a letter of May 24, 1943, he wrote that his career in letters had been "in absolute opposition to the main literary current" of his time. He had set himself against "the ideas, concepts, theories, sentiments, and superstitions of the official literature of the United States between two wars." His own significance began when he recognized that he had been wrong in writing early articles denigrating Utah (where he grew up) and right in reacting against Van Wyck Brooks "and his system of thinking about American culture."[15]

DeVoto's major charges against Brooks were not so entirely original with him as he seemed to believe: adverse comments may be found among the dominantly favorable reviews of *The Ordeal*. Critics said that Brooks was humorless, incapable of understanding Twain or of appreciating his merits, less than magisterial in his lay psychologizing, and gloomy in portraying the American past. Articles and books began to appear defending the cultures of Hannibal, Virginia City, and Elmira. No such blanket condemnation of Brooks was made, however, as that to be found in *Mark Twain's America*.

The immediate reception of DeVoto's book was perhaps as mixed as had been that of *The Ordeal*. In 1932 Brooks was still highly respected as a *penseur*, an arbiter of life and letters, and the tone of DeVoto's attack shocked even some of his own friends. Reviewers questioned the reasons for DeVoto's anger, called him volcanic and controversial, and, turning from Brooks to Twain, wished that DeVoto had written more acute, less limited critical passages on Twain's works. Nevertheless, most writers trusted DeVoto's scholarship and approved his favorable views of southwestern humor, popular art, frontier democracy, and Twain. Among the scholars who have in their several ways paid tribute to DeVoto are DeLancey Ferguson, Dixon Wecter, Walter Blair, and Henry Nash Smith.

For a time Brooks insisted that he saw no reason to change his positions on Twain by yielding to critics of *The Ordeal*, and he never issued a public reply to DeVoto. Brooks's sympathizers, however, had many edged comments to make about DeVoto both in 1932 and later. Lewis Mumford wrote to Brooks on December 27, 1932, that he had used the season of peace and goodwill to begin a murderous attack on DeVoto and was having a great deal of fun with it. He had waited three months pondering whether to speak out or not, one reason for refraining being that DeVoto was a jackass. He had finally decided to give DeVoto a few medicinal pellets that would make him more careful in the future of his citations and his tactics.[16]

The most virulent and insulting rejoinder to DeVoto came in 1944 from Sinclair Lewis and had reference to Brooks only as one among several whom DeVoto had attacked. Lewis wrote by arrangement with Norman Cousins, editor of the *Saturday Review of Literature,* who apparently wished to foment a controversy. Cousins published a cut version of the final chapter of DeVoto's *The Literary Fallacy* and followed it the next week with a featured reply by Lewis. Although the selection from DeVoto printed by Cousins was somewhat less contentious and wounding than parts of earlier chapters, he sharpened it by printing photographs of Hemingway, Lewis, Ludwig Lewisohn, Brooks, John Dos Passos, and Robinson Jeffers with a censorious caption drawn from DeVoto beneath each picture.[17]

Lewis had several reasons to dislike DeVoto. Lewis and Brooks were friends; DeVoto had ridiculed Dorothy Thompson (for a time Lewis's wife) in an essay in *Harper's* in December 1942; and in chapter 3 of *The Literary Fallacy,* DeVoto had included a vigorously condemnatory critique of Lewis's thought and writing. Lewis's diatribe was directed against DeVoto as an individual and against DeVoto's entire book, not simply against the version of the final chapter that Cousins printed.

The essay by Lewis is deficient in logic and fails to recognize that in *The Literary Fallacy* DeVoto was engaged in a continuing debate about the relationship of literature and life, the primacy of the inductive method, and the general health of American society and American art. Lewis also exhibited curious ignorances, as by grouping DeVoto, Howard Mumford Jones, Allen Tate, R. P. Blackmur, Yvor Winters, and Edmund Wilson. Worst of all, he derided DeVoto in ruffianly terms as a tedious and egotistical fool, a pompous and boresome liar with a froglike face. DeVoto was justified in writing furious letters to Cousins objecting to the publication of personal vituperation.

The two articles bred a small swarm of rejoinders. That Brooks did not join in did not mean that he took DeVoto's new attack placidly. He defended himself indirectly in his writings, expressed resentment to friends, and seventeen years after Lewis's essay appeared noted with satisfaction in one of his autobiographical volumes that Lewis gave DeVoto the literary trouncing of his life.[18]

One freakish by-product of the Lewis assault was that DeVoto made a conciliatory gesture in the general direction of Brooks. Malcolm Cowley, whom DeVoto had abused as the apologist for a coterie when Cowley published *Exile's Return* (1934) and as a distorter of American life and literature when Cowley edited *After the Genteel Tradition* (1937), wrote DeVoto dissociating himself from Lewis's defamatory paper. Cowley explained that his own forthcoming unfavorable remarks on *The Literary Fallacy* were motivated by difference of opinion, not rancor. DeVoto met politeness with civility, reason with understanding in a long letter reviewing his treatment of Brooks and the Young Intellectuals.[19]

Although scholars have continued to accept DeVoto as relatively sound on Twain's literary predecessors, his life, and frontier culture, they have, nevertheless, often followed Brooks—with or without acknowledgment— in seeing Twain as a divided man and the culture in which he developed as more repressive than DeVoto's optimistic view would have it. To think of Twain as psychically disturbed has become progressively more easy, not so much because DeVoto saw him thus in *Mark Twain at Work* as because this is the Twain who has been emerging in his posthumously published writings and in scholarly articles.

The significance of Brooks's revisions in the second edition of *The Ordeal* (1933) has been variously interpreted. DeVoto observed in a footnote that while *Mark Twain's America* was in galley proof, Brooks's publishers announced the new edition of *The Ordeal* and at first refused him permission to quote from the first edition on the grounds that some of Brooks's opinions would be reversed in the second.[20]

Gladys C. Bellamy believed that when Brooks revised *The Ordeal* his central position remained fixed. Robert E. Spiller similarly declared that Brooks "took back nothing." James R. Vitelli wrote that Brooks "softened a phrase or two, eliminated an outburst against New England, but altered his essential thesis not one bit": the new edition "may be taken as Brooks' calculated reiteration of his point of view." William Wasserstrom took what seem to be contradictory positions on the subject. First he remarked that Brooks only corrected a howler or two, toned down a few passages, and played up a few others: the changes were purely cosmetic. A few pages later he stated that the revision "represents a retreat from some hard-won positions. Far more ground is given up than is accounted for in a simple arithmetic of words changed or phrases dropped." Stanley Hyman produced a limited amount of evidence to support his opinion that in the second edition Brooks discarded a good part of his original major thesis. Hyman asserted that important changes turned up by a random comparison of the texts are "almost unbelievable" and "innumerable." He then discussed approximately thirty illustrative emendations that, he thought, soften exaggerated statements, hedge, back out of misstatements, weasel on contradictions, and delete slights to America, New England, and John D. Rockefeller, Jr. "It is not," he concluded, "a pretty picture."[21]

Brooks himself made discordant comments on his revisions. Writing to Lewis Mumford shortly after DeVoto's book appeared in 1932, he said that he improved *The Ordeal* by making approximately twenty-five hundred revisions, about a dozen of them occasioned by DeVoto. (It seems clear that Brooks did make most of his revisions before he saw *Mark Twain's America*.) In perhaps another dozen instances DeVoto was, Brooks added, simply mistaken; and he claimed "in the face of DeVoto" that in the first edition he gave full credit to the positive elements in the character of pioneer and Puritan, was correct in his interpretation of the effect of the West on Twain, and right about the relative freedom of mind that Twain found in the East as compared with the West.[22]

In *Days of the Phoenix,* Brooks reaffirmed that Twain had "made the great refusal" and that *The Ordeal* was substantially just, but he also made a large concession: he had portrayed only half of Twain. The reason for this, he explained, was an overconcern with psychology that reduced its subject to a type, a congeries of inhibitions, and left no room for literary or human appreciation. The real Twain was more the champion of justice, hater of shams, and lovable genius than he had pictured, and Twain's humor had a positive value that he had "all but entirely" neglected to suggest. How speak of failure in connection with a writer the most successful of his time? Brooks concluded that he saw these objections to *The Ordeal* clearly when he wrote his "literary history," *The Times of Melville and Whitman* (1947).[23]

Nearly fifteen years after the appearance of Hyman's critique, Brooks quoted from Hyman (without naming him) in the third and last of his autobiographical volumes and responded to some of his charges. He answered the allegation that he hedged and weaseled in reissuing *The Ordeal* by saying that he "had merely removed exaggerations, the result of the ignorance of youth," and he wryly noted that after he rebelled against the "fascist-communist alliance" he was called, among other things, a comrade-in-arms of Bernard DeVoto.[24]

An examination of the significant changes revealed by a collation of the two texts of *The Ordeal* appears to demonstrate that these revisions were less numerous and less important than Hyman said they were.[25] Hyman did not falsify the sense or the direction of the emendations that he listed; but he exaggerated their importance to the overall impression made by the book and also exaggerated the number of similar changes that he left unspecified. Brooks's revisions modify the biases of the book, but they do not reverse them.

Along with many instances of stylistic improvements and minor corrections, there appear to be fewer than one hundred important emendations. These emendations make *The Ordeal* more favorable to Twain's positive accomplishments, less condemnatory of his lack of artistic integrity and his defects of personality, less positive that he had no will of his own and never attained to creation in the proper sense of the word, less insistent about the defects of the genteel tradition and genteel writers, less vehement about the hideousness of the pioneer experience and the nonexistence in America of a folk art, and less absolute about America's conformist herd-life. Fewer adverse moral judgments appear. The West is now only unpropitious to the development of personality, not inflexibly opposed.

Even though Brooks wrote in 1957 that on "restudying" Twain he saw many reasonable objections to his earlier treatment in *The Ordeal,* in 1961 he declared contradictorily that no attempt had really been made to reply to the evidence that he had assembled in that book and that when he came to write *The Times of Melville and Whitman,* which contains his only other extended treatment of Twain, he repeated substantially the thesis of his original book. In fact, Brooks encountered friendly dissent from his theses before publication and a number of remedial criticisms afterward. Obviously, crosscurrents and confusions pervade this matter.[26]

An extended comment by Malcolm Cowley mingles fact and fancy. He reports that Brooks presented in *The Times of Melville and Whitman* a generally sympathetic picture of Twain and met the challenge from DeVoto to study the early American humorists and life on the frontier by writing absorbing accounts of both. Cowley adds that this approval of Twain is merely a shift in emphasis: in *The Ordeal* Brooks wrote for "those with a sense of literary vocation" and only "to be overheard" by the cultivated public; in the later book he wrote for the whole public.[27]

The truth is that Brooks continued to show little knowledge of the early American humorists or of the frontier, wrote impressionistically of them, and revised in a bizarre way his position on Twain. To say that the change between *The Ordeal* and *The Times of Melville and Whitman* is one in emphasis is misleading, and although Cowley's transmogrified echo of J. S. Mill's dictum ("Eloquence is *heard,* poetry is *overheard*") does not ring altogether false as an explanation of differences in the treatment of Twain in the two books, Brooks never argued in his own defense that he wrote *The Ordeal* for a special audience.

Among critics who have pointed out that Brooks and DeVoto grew closer to each other in their later writings on Twain are several who have suggested, too absolutely, that Brooks reversed himself. Dwight Macdonald, for example, came to this conclusion.[28] The actuality is more nuanced.

Two separate but related determinations concerning Brooks's recanting may be readily arrived at. First, at some time not fully agreed on (Lewis Mumford thought in 1925–26; Brooks suggested 1931–32), Brooks reversed his earlier "negative" and "pessimistic" social attitudes. Second, while freely acknowledging this general reversal, Brooks in some statements avoided any clear admission that he reversed himself on Mark Twain and in others denied that he wished to do so.

What Brooks actually did in *The Times of Melville and Whitman* was to paint two strangely contradictory portraits of Twain in two chapters which give the effect of a reversal followed by a reiteration, with modifications, of what was said in *The Ordeal*. They also give the effect of glorifying the West and, if only by implication, depreciating the East. "Mark Twain in the West," chapter 14, is widely separated from its sequel, chapter 22, as though an artist realized that he had painted two incompatible portraits of the same man and decided to hang them in separate rooms. One thing the two chapters have in common: they grasp whatever opportunities arise to rebut charges made by DeVoto, though without naming him.

Brooks liked to think that chapter 14 was an appreciation of the early, western Mark Twain who was "left out" of *The Ordeal*. In fact this chapter presents together with shreds of the old an unrecognizably different Mark Twain and an unrecognizably different frontier environment: the West is now akin to conventional images of the cultural Garden of the World. During Twain's stay in San Francisco (1864–66), Brooks writes, we have the first real public appearance of "a mind as original as Melville's or Whitman's and a character as marked and complex as theirs." In Twain's blood were the qualities of the West and South. He had a masterly grasp of the American scene, and his better work before 1885 constituted the germ of a new American literature "with a broader base in the national mind than the writers of New England had possessed, fine as they were." There is, then, Brooks notes, a measure of justification in Hemingway's remark that all modern American literature comes from *Huckleberry Finn*. Twain was "the serio-comic Homer of this old primitive Western world, its pathfinder in letters, its historian and poet."

Set against perfervid praise in chapter 14 are a few minor complaints or half-complaints. Twain was prudish: he permitted others to censor him, or he censored himself. He was an impulsive boy, tractable and rebellious by turns. But this was no more than DeVoto had said; indeed, Brooks cites DeVoto on the issues of censorship and self-censorship. He even finds excuses for Twain's Philistinism in *Innocents Abroad* (it taught writers to be honest in their vision and cleared a path for an American culture of the future) and for his ignorance (it was on the side of growth). DeVoto could not reasonably have asked for ampler homage.

Chapter 22—"Mark Twain in the East"—opens by recapitulating the praise and the minor complaints of chapter 14, almost as though chapter 14 did not exist. Brooks then wrenches Twain into a different perspective. Against the heroically creative figure of chapter 14, he balances a milder version of the failed artist he had portrayed in *The Ordeal*. Major theses of *The Ordeal* reappear. Twain's commercial and literary motives were inextricably mingled; Twain was a divided soul; he took little pride in his writing; he suppressed his more dangerous beliefs. His imagination never flowered freely in the world of the Gilded Age, and he was never successful as a novelist. Although a few of his writings are destined to live, he wrote hundreds and thousands of pages of undistinguished journalism. Because he feared to offend the public, he acted as a free mind and an artist only now and then.

Chapter 22 does not return us precisely to where we started in the first edition of *The Ordeal*. Brooks could not have said here as he did there, "A great writer of the past is known by the delight and stimulus which he gives to mature spirits in the present, and time, it seems to me, tends to bear out the assertion of Henry James that Mark Twain's appeal is an appeal to rudimentary minds."[29]

In neither of these chapters does Brooks try to explain why Twain was (if only to a degree) a failure. He attempts no psychoanalytic interpretations and incorporates no theory relating Puritanism and false humor to the frontier. Twain's deficiencies appear as discrete, undetermined, in no way coordinated, part of no ideological scheme.

Apparently Brooks did not fully understand what he had done either in revising *The Ordeal* or in composing *The Times of Melville and Whitman*. When he revised *The Ordeal*, he made changes that hinted at his large mental reorientation; but he left the ideological framework nearly intact: to have removed it would have meant a complete rewriting and rethinking. In books and articles published after he revised *The Ordeal*, he did abandon the entire ideological structure that had given solidity and point to the book. American Puritanism no longer dichotomized into equally unsatisfactory halves. The frontier became sanely, humanely humorous and possessed of a worthy folk art. America became a success story. Henry James, who had been the failed artist as expatriate, became a great writer. But Brooks, it seems, could neither bring himself to announce a surrender to DeVoto nor convince himself that Twain was an almost unqualifiedly successful major writer. He could not set Twain in entire analogical compatibility with his new, optimistic ideas.

Probably, then, because of rifts within the mind of Brooks, we find flagrant antitheses in his final treatment of Twain. Twain is an integrated human being who remains, nevertheless, mildly schizoid. As an artist he is both a success and a failure. He brilliantly transcends the regional and gives direction to American writing, but he is incapable of treating his own times in fiction.

The pretensions of the Young Intellectuals, including Brooks, as breakers of old molds, discoverers and interpreters of what Brooks called a "usable past," harbingers of a better future, were, like DeVoto's hubristic ambitions, decidedly inflated. Looking back, we see the discursive powers of all of these writers as less than irresistible, their work as too uninformed and ineffectual to have generated anything resembling a paradigm shift.

It seems likely that literary history will value DeVoto's books on Twain and Brooks's early writings on Twain above all their other work. In some important ways, these writings may be compared as well as contrasted. The two critics existed in the same cultural matrix and stressed much the same topics. Because they concentrated on similar topics from opposed points of view, their differences were accentuated.

Brooks derived his conceptions of Twain and of Twain's milieu from shaky theories and a minimum of facts, as DeVoto insisted he did. DeVoto declared an antipathy for theories, deductive reasoning, and ideological systems, claiming that he himself was a thorough inductivist who founded his Mark Twain and his America on facts, but his claim involved gross self-deception. With respect to the data of cultural and literary history, he was much less exact than he thought: as he himself sometimes remarked, he could make a fact go a long way.[30] His postulates were as dominating as were those of Brooks, and his Twain was as synecdochic as was Brooks's. His Twain, too, underwent puzzling changes: the Twain of *Mark Twain at Work* does not fill out the role of the hero of *Mark Twain's America*.

Whereas Brooks first used Clemens to illustrate our national psychopathologies, DeVoto conversely magnified him in *Mark Twain's America* as the greatest and most American of our writers. Given the workings of environmental determinism, in celebrating Clemens, DeVoto celebrated the American experience. Recognizing the metaphoric weight carried by Twain helps us to understand the ferocity with which DeVoto attacked Brooks and the tenacity with which he clung to the notion that his own interpretations of Twain did not change. And although the large public quarrel between the two critics concerned the nature of the American experience and the direction in which national salvation lay, a more hidden quarrel related to the virtues and defects that DeVoto saw in his inmost, most precious self, for he, like Brooks, identified himself with Twain.

A commonsensical but questionable dictum generated by the controversy is one often applied to critiques and biographies with which one is in disagreement. Sir Philip Magnus wrote that Gladstone's Homeric studies throw more light on Gladstone than on Homer; Charles Eliot Norton remarked of Mrs. Gaskell's biography of Charlotte Brontë that it "was almost as much an exhibition of Mrs. Gaskell's character as of Miss Brontë's"; and Lewis Leary believed that samples of the controversy over Twain which he collected tell "the story of how men's minds have reacted to Mark Twain": his *Casebook* "is really not about Mark Twain at all."[31]

Such dicta invite modifying comments. Important though it is to try to bring our images of Mark Twain into conformity with factuality, all images are received images, and these particular received images have interesting significances. Although the various metaphoric Mark Twains are inaccurate as portrayals of "the historical" Samuel Clemens, they are the materials of histories of judgment, taste, influence, and reception (*Urteilsgeschichte* and *Wirkungsgeschichte*).

Also to be taken into account are now commonplace refusals to accept notions of a stable, unitary reality. Mikhail Bakhtin helped to popularize the idea of a plurivocity of discourses, dialogical discourse, of a reciprocity between text and reader as opposed to an authoritarian literalness. Paul Ricoeur and many others have written to these points. Paul de Man notes that "the observing subject is no more constant than the observed," that "each time the observer actually succeeds in interpreting his subject he

changes it," and that "every change in the observed subject requires a
subsequent change in the observer." Roland Barthes asks, "How could we
believe, in fact, that the work is an object exterior to the psyche and history
of the man who interrogates it?"

Perhaps we may at the same time strive toward historicity and agree that
there can never be a definitive life of Samuel Clemens. A. B. Paine's official
biography (1912) won high praise as full and life-sized. Brooks's image of
Twain (1920) impressed many as an astute psychological likeness; and
DeVoto's apotheosized representation (1932) was widely accepted as pho-
tographically exact. In life and in death, Samuel Clemens has displayed
multiple selves.

Because for so long a time now DeVoto and the Tribe of Benny have
ostensibly carried the day, DeVoto's archfoe, Brooks, is the critic of this pair
who most needs an unprejudiced hearing. His early pessimistic view of the
American past and his analogical image of an unsuccessful, neurotic Mark
Twain do not today appear to be impossibly perverse in their bearing,
though ill-grounded in history and ludicrous in certain details. He seems
more or less right about American materialism and some of its effects:
America's disvaluing of art, Twain's divided mind, and Twain's waste of his
talent. His later portrait of Twain in chapter 14 of *The Times of Melville and
Whitman* is overcorrected. The sketch in chapter 22 conforms more nearly
to my interpretation of the assembled data of history by exhibiting a gravely
flawed American talent.

But it was in *The Ordeal* that Brooks raised in frequently original detail—
and with a certain irresponsible eloquence—questions that were taken up
antagonistically by DeVoto and have proved magnetic since. Fortunately,
Mark Twain has been peculiarly responsive to and enriched by the examination in his life and works of ideas about nature and civilization, nature and
art, East and West, rationalism and romanticism, censorship and independence, materialism and idealism, progress and regress, national identity and
personal identity. The contrasting, controverted, analogical Mark Twains
of Brooks and DeVoto have, like some Janus-faced personage carved on
Mount Rushmore, somewhat eroded. Twain is now more multifaceted, less
a confrontational duo, than he was; but he is almost equally synecdochic.
He remains, as Brooks put it, "an arch-type," a paradigm for a bewildering
variety of Americas.

AN ADAM

FROM THE

WESTERN

GARDEN

▲ ▲ ▲ ▲ ▲ ▲ ▲ ▲ ▲

In America the idea of the West, perhaps our dominant myth, incorporated in itself two opposed, multifaceted dimensions. The West—the frontier in general—enjoyed a metonymic relationship with ideas of great antiquity about nature. Nature represented freedom, virtue, and equality; it was the Magna Mater. But the idea of nature also encompassed the rude, the barbarous, that from which Western man was progressing in his grand, Condorcettian march toward civilization. William Bradford, in his *History of Plimoth Plantation,* wrote darkly of the Indians as "salvage and brutish men," little different from wild beasts; the country he called "a hideous and desolate wildernes," presenting "a wild and savage heiw."[1]

Conceptions which complicated and enriched the ideological implications of the idea of the West were associated with a variety of myths and
traditions, pagan and Christian, secular and religious. Of extreme importance were ideas of heavenly and earthly gardens, the biblical Eden, the
Golden Age, the Fortunate Islands, and the millennial forecast of Jesus as
quoted in John. *Eden* is associated with the Babylonian term for an alluvial
plain; *paradise,* probably Iranian in origin, denoted a (usually royal) park or
garden; in apocalyptic literature paradise was a heavenly counterpart of the
Garden of Eden, a place of rewards. In the Ugaritic Baal epic, God lives in a
cosmic paradise; and in the story of Gilgamesh, Utnapishtim is translated
to Dilmun to be in the garden of the sun. The Jewish Paradise of Delight
was roughly equivalent to Egyptian Elysian Fields. In Genesis the earth is a
waste before God plants a garden, which garden is, nevertheless, but a
shadow of the Garden of God. During the Middle Ages there were many
versions of the land of Cockayne (a thirteenth-century invention), of Pres-
ter John, of Ternangue; and the Earthly Paradise, a favorite topos, had
various analogues during the Renaissance and after.

The Orbis Terrarum—made up of Europe, Asia, and Africa—was believed to have been given to Adam's progeny as a habitation. Columbus
unknowingly added a new world which, not being part of the Orbis
Terrarum, should not have had inhabitants. What, then, of the Indians? By
applying the Christian principle of the unity of mankind, they could be seen
as descendants of Adam. On the other hand, they could be considered
strange creatures of nature or agents of Satan. More important, beginning
in 1492 man seemed to have broken out of the territory to which he had
been assigned into an Orbis Alterius. The discovery made way for a new
Adam in a restored Golden Age. The Earthly Paradise, traditionally distant
in space, in time, or in both, often on a mountaintop and usually in the
East, could be considered accessible by sailing west and might be identified
with the newly found lands: Gonzalo Fernández de Oviedo (1526) believed the Indies to be the Hesperides.

From the earliest of colonial times in North America, the edge of civilization, whether conceived as benevolent or desolate, was a constantly shift-
ing, mysterious, magnetically attractive line or space. Complications
abounded: to William Byrd, the line ran east and west rather than north and
south, or as well as north and south, and separated Virginian civilization
from North Carolinian barbarism. In the South, the idea of the Garden was
likely to be associated with plantation life, not with the pastoralist or the
yeoman farmer; but the appeal of the frontier was also strong.

Captain Arthur Barlowe, reporting on his voyage to Virginia in 1584, made the idea of the garden a controlling metaphor: approaching land, "we smelt so sweet, and so strong a smel, as if we had bene in the midst of some delicate garden. . . . I thinke in all the world the like abundance is not to be found." Humphry Marshall, a Kentuckian legislator, referred to Daniel Boone as a second Adam, entered into a second Paradise. The anonymous author of *Boone's First View of Kentucky* described that frontier region as the Garden of the West.

In New England a parley of voices confused—though certainly not for the first time—theological and secular impulses. The Garden of the World could be entangled with the City of God (Psalms 46:4–5), or the city that is set on a hill (Matthew 5:14–17), or the most glorious City of God (in Augustine). John Winthrop preached a famous lay-sermon in 1630 on board the *Arbella* in mid-Atlantic between Southampton and New England, assuring the congregated Puritans that by a strict performance of the articles in a covenant with God, "wee shall be as a Citty upon a Hill, the eies of all people are uppon us." Writing later to a friend, Winthrop entreated God, "Carry us into thy garden, that we may eat and be filled with thy pleasures, which the world knows not." And as the theocracy and the sense of mission faded, the good land to the west, a possible garden, remained— increasingly secularized, yet still capable of being a model for "succeeding plantations." In 1797 the Reverend James Smith wrote with the rapture of a Persian poet of the village of Deerfield, Ohio, "What a garden of spices! What a paradise of pleasures!"

To the minds of modern historians, opinions concerning differences between East and West have not depended entirely on notions about paradises: the observers' social position and wealth are among matters that have had bearing. Distinctions made have had to do with free land, furs, silver, gold, the labor pool, and decentralized banking. Nevertheless, distinctions have also concerned character, principles, morals, cultivation, self-images, and ideologies: the frontier "gave birth to distinctively American legends, myths, and heroes."[2]

Those who have taken the terms *East* and *West* seriously have ordinarily used them to establish simple dichotomous classifications which have had to be abandoned when empirically scrutinized. Each of the polarities has helped to define and constitute the other, and each has undergone vicissitudes. Timothy Dwight, Timothy Flint, Emerson, Thoreau, Whitman, and Henry James are among those who have explored supposed differences in the qualities that divided sections, replicating at points explorations of real or imagined differences between the Old World and the New. Long before 1893, when Frederick Jackson Turner pressed in an epochal paper the idea that the European, meeting the frontier, is born again, ambivalences about East and West beset the minds of William Dean Howells, who spent his youth in small Ohio towns, and his fellow westerner Samuel Clemens. (Neither writer seems to have become aware of Turner, nor does Turner, in this relationship, appear to have been aware of them.)

At times it is possible to unravel with some plausibility what Clemens thought about literature or society by examining the mind of Howells, whose ideas, in any case, had considerable influence on Clemens. The two men were alike in being intruding newcomers, making their respective ways in the East; then, too, Clemens, the newer and more roughhewn of the passionate pilgrims, read Howells's novels and critical essays, read or tried to read books that Howells recommended, struck out what Howells suggested that he cut from his manuscripts, and agreed to most opinions that Howells voiced. On his side, Howells, editor of the *Atlantic Monthly* and over a long period dean of American critics, liked Clemens and was captivated by his representational possibilities. For Howells, the idea of the West made plausible Twain's idiolects, his registers, and his apparent formlessness; and he gladly promoted his friend as a Great American Writer.

Clemens referred to Hannibal, Missouri, where he grew up, as the West (with a capital *W* in the Morgan Library's holograph copy of *Life on the Mississippi*) but also said that he was born in the South. When he went east in 1867, he had lived in Nevada and California for more than five years, was known for his western humor, and was billed as the Wild Humorist of the Pacific Slope. At the appearance of *Innocents Abroad* (1869), Bret Harte, writing in the *Overland Monthly* (January 1870) called favorable attention to Twain's "picturesque Western talk": and the reviewer of *Roughing It,* writing in the same periodical (June 1872), declared Twain's genius to be "characterized by the breadth, and ruggedness, and audacity of the West; and wherever he was born, or wherever he may abide, the Great West claims him as her intellectual offspring."

This heroizing tendency increased, turning Twain first into Adam out of the Garden in the West and finally into Man, protagonist in a modern morality play. A. B. Paine emphasized the universality of Twain's genius and proclaimed of his death, "Nations have often mourned a hero—and races—but perhaps never before had the entire world really united in tender sorrow for the death of any man." Bernard DeVoto, although aware that the frontier had moved beyond the Hannibal of Mark Twain's boyhood, nonetheless painted garishly colored pictures of the cultures of both frontier and river as enchanted, fructifying memories for the writer. John S. Tuckey takes a full, panoramic view: Clemens, he suggests, found "within himself . . . all the qualities that were present in the make-up of any member of his race. He was the representative man, the race in singular—Adam."[3]

Whether the influence of Howells on Clemens was for good or ill has been the subject of sharp disagreement. As Lionel Trilling put it, H. L. Mencken, Van Wyck Brooks, and others made Howells's timorousness a synonym for evasive gentility. On the other hand, DeVoto found little supporting evidence of damaging expurgation indisputably attributable to Howells. (During the 1930s, a hero of the virile West, which is how DeVoto saw Clemens, was not supposed meekly to accept bowdlerizing.) Similarly, Henry Nash Smith and William Gibson, editors of the Twain-Howells correspondence, wrote that publication of the letters completed the destruction of "the once widely held belief that Howells as an editor emasculated Mark Twain's vigor of expression and partially kept him from artistic fulfillment." They thought Howells's deletions of language "likely to offend *Atlantic* subscribers or the mass audience which bought subscription books," whether helpful or harmful, to be "negligible in the light of advice to Clemens in such larger matters as consistency of tone, verisimilitude, and the need to eliminate irrelevancy and to keep burlesque from becoming mere horseplay." It is true that we do not have many examples of excisions made by Howells. It is also clear, however, that Clemens accepted bowdlerizing by Howells (and by a good many others) and upon occasion suppressed items that Howells thought better left unpublished.[4]

In fact, Howells—an advocate of social and literary niceties—seems to have given relatively little advice to Clemens on larger matters. But, more important, like Olivia Clemens, he served as a genteel Presence, a censor acting not just in advance of publication but in advance of composition. He praised *Adventures of Huckleberry Finn* discriminatingly, but he may have preferred *A Connecticut Yankee*. He admired *The Prince and the Pauper* and wrote fulsomely of "A True Story" and of "The Turning Point in My Life." If Howells's taste in literature was better than Clemens's, it was, nevertheless, decidedly imperfect; and whether his general influence on Clemens was beneficial or not remains in question.

When the youthful Howells paid his first visit to the East in 1860, he brought with him an extravagant faith in the virtuousness of western society and a burning ambition to associate himself with the East, where culture had its established home. It was with an almost overmastering sense of awe that he made his initial social calls upon Lowell, Longfellow, Hawthorne, Emerson, and Thoreau. Any apprehensions were groundless; these American Worthies were in their different ways receptive: they opened their doors and minds to their visitor—he was appropriately humble, a devotee of High Culture, and he was western.

As America was Europe's dreamed pastoral, so the West was pastoral for easterners. An idealized West—the actuality could be another matter—was part of their vision of history. Dichotomies (New World-Old World, Nature-Civilization, Present-Past) teased and energized their thoughts as much as they did those of Howells. These demigods of New England were not of the party that frankly, obdurately despised the West. They might patronize the actual West, but they were not minded to upset notions of western primacy in matters of morality, equality, and truth. Indeed, they sought to capture in their own characters and writings a supposed American freshness and authenticity.

Emerson's favorable interest in the West was well known: he had fitted the wilderness snugly into his Neoplatonist, monistic scheme. In *English Traits* he commented characteristically that in America there "still sleeps and murmurs and bides the great mother, long since driven away from the trim hedgerows and over-cultivated gardens of England." Thoreau, Margaret Fuller, and others—like Emerson—held sentiments that accorded with Crèvecoeur's satisfaction when he assured the friend to whom he wrote that, though his letters would not be elegant, "they will smell of the woods and be a little wild."

Two years after Howells visited him, Thoreau wrote in "Walking" about the subtle magnetism of Nature: "My needle . . . always settles between west and south-southwest. The future lies that way to me, and the earth seems more unexhausted and richer on that side. . . . I may say that mankind progress from east to west." Hawthorne, no Transcendentalist, relished memories of the freedom he felt during youthful experiences in the woods of Maine and combined them with dualistic obsessions, Romantic antinomies, and the mirrored mysteries of human nature. He expressed to Howells approbative curiosity about the West, seeming to believe it "much more purely American" than the East. Howells reported him as saying that "he would like to see some part of the country on which the shadow, or, if I must be precise, the damned shadow, of Europe had not fallen." Lowell liked Howells's being proud of his western region and said he "had always fancied that human nature was laid out on rather a larger scale there than in the East."[5]

Although these venerated New Englanders saw Howells's West (Columbus, Ohio) as a contemporary version of a former, more innocent East, there were enough others who saw it as a drab, unmannered, almost savage postfrontier to keep Howells—and to a lesser degree Clemens—alert to the advantages possessed by men fortunate enough to have been born in Boston or Cambridge. As Howells affectionately describes the Cambridge that he lived in and loved, that tight little community (which is to say its culturally superior citizens, not the blacks or the Irish) could hardly have been more self-consciously given to preening itself on its moral, social, and intellectual elevation.

Howells sympathized *almost* completely with this self-infatuation. To him Cambridge was meritorious and welcoming. By contrast with Europe, it was innocently western. Literary men, men of letters, and scholars abounded. The guests at Craigie House on Longfellow's Dante Club evenings were those, Howells wrote, "whom of all men living I most honored." Money was comfortably, unobtrusively present. Aggressive capitalism and industry were for the most part absent. Neighbors who as likely as not could read Sanskrit or put Dante into exact prose or careful verse were as supportive as rustic Ohioans at the house-raising described by Howells's father in his memoirs. Cambridge seemed a better Ohio, an elevated *communitas,* a warm, sustaining gemeinschaft.[6]

Yet the essential America, America in its purest form, had moved to the West. A millenarian vision of western America lay behind the welcome that New England gave Howells and the warm reception that Howells accorded Clemens. H. H. Brackenridge, Timothy Flint, Daniel Boone, Davy Crockett, Bret Harte, Joaquin Miller, Fenimore Cooper, and Edward Eggleston are among those who have been identified as being, in their different ways, importantly western; but those who chose Mark Twain to be the exemplary natural man did well, for Twain has exhibited unique appeal and staying power.

Western though Twain was, his easternization and *embourgeoisement* proceeded apace after he arrived in New York from San Francisco, for, like Howells, he was enamoured of a myth of the East: he informed friends, editors, and publishers that he wished to purify his writings in order to conform. He could not object, however, to being considered the prototypical western humorist. His early success depended on that identification; and he did not altogether disbelieve what he wrote in 1862 while in the West: "This is a great country—wide—vast—and in the southwest unlimited. . . . Europe! what is Europe? She is no whar, nothing, a circumstance, a cypher, a mere obsolete idea."[7]

Nor could Clemens have been unaware of or hostile to the theoretical implications of what Charles Henry Webb, a friend, said of him in the Sacramento *Union* in 1865 relative to a favorable notice of Twain in the New York *Round Table*: "They may talk of coarse humor, if they please, but in his case it is simply the strength of the soil—the germ is there and it sprouts good and strong."[8] Although Webb would hardly have known it, John Neal, the novelist, and Alexis de Tocqueville had offered similar remarks about American writing. Neal, who favored "natural writing," said in *Seventy-Six* (1823), that the American should match the roughness of his country with "coarseness,—that other name for great vigor, wild power, and courageous peculiarity." Tocqueville (1835) held that democracy fostered disorder and wildness in literature but also made it strong and bold.

Such observations reflect the early Romantic notion of geographical determinism and carry the implication that genuine literature, authentic literature, arises from the environment like a vapor or a chthonic spirit. Ideas of language forged a special link between Mark Twain and ideas of naturalness, Eden, and Adam. When Thoreau was idealizing the primitive, he judged that for the growth of a new literature, America must look to the West: "Already there is more language there, which is the growth of the soil, than here." In a curiously inverted, historicizing passage in "Walking," he ties the ancients to the moderns: Atlantis and the Hesperides, a sort of terrestrial paradise, "appear to have been the Great West of the ancients, enveloped in mystery and poetry." Others, too, looked to the West for a national bard. Margaret Fuller, like a good Transcendentalist, hoped to woo "the mighty meaning" of the primitive, almost satanically disordered western scene, "perhaps to foresee the law by which a new order, a new poetry, is to be evoked from this chaos."

For, as it is said in Genesis, the Lord formed man from the dust of the ground and put him in the garden and brought the beasts and the birds to the man to see what he would call them, and "whatever the man called every living creature, that was its name." Clemens, like the original man in the garden, has been treated by admirers as though he possessed the power to name. Critics have seen him as a new Adam in an ahistorical Western world, burning away the falsities of polite rhetoric with a new language, giving things their Cratyllian names, their iconic names, names possessed of the character of their objects.

In *Mark Twain's America* (1932), DeVoto explained that his effort was to perceive where and how Twain's books "issue from American life." *Tom Sawyer*, it would appear, is an instance of iconic naming: what "finds expression here is an America which every one knows to be thus finally translated into literature." Members of the eastern establishment are false and shallow; Clemens, the westerner, is authentic and natural. Looking backward ten years later, after having occupied himself for four and one-half years with the Mark Twain Papers (he succeeded Paine as editor), DeVoto confirmed in *Mark Twain at Work* that "much of what was great and fruitful in Mark Twain's books was an expression of a national experience."

That Hannibal, St. Louis, and the piloting years were partly or mainly southwestern and southern was apparently of no moment. New York, New England, and Europe had no bearing on this tale of a mythical determinism. America comes into existence at the frontier line, the frontier is the West, and the West is in some sense the Garden of the World. Twain and his writings were, it seems, not too late to be purely western, magnificently representative of the essential America.

Among later Twainians, Henry Nash Smith most elaborately and influentially portrayed America of the second half of the nineteenth century as corrupted by a depraved value system that exhibited itself in the sapless, colorless language used by polite writers. Like others, he identified Mark Twain as a redemptive hero who devised a new literary language. Extended, this meant that Twain introduced a new vernacular morality, a democratic ethos concordant with America's agrarian promises. It may be objected that this view neglects the extent to which writers other than Clemens—Emerson, Thoreau, Whitman, Dickinson—labored to invigorate the language and to restore national virtue. This view also neglects ideas about the arbitrary nature of language, the moral neutrality of language, the unstable nature of linguistic sign systems, and intertextuality.

A source for nearly all characterizations of Twain as admirably western may be found, rather curiously, in Howells, for Howells's own early models were Heine and Thackeray and, once in the East, he strove successfully to acquire the literary manners and ideals of James Russell Lowell. Lowell represented the best of the Old and the New worlds. In Ohio life had been free and moral but dull and crude. Europe, Howells decided on first experiencing the Continent, possessed a certain seductive charm: it had polish and picturesqueness; but vicious social and political systems supported passive, victimized masses and idle, immoral upper classes—"the young men are beasts." Lowell and Cambridge occupied a kind of ideal middle ground between Rome and the wilderness.

If Cambridge was everything that seemed admirable, it was not exactly the heartland of America. Perhaps because the central purpose of Howells's life was to discover the essential America and to represent it in fiction, he related the actual Wests of Mark Twain to an imagined, wild, innocent West that bore some resemblance to a Terrestrial Paradise. Howells's own West, which he also idealized, was a land of small towns and quiet villages. It was not until the late 1870s and the 1880s that a broadened, darkened conception of America forced him to turn away from dramatic-psychological novels on the model of Turgenev toward Balzacian, Zolaesque social novels intended to give expression to the problems of the individual in an industrialized society, in a gesellschaft that was neither free nor innocent.[9]

A limited parallelism may be established in the relations of Howells and Clemens to the East. To Lowell, the young Howells's delicacy and refinement justified American democracy; once Howells improved himself by study and by experiencing Europe, his western qualities would be a benefit, not a hindrance. In his turn, Clemens, too, was like the young frontier beauties with whom aristocrats fell in love in novels in the Leatherstocking tradition. The young women could be reconstructed into suitable mates by periods of polishing in seminaries or in upper-class families. So Clemens's crudities could be filed away by marriage to Olivia Langdon and by experiences in the East and in Europe. That Clemens needed such treatment was generally agreed on. While he was in the West, Bret Harte improved him. Mrs. A. W. Fairbanks, a friend and mentor beginning in 1867 (Clemens liked to call her Mother), corrected him. Mrs. Thomas Bailey Aldrich, wife of the novelist and editor, thought him, as he first appeared in Boston, to be untamed. Livy's mother agonized over the prospect of losing her daughter to an unmannered humorist who had lived a disordered, possibly immoral life. He did not at all fit into her conception of secure gentility.

Howells played a double role as the critic who gave a theory to American literature (adherence to the truths of American life) and a writer who consistently worked toward the Great American Novel. His generosity was such, however, that he recognized from the publication of *Innocents Abroad*

(1869)—he reviewed the book in the *Atlantic Monthly*—that Clemens merited serious treatment: in the life he had lived and in the language he used, he was broadly, genuinely western, more so than Howells himself, and therefore more American.

That Clemens in his inner self and in his outward expressions represented a free, democratic West became a cardinal article in Howells's literary creed. *West* as synonymous with *Nature* was not the Nature of Hobbes's war of all against all, where man's life is poor, nasty, and brutish, but as in imagery of the Garden of the World, where a hazily roseate conception has virtue at its heart. So much were easterners possessed by ideas of this kind about the West that Howells could call Harte's factitious confections novel and enchanting art from the soil and the air of the newest kind of new world.

For Americans in general, as for Howells in particular, Clemens became the incarnation of an ideal type and served an important programmatic function—he is almost *natura naturans*. That he claimed to be relatively unread in the European masters of fiction could be interpreted as indicating not ignorance but a fruitful innocence which enabled him to see the world as if he and it were newly born. His books were compact of morality, humor, and democratic candor. This conjoining of Mark Twain, the West, and Nature is Howells's great ideological legacy to later Twainians.

Howells published appreciations of many of Clemens's books as they appeared and added brief comments on some of them in several general essays, especially in his culminating tribute, "My Mark Twain" (1910). The effect of that ceremonious reminiscence is to draw attention away from the individual texts and to focus retrospective consideration on the man and the canon. More precisely, Howells describes and honors the spirit of the author and of his writings in their quintessential unity and westernness. Single works are subsumed under more comprehensive headings, alluded to from wider perspectives as illustrating the patriotic hopes of the nation. Twain's volumes neither exist nor need to exist in any literary tradition; their separateness is indicative of their uniqueness, their New World origin. The oeuvre, from *Roughing It* to *Joan of Arc,* is permeated by the American spirit, is sui generis.

Strains of Romantic primitivism mark what Howells has to say on order and unity in Clemens. When considered from logical or mechanical perspectives, Twain's individual texts lack coherence. Considered in the light of an implied version of the organicist conception of free order, his works are all the truer and more entertaining for their apparent disorderliness:

nature condones the apparently formless. Twain was simply not enslaved to consecutiveness; he practiced an inviting libertarianism in his sentences, his chapters, and in "the ordering or disordering of his compilations." When the parts are dissolved into the whole, which is how Howells presents the writings, a critic attuned to essences will see that whole as beautifully expressive of the author and of America. Writer, works, and nation come together in spiritual oneness. John Neal and Tocqueville would have approved this argument.

As Howells's ideas about American society shifted, he tended to assume that those of Clemens shifted in similar if not identical ways. It was not necessary, therefore, for Clemens to tug very hard at the strings of friendship to elicit from Howells the series of favorable reviews that helped to establish Clemens's literary reputation.

In fact, the thoughts and habits of Clemens were not always comparable to those of Howells. For one example, the East that compelled the devotion of Howells and the East that, together with some small contribution from Europe, reshaped Clemens were very different. In a sociological phrase, the two men subscribed to the values of different reference groups. Clemens did not dispute the eminence of the *littérateurs* of New England, though critics have thought he did, but he never made literary models of them nor was he much inclined to seek them out. He preferred the company of James Osgood, a small-town boy from Maine who became a Boston publisher and bon vivant, and of Henry Huttleston Rogers, the self-made millionaire, yacht owner, raconteur, and poker player. Howells mastered the *politesses*. Clemens retained evidences of the West in speech, manner, and personal habits even though his views were usually those of easterners of wealth and position or the sometimes warring views of the "enlightened" middle class—the closest thing that America had to an intelligentsia. Howells wrote for the sake of the writing and to make a living; Clemens often wrote—much as he speculated—with the accumulation of a fortune in mind.

Clemens was always ambivalent about easterly and westerly characteristics—the vernacular and the genteel, liberty and conformity—but the influence of the East on his writings is particularly manifest when his work is considered in social and intellectual rather than in purely formal terms, manifest though it is in the formal connection, too. The East meant, for example, the *Atlantic Monthly,* which Howells referred to not as a magazine in which good writing appeared but as a guardian of taste, "the most scrupulously cultivated of our periodicals," as though it were a normative social handbook.[10]

The West had encouraged Clemens to perfect himself in modes suitable for inclusion in newspapers in Nevada and in California, sketches that were audacious, humorous, and easy to read. But the West also encouraged in him a predilection for the forcedly clever, for Milesian tales, the irritatingly buffoonish, the flippant, the jejune, the bombastic, and the vulgar. The resulting oppositions in Clemens often produced a blurring of artistic vision, a failure to make lexical, rhetorical, and tonal distinctions, and a failure to balance or reconcile.

Eastern influences, like those of the West, were both good and bad. The East extended Clemens's literary, social, emotional, moral, and intellectual range. It encouraged book-length publications and moved him to prune vulgarities and to improve his diction and syntax. Traditional literary virtues were not well established, however, in the East, certainly not in the intellectual milieus that Clemens most frequented. Hawthorne, Emerson, Thoreau, Melville, Whitman, Dickinson, and James meant little or nothing to him; unless one takes his Nook Farm neighbors in Hartford to constitute a literary circle, he belonged to none. Howells was his only close associate who demonstrated anything like practiced critical intelligence.

The pernicious effects of genteel culture made themselves felt before Clemens left California—the West, too, had its fastidious inclinations. Early and late, the East bent him toward the timid, the pompous, and the pretentious, toward Landseerian sentiment, a showy rhetoric of declamation, and the false-sublime.

In part because Clemens actually was, as Howells indicated, the most nearly without great antecedents, great challenges, of all America's important writers, he was the most open to bad influences. As Harold Bloom has emphasized, writers contest against and feed upon other writers (no matter what objections an Emerson or a Howells may make to that practice), and Clemens's chief models for style, structure, and tone were all too easily mastered and surpassed: his roots were in southwestern humor, newspaper wit, cheap melodrama, stories for boys, commonplace magazines, and platform clowning. When he presented himself to the East in 1867, he had perfected his pastiches in the minor forms (tall tales, anecdotes, diatribes, hoaxes, pseudoletters, comic sketches) that were the standard products of the almost nameless writers and entertainers who preceded him. He had reached a point at which he was ready to authenticate a personal style, an authorial signature, and to attempt works of magnitude. His rate of prog-ress—except in money-making—was not, however, spectacular. After the enormously successful *Innocents Abroad,* an extended pastiche, he floun-dered until he hit by accident on the connected sketches for the *Atlantic* called "Old Times on the Mississippi" (1875).

Although Clemens kept a close eye on important eastern periodicals and was a voracious reader, his interest, as he and Howells both said, was not in fiction or in poetry. When he browsed in the supreme novelists of Britain or of Europe, he seems to have felt no compulsion to measure himself against them. He tended to dismiss them out of hand or to judge that they had nothing to offer him, and his loss was great. Bereft of a major tradition, his recourse was to the second-rate and the third-rate. This turned him toward burlesquing, hit or miss improvisations, self-plagiarism, and exploiting the qualities in his personae that lent themselves to caricature.

Yet, to have no masters (other, perhaps, than Cervantes) was not al-together a misfortune: Clemens could not suffer the enfeebling effects of possible subjection. Because he was not bound by exacting constraints, he could be spontaneous and, within limits, experimental. The best of his southwestern comic forebears, seeing themselves as recorders of social history, had striven to capture for the delight and instruction of future generations the passing manners and the speech of yeomen and frontiers-men. Their convenient, comfortable example helped validate for Clemens aspects of American life and American speech.

He defended rambling in his autobiographical writings, but he probably paid no substantial allegiance to theories favoring disorder in fiction. In his longer works, the coherence that may be achieved in ways that were standard tended to elude him; no impulse pressed him strongly toward integrity of plot and theme. His travel books and his fictions relied heavily on discoveries made when he stitched together *Innocents Abroad* from letters he had written for the San Francisco *Alta California,* the binding effect of the trip, of a vividly humorous persona, tonal alternations, and architectonic improvisation.

The quality of American individuality said to exist in Mark Twain could hardly be presented more admiringly and emphatically than it was by Howells when he wrote of Clemens's funeral,

> I looked a moment at the face I knew so well; and it was patient with the patience I had so often seen in it: something of puzzle, a great silent dignity, an assent to what must be from the depths of a nature

whose tragical seriousness broke in the laughter which the unwise took for the whole of him. Emerson, Longfellow, Lowell, Holmes—I knew them all and all the rest of our sages, poets, seers, critics, humorists; they were like one another and like other literary men; but Clemens was sole, incomparable, the Lincoln of our literature.[11]

Howells was abetted in these opinions by American, British, and European readers who saw Mark Twain as the prototypical American at his wisest and most humorous: by the time of Twain's death in 1910 he was established as a deity arisen from the Mississippi, brought to maturation in the Far West.

Many early reviewers who found offending traits—coarseness, ignorance, and irreverence were prominent among them—in Clemens attributed them to his western origins. Howells accepted no such charges. He omitted from his portrait of Clemens any elements of vulgarity, neuroticism, and aggressive self-seeking; he minimized an extravagant striving for effect, the insistently macabre, the cruel, and the mindlessly boisterous. His emphasis was on naturalness, truth to reality, generous humanity, good sense, love of justice and equality, hatred of arrogance and humbug. His Clemens is frank, manly, and shrewd.

In opposing allegations of western crudity, Howells spoke of morality and sensitivity: Clemens draws on life, not on Thackeray or on Dickens, for a serious humor with little or nothing in it to harm any reader. His very profanity was excited by such despicable objects that it had a kind of piety about it. The writings project the author's self, and "Clemens's central and final personality was something exquisite"; his strength and originality are softened by refinement; his instinct for right and wrong reminds one of the superior moral sense of women.

Most modern writers have portrayed Mark Twain and the West as vigorously masculine, but the elements of the feminine mentioned by Howells were not extraneous. Turner's "good" West, too, was feminine. The West that Howells pictured was, in fact, of its era in combining the virtues of the masculine and of the feminine. His Clemens, like a figure out of Shelley or like Tennyson's new man who is yet to come, was miraculously, pleasingly androgynous. This insistence on femininity was defensive, but it also reflected a standard feature of enlightened Victorian discourse about "the Woman Question." Each sex, it was said, should cultivate traits usually attributed to the other as primary. Thus they would draw closer together, would begin to approximate the unified moral being described by Plato when he depicts Aristophanes' myth of the primeval androgyne.

The closing lines of "My Mark Twain," quoted above, might be read as an undispassionate, emptily elegiac magnification of the merits of a friend, but in context they are the culmination of a determination that evolved over four decades to use Mark Twain in defining America. Howells's initial view of Clemens was, naturally, less firmly laudatory than was his final estimate. On May 13, 1876, for example, he wrote to Oliver Wendell Holmes praising Clemens; but he was at least semihumorously prepared to retreat if Holmes accused him of lack of discrimination. "What will you think of my taste," he asked, "when I tell you that I think Mark Twain's last, one of his very best? . . . It seems to me to go deeper than anything else he has written, and it strongly moved me from its serious side." If necessary in order to get a poem from Holmes for the *Atlantic,* however, he was prepared to revise his opinion of Clemens: "I felt obliged by my conscience to so much candor, but if what I say impeaches my judgment of your poem, pray believe me joking."[12]

At the end, Howells fitted Twain with an ideological halo that had been long in the making. He saw Twain not as necessarily greater than Emerson and his fellows but as superbly different, autochthonous; he was our American fabulist, our epic historian, our mythological romancer, our western self in all of its originality and universality.

How much or how little Clemens was western or eastern, a hero of the folk or an intellectual, relates to opinions on the depth and extensiveness of his reading; and our conclusions about his reading affect our notions about his general culture. Most of the early British reviewers, and many of the American, assumed that Mark Twain and other western humorists were ignoramuses in the world of letters—they belonged to a primitive stage of society. The humorists lent credence to a belief in their deficiencies by boasting of their lack of and distaste for eastern delicacies. In the case of Clemens, the supposition that he was unread has been strongly contested; yet it has also been argued that although he was rich in experience, he was deficient in culture, including the culture of books.

Clemens himself was responsible for some of the popular beliefs concerning his cultural impoverishment. He made depreciatory remarks about his reading and promoted the special value of knowledge acquired through experience. He did not, he said, care for fiction or read it, but he did like facts and statistics.[13] He read, he claimed, "little but the 'heaviest' sort of literature—history, biography, travels." After reading a novella by Grace King, the New Orleans writer who was also a family friend, he flattered the author by telling her that if he could have stories like hers to read his prejudice against fiction would die a swift death. He proclaimed to Howells his ignorance of standard literature: "You are really my only author; I am restricted to you; I wouldn't give a damn for the rest."[14] When Howells recommended novels, Clemens might try to read them, but he earnestly resisted writers as diverse as Jane Austen and George Eliot.

Apparently Clemens was correct when he claimed that he had little affection for fiction or poetry and that he was not well read in them. Observers who said much the same thing bolstered Twain's image as a natural man. When Howells asserted that Clemens remained for him the most unliterary in make and manner of all the literary men that he had ever known, he was construing *unliterary* to be creditable: Clemens possessed a precious kind of intelligent simplicity, and he mirrored life.

Clemens's attitude toward reading entered into his theories of composition. The writer, in his opinion, must not rely on books for his materials but on lived experiences, on "absorbing," and on devoted service to his craft. Making notes in 1888 for an (ultimately unwritten) article for the *New Princeton Review,* he decried building on totally imaginary incidents or situations. The writer should instead found his work on a *fact* in his personal experience and expand on that.[15] This recommendation implies strong positions on both art and reality; as Clemens informed a correspondent about 1890–93, he could have written novels for adults instead of books for boys: "I surely have the equipment, a wide culture; and all of it real, none of it artificial, for I don't know anything about books."

The "I don't know anything about books" disclaimer, unless narrowly interpreted to mean that he was not deeply read in the classics of English and continental belles lettres, is thoroughly misleading. It runs contrary to what he said at other times and, more important, to what is known about him.

Friends and reporters were sufficiently interested in Clemens's reading to set down remarks about it. Carlyle Smythe, who was a companion during part of Twain's tour around the world in 1895–96, wrote, "He has a gluttonous appetite for books, but his taste is the despair of his family and friends." Smythe noted that Clemens liked Browning but not other poets, admired Stevenson, read Kipling, and had no affection for Thackeray, Addison, Goldsmith, or Meredith. Perhaps significantly, Smythe blamed Clemens's failure to appreciate "the masters of literature" on his devotion to newspapers, for Clemens does seem to have given an inordinate amount of time to newspapers and magazines. Brander Matthews, in "Memories of Mark Twain" (1919), remarked that he was not surprised to find that Twain had not read *Gil Blas,* for he knew that Twain "was not a bookish man," not fond of fiction. To alleviate the "not bookish," Matthews added that Twain was a constant reader of history and autobiography.

Shortly after Van Wyck Brooks brought to a critical head doubts about Twain's general culture, a long string of rejoinders began to appear. Advocates arose for everything from the richness of folk art and the literary sophistication of the Mississippi Valley to the extent and depth of Clemens's reading. In 1922 Olin H. Moore declared false the notion that the writer's genius just grew, like Topsy, or that he was a self-made man, "self-made" being understood to mean "lacking in book learning." Americans, according to Moore, "like to think that Mark Twain, above all other authors, dug into the virgin soil of his native country, and brought forth rich treasures which could be found nowhere else"; but the truth is different. It will shock those, Moore said, "who have habitually fled to Mark Twain as a refuge from Europeanism to know that their favorite drew much of his inspiration for his most American books from European models." And because Twain's reading may be assumed to have made up in intensity for whatever it may have lacked in extensiveness, "he was therefore all the more likely to be influenced by his favorite authors." The evidence presented by Moore was slight, however, except as it touched on *Don Quixote*.

Minnie M. Brashear noted that Twain tried to create a legend of himself as an original. Dewey Ganzel remarked that Twain fabricated a persona as the natural man of the frontier; and Hamlin Hill indicated that Twain's popular persona was of "a groundling with some literary aspirations." Alan Gribben—after compiling a remarkably complete list of books owned, borrowed, or mentioned by Clemens—explained that Clemens's affectation of being an unread man may be attributed to his notion of what was expected of him and to the pleasure he took in having his public think his artistry spontaneous.[16]

Clemens was, in fact, widely read in a variety of fields. He at least looked at a great many books in English, a few in French, German, and, possibly, Italian. Most of his reading in French and German authors was in translation, to be sure, and the profundity of his reading in any field remains debatable. He has not been established as a close student of literature or as a *maître à penser*. Scanning the accounts of his reading or possible reading, one is struck by how few marginalia there are, by how little interest these scholia possess, and by how high a proportion of the books he knew were rubbishy and deservedly ephemeral.

Nor do Clemens's writings, including his letters, indicate that he was a highly discriminating reader, that he absorbed many difficult or important works. Everything suggests that his reading, though voracious, was hasty and intermittent: a favorable interpretation could be that he read, in Emerson's phrase, "for the lustres." The three volumes of Clemens's notebooks now in print bear witness that he kept voluminous notes with many of them intended for possible use in future publications but had, nevertheless, little of critical interest to say about his own work or about that of others. He mentions writers, alludes to books, but is almost never seduced into the briefest of contemplative, devotional, analytical, or combative remarks. His notes—whether on anecdotes or epics—that relate or could relate to his own writing are likely to have to do with theatricalities, as in a Greek romance: comic complications, strangely sentimental occurrences, melodramatic happenings, extraordinary coincidences, and astounding reversals.

In the bulk of these notes Clemens shows himself as having, if not inveterately, more regularly than one would wish, the habits of mind of the journalist and jokester. He excelled, of course, in mimicking the vulgate, and the most aesthetically reputable and potentially useful among these hundreds of notebook entries are a small number of phrases, sentences, and conversational exchanges transcribed from speech.

If any American writer stands as the principal hero of the myth of the West, that writer is Mark Twain. Popular images have borrowed, nevertheless, only vaguely from the strictly pastoral tradition or from legends of the frontiersman, more wildly anarchic than an Indian. Early notices presented him as a rough far-westerner, a Nevadan, a Californian. Later images tended to modernize him, to connect him with the excitement of silver mining, with technological marvels, gingerbread steamboats, and the agrarian postfrontier. These portrayals relate him to the conspicuousness of authorship, the lecture platform, inventing, and publishing. They show awareness that he was a comedian, wit, and, in the popular mind, social philosopher. Yet, the corrections do not obliterate the mythic figure. Twain has never lost the auricular proportions of nostalgically cherished heroes of the frontier.

AFFINES

AND

BUSINESS

3

▲ ▲ ▲ ▲ ▲ ▲ ▲ ▲ ▲

Little has been said—other than by familial memorialists—about Samuel Clemens's attitudes toward his wife's family, the wealthy Jervis Langdons, first citizens of Elmira, New York, but what has been said tends to be curiously contradictory and to take on wide, unjustified biographical and social significances. It is regularly assumed that Clemens's relationships with his Langdon affines were affectionately tensionless and that the Langdons had little or no lasting influence on him as man or writer. Paradoxically, it is also believed that he viewed with humanitarian horror the policies and practices of the coal business founded by his father-in-law. Each of these beliefs is mistaken.

In order to preserve the image of Mark Twain as the independent western hero, defensive critics have thought it important to insist that any influence exerted by the Langdons was minor and temporary. The point is accurately made that although during the period of his courtship Clemens tried to please the Langdons by assuming all of the conventional values and habits he soon neglected regular readings in sermons and the Bible, drank old-fashioneds, and returned to swearing, at least in private. It is also true that Olivia Langdon, who became his wife on February 2, 1870, edited from his writings little or nothing that he did not wish to be censored. But this is not the full story. When Clemens pursued his courtship of Livy, he confirmed that wealth and gentility were among the central choices of his life. Insofar as he had not already done so, he attempted to adopt the major secular ideals by which the Langdons lived. He probably never accepted their more conventionally religious views, although for a time he tried to.

Badly informed as Van Wyck Brooks was concerning the life and background of Clemens, when he wrote *The Ordeal of Mark Twain* (1920), his guesses about *mentalités* and pathologies, both personal and social, were in some large ways more accurate than have been many later portrayals. Clemens was, as Brooks argued, continuingly influenced by the Langdons; but this influence operated because Clemens was never a consistent social rebel; like the most bourgeois of the bourgeois, he delighted in money and high living, and he fervently wished to become a member of the eastern establishment. In many ways he could get along comfortably with the innocently provincial Langdons. They seem to have been unsophisticated but less socially and religiously hidebound than many have thought.

Although Clemens exaggerated when he said that he spent the larger part of his life on his knees making apologies for having offended against social conventions, his complaints about Livy's having to correct him and rein him in did become a rather bad, reiterated joke. Where money was concerned, he had in theory no need to apologize to anyone: he constantly sought riches, sought to be worthy of his own ambitions, of American ideals, and, following his marriage, of the Langdons.

To the tensions that existed because of Clemens's impieties, deficiencies in manners, western background, and comic sense, there must nevertheless be added those which arose simply because the Langdons were relatives-by-marriage. In this instance, the ordinary frictions recognized by anthropologists were probably intensified by what Clemens saw as the very solidity of his wife's family. He, himself, made quantities of money, but he was nearly always in debt. After Clemens came to know them, the coal-based, monumental, invulnerable Langdons never were.

Clemens, his daughter Clara, and A. B. Paine laid the groundwork for the assumption of untroubled family relationships by what they wrote and by what they refrained from writing; but they had no hand in promoting the idea that Clemens condemned Jervis Langdon and, by extension, American industrial capitalism. Those who have generated this misapprehension make Clemens out to have been, if not a kind of American Leveller, a sensitively ethical, discerningly compassionate analyst of capitalist society.

The marriage of Clemens, at thirty-five, to Olivia, then twenty-five, has been represented as the mating of a boisterous demigod out of the democratic West with an ethereal eastern gentlewoman—a miraculous combination of the physical and the spiritual. Most biographers from William Dean Howells forward have vied in portraying the blemishless nature of the marriage. Edward Wagenknecht, for example, writes that "the marriage of the Clemenses was a complete union of body, mind, and spirit. . . . If any man ever learned that marriage is both a physical and a spiritual relationship, the two elements blended in a perfect whole which excludes all thought of shame, that man was Mark Twain."[1] A sunny view of the Clemens marriage—though not quite this sunny—was one of the requisites for the protection of the image of Mark Twain: to be western and libertarian was essential, but from the middle of the eighteenth century forward, it helped if a hero was, among other things, a man of *sensibilité*.

Structural relationships in families, many of them involving gifts, tribute, debts, or dependency for housing, ensure that a husband's feelings toward affinal relatives are likely to be highly ambivalent.[2] In our own culture structural associations may be fewer and less obvious than in tribal societies, but they do exist. Young men who marry upward in the social hierarchy are made to feel the difference in status; marital relationships often extend to business relationships: money and authority are passed from one to another. Mother-in-law jokes and caricatures of mothers-in-law have wide currency; and Oedipal-like conflicts are transferable to the wife's father.

Freud notes, one-sidedly, that as the period of the honeymoon wanes, tensions will ordinarily arise between the husband and his bride. While the man is an infatuated suitor, he characteristically overvalues the mental achievements and perfections of his sexual object and accepts her judgments with a "credulous submissiveness resembling that of a hypnotized

subject," then has to modify his overvaluation and its effects on his behavior. Early passivity on the part of Clemens was, however, powerfully
reinforced by his social and professional desires—Livy was as much a
cultural symbol as she was a love-object. Publicly, Clemens never ceased to
idealize Livy.

Although the father-in-law commonly takes on the role of the repressive
father, this was not true for Clemens. After Langdon dismissed his early
doubts about Clemens, he became a friendly and permissive father. Mrs.
Olivia Langdon filled—certainly initially—the role of the depriving parent.
As Freud observes, anthropologists think the incest taboo explains stringent tribal customs having to do with avoidance of the son-in-law by the
mother-in-law. The institution of "marriage-by-capture" contributes to this
attitude of aversion, and it was by something like capture that Clemens
took the much-petted Livy. In "civilized" communities as well as in "savage" ones the relationship between son-in-law and mother-in-law may be
the most delicate point in family organization. The woman may be reluc-
tant to give up her daughter; she distrusts the stranger to whom she is
relinquishing the girl. The man wishes autonomy and is jealous of the
woman who possessed the affections of his wife before he did. Because the
similar features of the mother-in-law lack the charm of youth, it becomes
difficult for the man to continue in the illusory overvaluation of the wife
that arose from his sexual feelings.[3]

Clemens suffered from almost paranoid insecurity as well as mild megalomania; therefore, his expectable anxieties must have been heightened by
the extraordinary lengths to which he had to go to explain and defend
himself to the Langdons before they considered him to be possibly good
enough for their daughter. In a relatively placid part of his *Autobiography*
composed in February 1906, well after Livy's death in 1904, he remembered that his wooing had not been easy, swift, or unobstructed. "There
was a deal of courtship," he wrote; "there were three or four proposals of
marriage and just as many declinations."[4]

Letters exchanged with Olivia in March of 1869 touch on a revelation
that deeply wounded Clemens's amour propre. Livy informed him that on
his first two-weeks' visit to Elmira he had come close to wearing out his
welcome. He answered, "But for that remark of yours, I would always have
fancied that I was quite a pleasant addition to the family circle at that time."
While still brooding over Livy's reminiscence, he had a dream in which she
appeared to snub him. "The dream brought back to me," he wrote, appar-

ently contradicting himself, "my desperate temerity in venturing to locate myself for two weeks in a house where I was a stranger-& in what strong anxiety and dread I was at some times, that some humiliation might visit me in my defenceless position."[5]

Morality was more important to the Langdons than social status, but Clemens's crudities in dress and manners created problems for him as suitor. The family thought him to be a very rough diamond indeed before Olivia took him in hand; and the opinion of some easterners was much the same. Clemens was not simply western, he was vulgarly western. To the ineffably refined Lilian Aldrich (Mrs. Thomas Bailey Aldrich), he was a "novel Westerner"; he dared immeasurably in wooing a "white and fragile flower" who seemed so lightly to touch the earth that she belonged to "another sphere."[6] Clemens himself accepted the judgment that he desperately lacked cultivation; nevertheless, he was not always happy about the cutting and polishing that he—a rough diamond—underwent.

The Langdon money presented both attractions and problems. At the time that he married Olivia, the household expenses of the Langdons, living in inexpensive Elmira, ran to forty thousand dollars a year—ten to fifteen times the earnings of most middle-class persons. That Livy moved in an aura of money was one of her charms, for, as his correspondence shows, the idea of money was endlessly present in Clemens's thoughts. Yet Clemens—a proud, sensitive man—in theory at least disliked intensely the idea of dependency; and during his courtship he repeatedly denied that he was marrying for money or that he wanted money.

The second protestation ran strictly contrary to fact. Clemens paid extraordinary attention to money-making, spent lavishly, speculated wildly, and was almost constantly in need of Livy's money. It would be strange, indeed, if the Langdon bounty, received by way of Livy, would at all times have seemed to him to be a blessing and familial emollient.

The bulk of published evidence in letters, documents, and reminiscences would support the comfortable view that once the Langdons persuaded themselves that the Wild Humorist of the Western Slope might be a satisfactory suitor for Livy's hand they and Clemens came promptly and forever to satisfactory terms. Clemens is supposed to have fitted easily into the Langdon household as he spent periods there conducting his long-drawn courtship. It is assumed that he established himself on a footing of respectful camaraderie with Jervis Langdon, was suitably fond of Mrs. Langdon, and looked upon Livy's brother, Charles J. Langdon (nearly five years younger than she), with warmly avuncular affection.

Biographers who accept this portrayal of familial relationships are capable of accepting concomitantly the discordant supposition, referred to above, that a passage in a letter of February 27, 1869, from Clemens to Livy and the whole of one cuttingly ironic pseudo-letter directed against Andrew Langdon, Livy's first cousin, constitute evidence that Clemens was appalled at the heartless way in which Jervis Langdon and his associates conducted the affairs of J. Langdon & Company.[7]

An examination of essential details in Clemens's relationships with Langdon, his wife, and their son, and scrutiny of the documents that are supposed to reveal his humanely reformist distaste for the Langdon business enterprises demonstrate the inaccuracy of these widely received views.

Reasons for Clemens to have had mixed feelings toward the Langdons may be guessed at from general anthropological and psychological observations and from the barest outline of his association, especially his early association, with that family. About the middle of 1867, when he and Charles Langdon were fellow passengers aboard the *Quaker City*, he saw a miniature of Livy which allegedly moved him to fall in love. In a letter of March 1, 1869, he declared that it was revealed to him "in a single instant of time" when he first saw Livy—whether he means in fact or painted on ivory is not certain—that she was the only woman he could love with his whole heart. He first met Livy in person in New York on December 27, 1867, but approximately eight months elapsed before he got around to visiting the Langdons in Elmira and began to sue for her hand.

The Langdons turned him off, at first firmly: he was not the settled, dependable, religious kind of suitor they would have preferred. With what was for Clemens surprising patience, he went about the task of overcoming their stiff objections. His letters to Livy and to her parents are for the most part models of restraint, conciliation, agreement, and devotion. He assisted the Langdons in their investigation of his character and his past; he professed eagerness to give up his vagabond life, buy an interest in a newspaper, reform his habits—especially his drinking and his use of profanity—and learn to be a true Christian.

He propitiated the Langdons not because he was in love with love, as Dixon Wecter described his condition, but because—if it were not too painful for him—he wanted to be what they wanted him to be; he wanted their ethos to be his ethos, and he probably believed that their values were his values, as in fact most of their social values were. He intended to reconstruct and broaden the appeal of the Mark Twain he had invented—to modify his western buffoonery, add seriousness, and gain respect. This period of self-abasement was not, however, a placid one. In some ways, revising himself was neither easy nor permanent; he clung to certain habits and attitudes. He resisted with passion wearing a flower in his buttonhole in public, and he rebuffed suggestions that he stop smoking.[8]

Indeed Clemens may not have thought himself to be as blameworthy and inferior as he often said he was. As quoted by his friend George Wiley, he remarked during the period of the courtship that he was too rough for Livy but expected to persuade her to have him: "I never had wish or time to bother with women, and I can give that girl the purest, best love any man can ever give her."[9]

According to Annie Adams Fields, wife of James T. Fields, the Boston publisher, Clemens became angry when the Langdons tried to bribe him to give up smoking and drinking.[10] He also reacted strangely to what seems to have been a request that he help Susan Crane (Livy's sister-by-adoption) prepare a memorial tribute to a young neighbor. Instead he made a number of savagely burlesque recommendations for the memoir in a letter to Livy. His taste did not run along the required sentimental lines: "I'm no compiler of Wm Lord Noyes bosh. When *I* get up memoirs I make the deceased get up too—at least turn over."[11]

There were times, also, when surface calm concealed wounded pride and seething emotions. Following rejections of his suit by Olivia and her parents, Clemens wrote to his sister, Pamela Moffett, "*Now* you know why I was so savage & crazy in St. Louis. I had just been *refused* by my idol a few days before—was refused again afterward—was warned to *quit* after that—& have won the fight at last & am the happiest man alive."[12]

He had not at the time actually won the fight; he had won the provisional right to be a suitor. The Langdons were still uneasy about his character, his habits, his lack of a conventional occupation, and his brand of humor. Jervis Langdon apparently wrote asking Clemens to proceed slowly with his courtship while Langdon corresponded with persons who had known Clemens in the West. He also indicated that a joking allusion in one of Clemens's letters about going off into a drawing room with Livy was improperly suggestive. Clemens answered that he had been hurt by the reprimand: "I see that you mistook the harmless overflow of a happy frame of mind for criminal frivolity. This is a little unjust—for although what I said may have been unbecoming, it surely was no worse. . . . But I accept the rebuke."[13] This appears to have been the only exchange between Clemens and Langdon that was not genial.

Clemens's problems with Mrs. Langdon were thornier than those with her husband. On November 27, 1868, he wrote to Mary Mason Fairbanks asking her to visit the Langdons: "They want so much to question you about me." Four days later Mrs. Langdon extended her inquiry into Clemens's character by addressing confused questions to Mrs. Fairbanks. She did not wish to ask about his standing among men or to be assured that he was a man of genius or to know what kind of man he has been or is or is to become, but "from what standard of conduct, from what habitual life, did this change, or improvement, or reformation, commence?" Does the change make of an immoral man a moral one?[14]

Clemens thanked Mrs. Fairbanks for her reassuring reply to Mrs. Langdon; and, after he and Olivia had become "irrevocably" engaged on February 4, on February 13 he, too, addressed a long, defensive letter to Mrs. Langdon. He insisted that he neither drank nor swore, claimed to be a Christian, had been unjustly defamed simply because he was a public man, did not wish to marry Olivia for her money, and would not be depraved enough to ask her to marry him yet awhile if he could not support her comfortably. He intended, moreover, to paddle his own canoe. A passage in this letter alludes to what seems to have been heavy-handed jesting by Charlie: "We won't come back & billet ourselves on the old home, & have Charley charging us for board 'on the European plan' as he is always threatening to do with me when I linger there a few days. That's a shot for Charley!"[15] In later years Clemens's letters to his mother-in-law tend to be playful but respectful in tone and include many protestations of affection and gratitude.

Clara Clemens, who was too protective of the family's reputation to be a reliable witness, may nonetheless be partly accurate in saying that Mrs. Langdon was "a strong and lovable personality. She ruled in the house, but she carried a scepter of love. . . . Generosity was one of her salient characteristics."[16] Others have testified that Mrs. Langdon had a strong personality and that her preoccupation with her own ill-health verged upon the neurotic. She was, indeed, generous with gifts, including gifts of money; and Clemens was compelled to borrow ten thousand dollars from her in 1890.[17] Everything considered, it seems possible that she grated on Clemens; and one may be sure that he did not enjoy having to ask her for money as his publishing house, Webster & Company, moved toward bankruptcy.

Except for two possibly antagonistic references, Clemens is noncommittal on the rare occasions when he mentions Mrs. Langdon in letters written not to her but to others. In view of the affection that he expressed for several women that he called mother, this in itself may indicate a lack of rapport. That Mrs. Langdon was difficult may be hinted in letters of September 2, 1870, and of December 12, 1886. In the first, written a little less than a month after Jervis Langdon's death, Clemens tells Mrs. Fairbanks that "Mrs. Langdon is with us & is reasonably well contented."[18] In the second he explains to William Dean Howells his inability to introduce a speaker in Boston. It would, he says, be unsuitable for him to do so; in addition, there would be company in the house, "& among them a relative whom I must fairly & honorably divide up with Mrs. Clemens: to place that whole burden on her shoulders for twenty-four hours would not be a slight thing but a cruelty." The relative was Mrs. Langdon, supposed by editors to have been at this point almost an invalid.[19] Assuming that Clemens is not using Mrs. Langdon in place of some less acceptable excuse and that Mrs. Langdon was in fact almost an invalid, it is unlikely that Livy needed physical help: the house was as usual swarming with servants.

Clemens's emotional situation vis-à-vis Charles Langdon must have been decidedly clouded at times. When the two first met on the *Quaker City* in 1867, Charlie was not quite eighteen, and Clemens considered "the Cub," as he called him, to be "pleasant, & well meaning, but fearfull green & as fearfully slow." An attempt by Charlie to advise Clemens at the card table is said to have caused Clemens to say, for example, "Young man, there's a prayer-meeting forward in the dining saloon and they need you there." During the voyage, however, Charlie's admiringly persistent intrusiveness is supposed to have won Clemens over.[20]

Travel letters to the *Alta California* suggest that in Clemens's view the early relationship remained very much one of superior and inferior. In the *Alta* the young man nicknamed "the Interrogation Point" (whom scholars identify as Charlie) is called "a born ass" and is classed with the ridiculous "poet lariat" as an annoyance to everyone on board. He is "not forthcoming" when the time comes to pay a mule driver in Gibraltar; and he "dickered and fussed" over paying "a poor devil of an Arab" for some fruit until "some of the passengers snatched him away and threatened to hang him."[21]

Clemens made extensive changes in letters to the *Alta* as he converted them to use in *Innocents Abroad,* and Livy censored many, possibly all, of the proofsheets. Nevertheless, in chapter 7, using language from his notebooks, Clemens describes the Interrogation Point as "young and green, not bright, not learned, and not wise." He also makes the youth the butt of two anecdotes, one as a naif taken in by a tall tale, the other as a foolish chauvinist badgering educated British officers at Gibraltar with braggadocio about America. The characterization is only slightly less derogatory than that offered in the *Alta*. Could the identification of Charles as the Interrogation Point be an error?

In Elmira, at any rate, the tables were rather turned. Charles, a pampered only son, was happy to introduce his rough but famous friend to his family; but if recollections in the community are correct, he opposed the engagement of Clemens to Livy. He would not, it is said, have invited Clemens to Elmira if he had known that his friend would fall in love. He was taken aback at the thought of Clemens "as the life companion of his adored and precious sister," and when Clemens first declared himself to be in love, Charlie encouraged him to leave.[22]

The year after Clemens's marriage the positions of the two men underwent a definitively hourglass reversal. Charlie became an authority-figure. Although only twenty-one, at the death of Jervis Langdon he took over almost complete control of the family's business interests. He was paymaster to Olivia and protector of her capital. Additional stresses became inevitable beginning during the late 1880s as Clemens's financial difficulties mounted and he turned to the Langdons for money.

Charlie was prudent and skeptical. He was unwilling to risk his capital in the losing ventures that fascinated and ultimately ruined Clemens; and he is said to have looked with anguish on the uses to which Livy's shrinking patrimony was being put. Opposition of the kind offered by Charlie was almost sure to have been keenly resented by Clemens.

A few details will suggest the problems that arose about money. According to Clemens, "Toward the end of Feb. '89" he offered Charlie a one-hundredth interest "in the U.S. business of the Paige Compositor for $25,000, or a lesser share at the same rate; same offer to Theodore Crane." (Clemens has been said to have thought Theodore, husband of Olivia's adopted sister, Susan, to be a mediocrity. Susan later invested five thousand dollars in the typesetter.) Although Charlie eventually put up three thousand dollars, he resisted making any loan or investment. On August 31, 1890, he pointed out that over a period of three summers Clemens had repeatedly been wrong about when the machine would be ready to operate, and he sailed with his family for a stay in Europe, leaving a frantic Clemens to continue his search for assistance. On August 15, 1893, after securing

Charlie's promise to "take up" two notes and to endorse another, Clemens wrote to Fred J. Hall, then in charge of his publishing company, that he was grateful to Charlie, "but heaven knows, I am sorry we had to ask him."[23]

It must be said, however, that Clemens's letters to Charlie, like his letters to Mrs. Langdon, do not show anger or acrimony. They do suggest that in the end Charlie became a father-figure to whom Clemens felt it necessary to justify himself. In a letter written during Livy's final illness, Clemens reported on the care that she was getting. After her death he expressed contrition for the poverty that he had brought upon her and spoke of her forbearance; but in the end he worked himself around, as he usually did, to suppressing his guilt and expressing a generalized spirit of bitterness and rebellion.[24]

In 1893, during one of Clemens's many financial crises, Henry Rogers advanced him the eight thousand dollars that he desperately needed to fend off creditors. Because of this help from Rogers, Clemens was able to tell Sue Crane that she need not send him the five thousand dollars in negotiable bonds that she had managed to raise in answer to his plea for eight thousand dollars. He could also release Charlie from a promise to endorse one of his notes. Clemens was forced, nevertheless, into bankruptcy in 1894. On June 27, 1895, Livy wrote to Rogers, who had taken over the direction of Clemens's muddled affairs, suggesting that thirty thousand dollars coming to her from Charles be used to settle things with Clemens's still importunate creditors but added that Charles "would not approve of this plan I know because he has felt very sorry to have my income so cramped as it has been by the machine and Webster & Co."[25]

In 1898—with creditors more or less paid off—Clemens exhibited an almost hysterical enthusiasm as he turned again to speculating. Just at this point Charlie made a nine-day visit to the Clemenses in Vienna and proved to be as unsympathetic to Clemens's new speculative interests as he had been to the prebankruptcy ventures. Charlie, as Clemens informed Rogers, was not attracted by the carpet-design machine that was to make the Clemenses (and Rogers, too, if he would only invest in it) spectacularly rich. So indifferent was Charlie that Clemens did not even try to encourage him to buy shares in a second invention, one that had already begun to engage Clemens's rapt attention.[26]

Clemens's repeated assertions of his intention to be financially independent contrast sharply with his actual situation. Before he and Livy were married he accepted from Jervis Langdon a loan of $12,500 to pay for one-half of the interest that he bought in the Buffalo *Express,* accepted the gift of a furnished house at the time of his marriage, attempted to interest Langdon in the large tract of Tennessee land that the Clemens family long hoped would make them wealthy, and after the death of Langdon regularly received sums due to Olivia from the Langdon coal properties. And, of course, during Clemens's various financial crises, he petitioned the Langdons for loans and endorsements.

A letter of June 27, 1878, to Howells written from Heidelberg contains a barely legible cancellation that appears to be evidence that even at that early date Clemens was sensitive about his dependence on the Langdons. He had, he wrote, good news: after having been in need off and on for two years, "we've quit feeling poor!" Then came the canceled passage: "Well, the annual report of the coal firm came yesterday, & with that as a basis . . ." This was followed by the information that the Clemenses discovered that they had more than enough income from investments to live in Hartford on a generous scale and concluded, "Well, now that we are fixed at last, of course the communists & the asinine government will go to work & smash it all." Livy had inherited "a substantial interest" in her father's company upon his death, and the company was probably recovering from effects of the panic of 1873. The reason for Clemens's cancellation would appear to be obvious: he preferred not to reveal his dependence on the Langdons even to Howells.[27]

Apparently Clemens's marriage to an heiress deepened an ambivalence about money that existed earlier. He regretted the national lust for gold, but he inveterately sought wealth. It has been said that what he knew of the Langdon enterprises fostered in him a strong ethical antagonism for them and that although he might for personal reasons praise Jervis Langdon or Henry Rogers, he took on principle a sharply critical view of industrial capitalism. As I have said earlier, evidence does not support such suppositions.

Clemens addressed a somewhat puzzling letter to Livy on February 27, 1869, fourteen days after he had written his vigorously defensive epistle to Mrs. Langdon. In the interim he had visited the Langdons in Elmira (February 19–22), gone to New York City with Jervis Langdon, and begun a lecture tour. The ambiguously teasing passage in his letter follows a humorous paragraph in which he speaks of not finding Mrs. Henry Brooks, a friend of the Langdons, at home in New York. Not seeing Mrs. Brooks suited Clemens, because he "preferred to talk to Mr. Langdon, anyhow—for I love him, & I only *like* Mrs. Brooks." Possibly with the idea in mind of familiarizing Clemens with the family business, Langdon had invited his prospective son-in-law to sit with him in his hotel room and meet some of his associates. Clemens makes the occasion one for humor, speaking of the men he met as "abandoned coal-heavers," "suspicious looking pirates," and "a notorious character by the name of Slee, from Buffalo." Then follows an account of "the Captain's case." The Captain wants his salary raised, simply because he has a large family to support and because his rent is being raised. "It is plain enough," Clemens argues, "to *any* noodle that that family has got to be reconstructed. Therefore, the salary will remain just as it is, & Mr. Slee will proceed to cut down the Captain's family to fit it. Business is business, you know.

"Mr. Slee gave me a very cordial invitation to visit his home in Buffalo, & I shall do it, some day. I like him first-rate."[28]

Dixon Wecter had no doubt about the interpretation of the central passage, remarking in a footnote, "For Mark's later reflections on the ruthlessness of the coal business in Buffalo, see 'Letter from the Recording Angel.'" (I turn to those "later reflections" below.) It is difficult to suppose that Wecter would have misread the first sentences of this letter. All is standard Twainian fun (anticipatory in mode of the Whittier Birthday Speech of December 1877) until we reach the mention of the Captain. Wecter seems to have supposed that at that point Clemens shifted to satire of a Swiftian kind, seriously condemning the inhumanities practiced by managers of the coal business, and continued, paradoxically, by saying that he liked Mr. Slee.

This reading would validate the unbelievable argument that Clemens, the eager probationer, threw caution and propitiation to the winds and, moved by humanitarian sentiments, followed up his earlier, glancing "shot for Charley" with a mortar shell aimed directly at the sacrosanct chief of the Langdon family, Clemens's ally and a man for whom in this same letter, in the *Autobiography,* and elsewhere he expressed respect and affection. If Olivia and her parents had taken this letter to be a satiric attack, Olivia could not have married Clemens. And for Livy to have concealed the letter from her family is equally unthinkable.

Other interpretations are easily conceivable. For Livy's possible bewilderment and for Jervis Langdon's amusement, Clemens could have fantasized a scene that never took place. Or the Captain may have been offered an increase. Or the Captain may have had no family. Or the passage may extend a joke that began in family conversations in Elmira. Another possible explanation is that an actual Captain performed his duties inefficiently or corruptly, for the letter carries on with additional ambiguous remarks, saying that the Captain "is altogether too valuable. He not only transacts all the duties that belong in his department, but he transacts a little of everything that comes along. And maybe you won't believe it, but he has been selling hundreds of dollars worth of coal on *tickets*—(hence the term 'on tick').—He sold a lot of Demurrage & other stuff on tickets to a Canadian mining company years ago, & they have got that plunder yet."

The probability is strong that by burlesque dispraise Clemens stresses the respectability of the coal merchants; by burlesquing Swiftian satire in support of the Captain, he attacks the ignorance and sentimentality of those who think that J. Langdon & Company has no heart. Without more knowledge of the immediate context, it is impossible to say with certainty how the letter was meant to be read in detail, but in the light of the whole and of Clemens's later actions and attitudes toward Langdon and his business dealings, we may be positive that it is a mistake to interpret it as an attack on a rapacious Jervis Langdon or on his coal business or on capitalistic enterprise.

Langdon and his company had their foes and may have deserved condemnation, but Clemens made plain that he did not stand among the hostile critics. He spoke with respect of Langdon and of Slee in letters and in his *Autobiography*. As an editor and part owner of the Buffalo *Express*, he tried to help Langdon collect $500,000 allegedly due him from the city of Memphis, Tennessee, on a paving contract. By promising to return the favor, he cajoled Whitelaw Reid, of the New York *Tribune*, into editorializing on this paving matter.[29] The Anthracite Coal Association, a regional cartel dedicated, it is said, to keeping prices up, consisted of J. Langdon & Company and the Delaware, Lackawanna & Western railway. When critics of the practices of the cartel sent condemnatory letters out to newspapers, Clemens made clear to his fiancée in a letter of September 3, 1869, that his sympathies were with the cartel and that as a part-owner of the *Express* he, too, was a businessman:

> Another of those anti-monopoly thieves sent in a long gratuitous advertisement to-night, about coal "for the people" at $5.50 a ton—I have deposited it under the table. . . . Day before yesterday there was a sneaking little communication in one of the other papers wondering

why the Express had become so docile & quiet about the great coal monopoly question. If Mr. Denther don't go mighty slow I will let off a blast at him some day that will lift the hair off his head & loosen some of his teeth. Good-bye little sweetheart—I've lost my temper now.[30]

Clemens also defended the cartel directly in an article entitled "The Monopoly Speaks" that calls the public naive and attributes the high price of coal to market pressures. Dixon Wecter, without attempting to explain why Clemens would, as Wecter assumes, satirize Langdon and condemn J. Langdon & Company on February 27 and defend them on September 3, comments, "Mark's loyalty to persons always transcended his comprehension of business principles, as he demonstrated many years later in defending Standard Oil against all comers because its ruthless Henry H. Rogers had befriended him in an hour of need." In fact the temper of Clemens's mind with respect to capitalism and social inequity was elitist and simplistic, as may be seen from his animadversions in 1879 on communism and on the people of South Ireland as contrasted with Jews.[31]

The pseudoletter mentioned above attacking Andrew Langdon is repeatedly cited as helping to demonstrate Clemens's shocked distaste for Jervis Langdon's supposedly remorseless profiteering. Bernard DeVoto, who put the piece into print in 1946, gave it the title "Letter from the Recording Angel."[32] (Clemens read—or read in—*Tristram Shandy*; so it seems likely that the Recording Angel comes from Sterne.) In 1939 Clara forbade the publication of a small collection that included this item; and it is not likely that she approved the first printing in 1946. Nor could members of the Langdon family have been pleased to have their cousin Andrew called among other depreciatory things "the meanest white man on the face of the earth."

The letter was probably composed in 1887. DeVoto established 1888 as the latest possible date for its composition, as Clemens (changing the name of the man attacked to Abner Scofield) then tried unsuccessfully to work the piece into the manuscript of *A Connecticut Yankee in King Arthur's Court* (1889). DeVoto misidentified Andrew Langdon as Livy's uncle (he was her first cousin) and was followed in that error by Wecter and others. And although DeVoto did not say that the letter was an attack on J. Langdon & Company as well as on Andrew Langdon, he gave indirect support to that idea by suggesting that the letter might be connected with an entry in the notebooks (August 1887) in which Clemens expressed surprise over the recent high profits of a Langdon colliery.

The "Letter from the Recording Angel" flaying Andrew Langdon must be accounted one of Clemens's small literary triumphs. The castigation of an individual is an antique minor mode in which Clemens excelled, practicing it assiduously in letters, newspaper sketches, the Autobiographical Dictation, and elsewhere. A number of his diatribes succeed (even when we know nothing of the individuals abused) because of their energy of language and their biting imagery. These diatribes are, as a rule, sufficiently brief to give the impression of being impromptu. The humor of schadenfreude entails hazards, however, as when we recognize that the sound and the fury exceed what is appropriate. Although we may laugh, we are also embarrassed when Clemens lets himself go to irrational extremes. We draw back from the excess, for example, when he condemns a proofreader as a goddamned ass, an idiot, blind, and partly dead, who can't see anything, because "he is blind and dead and rotten and ought to be thrown into the sewer."[33]

The "Letter," which gives the impression of originating in personal emotion and of being clarified by a systematic working out as a literary exercise, becomes a criticism of society in selected aspects and has a touch of maxim-writing about it. More than a simple eruption, it runs to approximately nineteen hundred words and cannot depend solely on boldness and spontaneity. Lacking a known, concretely significant object, it relies for its effect on its literary excellence and our general approval as it opposes religious hypocrisy, miserliness, and gouging in business.

By ironic inversion—generosity is equated with miserliness, praise with blame—and by letting the Recording Angel review the prayers and deeds of Andrew Langdon, accusations and implied depreciations are set at a distance. Langdon is indicted for his secret maledictions voiced against those who would encroach upon his business or prevent his making excessive profits or otherwise annoy him; for hypocritical expressions of piety; for pretended sympathy for the poor and distressed; and, as a climactic charge, for the niggardly assistance he, a wealthy man, has rendered to a destitute female relative and her family. Heaven, knowing Andrew and expecting absolutely nothing good from him, rejoices at his grudging donation to the widow. Irony enough, but in the last words Clemens manages a characteristic heightening: "Abraham, weeping, shook out the contents of his bosom and pasted the eloquent label there, 'Reserved'; and Peter, weeping, said, 'He shall be received with a torchlight procession when he comes'; and then all heaven boomed, and was glad you were going there. And so was hell."

The compounded irony of the four concluding words is the economical contrivance of an accomplished showman. The final turn, the jokesmith's snapper, resembles the conclusion of Clemens's Golden Arm story, a platform gem with which he regularly brought edgy front-row members of an audience to their feet. The climactic ending may be criticized as lacking in subtlety; sophisticated critics could think that a crudity in structure parallels a coarseness of purpose; it is too easy, too melodramatic. It would not satisfy the demands posed by Baudelaire in "De l'essence du rire" for the *dédoublement* of the *comique absolu*. In the literary and social context, however, the final sentence may hardly be censured.

Clara eventually withdrew her objections to the volume of short pieces containing the "Letter" that DeVoto wished to publish in 1939; and the volume was published as *Letters from the Earth* (1962). In 1952 Wecter included the "Letter from the Recording Angel" in a collection of short pieces and attempted to prove what he had only implied earlier, that Clemens was unhappy about the excessive profits made by a subsidiary of J. Langdon & Company. To establish this interpretation, Wecter, like De-Voto, quoted notebook entries showing sums paid to Livy and mentioning the success of a new colliery, but this evidence proves to be diaphanous.[34]

Paul Baender, the most recent editor of the "Letter from the Recording Angel," points out that the DeVoto-Wecter argument is both weak and "irrelevant in light of the fact that Andrew Langdon had no connection with J. Langdon & Company." Langdon, a successful man with many business interests, was also something of a philanthropist and is not likely to have been at all well known by Clemens. Two brief notes from Clemens to Langdon have turned up, one dated November 2, 1900, the other January 21, 1901. They have bearing only because of their cordial tone. In the first, Clemens declines an invitation to an unspecified event; and in the second he apologizes for being out when Langdon called.[35]

To explain the attack on Andrew Langdon remains a problem. If Andrew had nothing to do with J. Langdon & Company, Clemens would have known this; and the attack would have been a very confused way of reflecting adversely on that company, on the long-dead Jervis Langdon, or on Charles Langdon. Clemens expressed satisfaction, not shock, as we shall see, at large profits made by J. Langdon & Company. A possible occasion and a motive have been suggested by Andrew Langdon's grandson and namesake, who believes that in 1887 Clemens tried to enlist his grandfather among backers of the Paige compositor and was angry at being refused.

Baender remarks that if Clemens did approach Andrew Langdon and was turned down it would have been typical for Clemens "to characterize Langdon as a gross egotist and hypocrite, already a common sort of figure in his vilifications after real or imagined insults."[36] If good reason for personal animus existed in 1887, Clemens seems to have forgotten it by the time of his note of November 2, 1900.

By accepting and expanding on misreadings of the letter as an attack on Jervis Langdon and J. Langdon & Company, Wecter, Justin Kaplan, and others adjust Clemens's mind and, in this instance, one of his better pieces of abuse to the support of an image of the writer as warmhearted, sometimes angrily equalitarian, and quick to perceive faults in profit-oriented capitalism even when the faults appeared in members of his wife's immediate family and in the business on which he and Livy depended for a substantial portion of their income.

The optimistic image of Clemens thus projected provokes significant misapprehensions concerning his attitudes toward important aspects of capitalism in America. DeVoto's small error in interpretation becomes a grave biographical misconception. Even Kaplan, a relatively revisionist biographer, so misconstrues the case as to suppose that Clemens from the year of his engagement saw the family business as exploitative and was troubled by the implications of his approaching membership-by-marriage in the minor plutocracy. This is an inversion of the actual situation: Clemens was desperately eager to join that plutocracy.[37]

As invented by his biographers, Clemens has been converted to agree with protective and heroizing postulates. If the usual portrayals were accurate, they would imply that from 1869 to 1887 and beyond he hypocritically concealed his anger at the cruelty and rapacity of kinsmen and that he was willing to make use of money derived from sources that he condemned on ethical grounds. In truth, he was neither antibusiness nor a populist hero.

He suffered from extraordinary tensions, but they were not those one might expect to find in a thoughtful critic of an unbridled market economy. To him, capitalism as represented by Jervis Langdon was the reverse of deplorable; it was a necessary aspect of the ideal social order. Despite his asserted liking for a simple, natural life and his expressions of nostalgia for a time when individual heroism was possible, over much of his life Clemens believed in a version of the Idea of Progress, grounding his faith principally in technological innovation. His conception was more conservative than liberal; innovation would make shrewd men wealthy and would bring old-fashioned order back into a disorderly world. The tensions between him and the Langdons had nothing to do with the Langdons' hypothesized deficiency in business rectitude. The humorist seriously assured and reassured his future parents-in-law that his ego ideal was identical with their ego ideal, his ethos with their ethos. Although he could not live up to these ideals completely, at conscious levels his protestations and guarantees were sincere.

Clemens was what Freud would call a narcissistic suitor: he ardently wished to marry a woman who typified not what he was but what he wished to be—rich and possessed of status, a member of the eastern social order. In pressing to win Olivia, he abased himself in ways that were demeaning to his ego. So long as the Langdons doubted his worth, they played the role of castrating parents; and his resultant moods could be savage. They made his wounded narcissism whole again only when they removed the obstacles that they had put in his way and, by giving him his object-choice, indicated that they esteemed him.

Continuing shocks to Clemens's narcissism arose from causes inherent in being a son-in-law, particularly a son-in-law who asserted independence but was in fact dependent. The family of the wife is inevitably in certain fashions taboo to the husband; and that which is taboo is sacred, powerful, and dangerous, a focus of special interest and anxiety.[38] New as the Langdon fortune was, it had been achieved before Clemens met the family. Fortune and the affinal relationship made the Langdons in Clemens's eyes potent and impregnable, a caste apart. Through their benefactions he became, as he remarked, following the gift of a house in Buffalo, "little Sammy in fairyland," but he found it difficult to see his fairyland as substantial and permanent. Because in many ways he never matched the Langdons, emulation of them probably reinforced his drive toward wealth and his tendency to wallow in guilt.

By contrast with the Langdons, Clemens was forever the arriviste. As his business affairs went all awry, even Livy's generosity and sympathy—in certain respects she *was* an ideal Victorian wife—could not blank out the affective significance of his monetary indebtedness to her; he reiterated his shame and guilt. As Livy lay dying in Florence, he felt impelled to give repeated assurances to Charlie that no expense was being spared in his efforts to care for her. Yet, strangely, his grief at her death did not prevent his quarreling with the physician who attended her or his refusing to pay the full amount of the bill.[39] As *he* lay dying in his Connecticut mansion, he insistently spelled out to his only surviving daughter, Clara, who returned from Europe in time for the death, the elaborate financial provisions he had made on her behalf, provisions which in fact ensured that she would be rich, for his estate was valued at over $541,000. "He was pathetically anxious to inform me about the financial state of affairs, expressing regret that there was less than he had hoped there would be," Clara wrote. "He appeared skeptical also as to whether the sale of his books would continue for more than a brief period after his death. I was too much moved by this evidence of his lingering care for me to trust myself to speak."[40]

Gestures like these toward financial competence and emotional probity must have signified to Clemens that—contrary to what the course of his life might have led others to think—he was responsible as he and presumably the Langdons conceived of responsibility. Despite his continuing speculations and thanks in large part to Henry Rogers, his business affairs did fall into a semblance of order. He was no longer in debt to anyone, except in a sense to Livy, for part of his new fortune came from her. His royalties mounted. He could act as an authority-figure himself: indeed, he tyrannized, and not always mildly, over Isabel Lyon, Paine, and others under his dominion. To his satisfaction, it seems, Miss Lyon and a few additional intimates called him the King. To the public he was a larger-than-life, drawlingly genial social philosopher, an amusingly cantankerous national icon.

Yet Clemens was not the confident, autonomous individual that he appeared to be. He was oppressed by searingly guilty memories of inferiority, borrowings, and failures. His daughter Jean could consider him to be horrid; Clara could at once make free with his money and flout his desires. Up to the end he seems to have been trying to live up to what he took to be the Langdons' expectations of him, to realize the role he had chosen. But even though he chose to be rich and genteel, a case might be made for thinking that his mature life was a mélange of tensions or, in Eriksonian terms, one extended identity crisis. He was a poor boy who married into a rich family, a recovered bankrupt, a transplanted savage, a western comedian wooing readers accustomed to the unruffling humor of Lowell and Holmes. It could be argued that he remained a culturally marginal man.

Although he approximately achieved the aspirations to wealth, fame, and love that he entertained as a youth and pursued throughout his maturity, from the 1870s on he doubted the justice of God, if there were a God, and from 1896 to the end of his life he believed that he, solitary, not certain whether he dreamed or woke, faced a hostile universe. When his daughter Susy was six and was oppressed by dreams of a ferocious bear, she complained that she was never the one that ate, but always the one that was eaten.[41] Clemens became in his own eyes a heroically rebellious, interminably suffering Promethean figure, forever being eaten, not like a little girl by a bear in a passing dream, but mythically, by the eagle of Zeus. His transformation from being a bold new Adam irrupted from a prelapsarian paradise was complete.

ART

AND

MONEY

▲ ▲ ▲ ▲ ▲ ▲ ▲ ▲ ▲

That western American comedy should distress conservative critics during the middle of the nineteenth century was inevitable. Art was usually seen as distinctively a product of high civilization: western comedy was barbarously of the Pacific Slope. Mark Twain could be classified only as vulgar; and vulgarity and art were incompatible. But as applied to Mark Twain, such conservative doctrines were never universal; taste changed and relaxed, and in time, by a reversal of doctrine and of polite opinion, *Huckleberry Finn* was placed among the masterworks of the immortals and Twain's writings in general gained respect.

Although the question of the vulgarity of Clemens's art is not now much debated, his personal characteristics, literary reputation, and image as a hero are far from being fixed. The problematic of the relationship of the man to his art has several centers, one of them being money. At issue are the reasons for his passionate pursuit of money, the effect this preoccupation had on his life and writings, and the bearing that it may have on his currently received image as a saint of the vernacular.

Some historians have supposed that Americans (almost like Australians) are lonely, bereft of comforting traditions, facing a land more hostile than welcoming, surrounded by persons who, like themselves, incline to be more discrete, predatorial, and acquisitive than associative and supportive. Opinions differ as to when and to what degree pre-Revolutionary and post-Revolutionary Americans were "Whiggish," "liberal," or some combination of the two. Quantitative analyses show, however, that in some localities early settlers were decidedly liberal, valuing individual freedom and material gain over public interest. By the time of the Revolution, land speculation and individual venturing were, some think, a way of life.[1] Clemens not only accepted this liberal acquisitive mode but intensified it.

In *De la démocratie en Amérique* (1835–40), Tocqueville declared that in aristocracies writers labor diligently for little gain, other than reputation, in order to please demanding readers. In democracies the number of readers is prodigious, but they are undemanding; a writer can readily win a mediocre reputation and a large fortune. Democracies therefore breed writers who make literature not an art but a business, who are less artists than merchandizers of ideas: "Les littératures démocratiques fourmillent toujours de ces auteurs qui n'aperçoivent dans les lettres qu'une industrie, et, pour quelques grands écrivains qu'on y voit, on y compte par milliers des vendeurs d'idées."[2]

Critics and theorists have long decried the contamination of art by commercialism—Horace deplored the money-grubbing of young Romans—but so liberal, so little Tocquevillian were Clemens's early critics that the compatibility or incompatibility of money and art seems hardly to have existed as a question in their minds. Nor did Clemens's friends, relatives, and readers complain that his marriage to Olivia Langdon turned him from his true vocation of artist and forced him into money-making. Clemens was in fact not regularly thought of as an artist; he was a western comedian, a journalist, a platform reader, and a businessman. Eventually he became an indispensable public figure, a quizzical shaman crowned with white hair who told the civilized world what to think on all topical subjects and made his instruction palatable by exercising a wit that his admirers liked to consider homespun. Howells did tend to treat Clemens as an artist; but he, as a man who made his own living by writing and editing, managed to be remarkably suggestive and in the next breath amiably unanalytical in what he said about Clemens and money. At his most provocative, he remarked that Clemens was "never a man who cared anything about money except as a dream, and he wanted more and more of it to fill out the spaces of this dream." Though he recognized the expansive, excessive strain in his friend, his comment in his chief essay on Clemens was flatter: "He did not care much for money in itself, but he luxuriated in the lavish use of it, and he was as generous with it as ever a man was."[3]

A. B. Paine, perhaps because he knew well what Clemens's speculating had done to him and his family, stressed the innocence and playfulness of the writer's attitude toward money. Clemens, he said, "with money was like a child with a heap of bright pebbles, ready to pile up more and still more, then presently to throw them away and begin gathering anew."[4] The hagiographical Paine preferred to record only the unclouded aspects of his saint; yet his optimism resembles the views that have seemed acceptable to such scholars as DeLancey Ferguson, Edward Wagenknecht, and Walter Blair. It has been said that tales of fortunes to be made in Nevada inspired Clemens; to catch the fever for speculating was normal. For him to take a deep interest in the money to be made from articles and books is also said to have been normal: he was primarily interested in money as a protection for his family; although he enjoyed good living, he was not devoted to power or display; he tended to see money idealistically and romantically; and if he could not resist speculating, he bore his losses stoically. That Clemens's speculating was neurotic does not seem to enter into these often inexact descriptions; nor does the complexity of the role played by money.

Van Wyck Brooks was the first to make much of Clemens's pursuit of money and neglect of art, but Bernard DeVoto so thoroughly discredited Brooks with academic critics that his lead was not followed. On this question, as on others, Brooks was wrong at many points—though not the main one—and was, therefore, easy to dismiss. He inextricably entangled his topic with dubious observations on American materialism, Puritanism, the frontier, the expectations of the Jervis Langdons, and the culture of Elmira, New York. Most destructive to art, Brooks believed, was Olivia, considered in her own person and as representative of a culture. By winning Olivia, Clemens pledged himself to the goddess success as worshipped by Elmira, became an artifact of the culture. Jervis Langdon, a doting father, fairly shanghaid Clemens into a money-oriented way of life by presenting him with a splendid house, furnishings, and servants. Livy magnified the problem: far from being a votary of genius, and not quite the votary of love, she was the unquestioning daughter of a rich father. When Clemens "fell behind in the race of pecuniary emulation she could not help applying the spur."[5]

In his sharp answers to Brooks's various charges against Clemens, DeVoto disregarded almost entirely the possible ill effects of money on art and the question of responsibility for Clemens's dedication to money-making. To DeVoto the plutomania of the mining West was no more than a congruent part of a magnificently large-scale, tumultuous culture created by men who were "hammering out an epoch." As for the commercial, cultivated East, DeVoto (in the face of mountains of data to the contrary) believed that Samuel Clemens, unlike the deferential Howells, did not think the difference between the East and the West "amounted to a damn. He was, that is, a savage." Moreover, DeVoto associated money-making with a desirable professionalism. He himself wrote profitable novels (pseudonymously), did potboiling magazine work, and despised the aesthetic inclinations of his literary enemies. To DeVoto, Clemens was simply, admirably, and successfully professional.[6]

Clemens himself was of two minds about money. He often wrote of the destructive effects of a lust for money; yet profits had an inordinate importance for him, and he used money frequently in his writings as a reward for merit. The question of Livy's responsibility for his concentration on profits (and thus, perhaps, for the stunting of his artistic growth) requires reexamination. This reexamination necessarily involves consideration of Clemens's speculative ventures, their psychological implications, and the meaning money had for him.

By scrutinizing the psychological bearings of Clemens's speculations we see that his greed for money went far beyond his needs and beyond what was normal for the culture. This judgment, though contrary to most scholarly opinion, is not altogether revolutionary. Signs of severe personality disorders have been noted in Clemens. The sum of such signs does not mean, to be sure, that there is no truth in favorable accounts of Clemens. What the evidence does indicate is that he suffered from a form of psychoneurosis and that significant modifications of received views of the man and of his work are in order.

Speculating was never forced on Clemens, as some have suggested, as a desperate attempt to escape poverty or to protect his family. He and his family lived very well. When his fortunes were at their lowest ebb, he wrote a self-pitying letter to Henry Rogers calculating that his income for 1895 would be only $7,500—approximately twice what most middle-class wage earners would make. (It has also been calculated that at this lowest point in his fortunes the family income came to no less than $12,500.) A notebook jotting seven years later indicates that his income for 1902 was up to $100,000. His speculating was not either brave or necessary, as it has been called, but neurotic; and his neurotic speculating may be interpreted as an attempt to obtain affection, power, reputation, and relief from anxieties. For the compulsive gambler, a lust for money—usually one among a constellation of greeds—may never be satiated; the hostilities, the anxieties, and the needs return.

Clemens habitually thought of his writings as objects made to sell. The partial obscurity that had veiled this topic was unintentionally lightened in 1946 by Clemens's great-nephew, Samuel Charles Webster. Webster wrote in reply to the publication of railing passages from Clemens's Autobiographical Dictation that blamed on Webster's father, Charles L. Webster, the husband of Clemens's niece, Annie Moffett Webster, the failure of Webster & Company, the publishing house that Clemens established and owned. S. C. Webster printed with comments and connecting links letters and documents intended to demonstrate that Samuel Clemens was the author of his own bankruptcy. Although Webster was not entirely right about this, he was accurate in portraying Clemens as an inept businessman—whimsical, irrational, and sometimes vicious in his attacks on associates and subordinates. Incidentally revealed was the absorption of Clemens in the money-making process.[7]

Clemens's letters to his publishers and to Henry Rogers helped complete the demolition of any assumption that Clemens's pursuit of money was playful, casually intermittent, or necessary. He was grindingly absorbed in profits, ardently disposed to speculate, hyperbolic in his protestations of guilt when he lost, and zealous to find scapegoats on whom to blame failures. In this context, his sporadic generosities lose the simple, wholesome preeminence given them by Howells and by Paine, and much of the comedy goes out of his sometimes splendidly vituperative abuse of his associates. Many of his associates were in truth both incompetent and venal; but it has been noted that he complained of the venality of his publishers only when he thought that they were cheating *him*.

Clemens was not a blind devotee of the materialist, acquisitive West: his portrayals of American money-madness could be both shrewd and hilarious. He described the California gold rush as marking a moral watershed dividing an age of high ideals from one of corruption and greed; and he castigated a few notoriously dishonest eastern magnates. Although he (unoriginally) called gold the root of all evil, Justin Kaplan is right when he observes, "It is hard to think of another writer so obsessed in his life and work by the lure, the rustle and chink and heft of money." And Hamlin Hill correctly judges that the marketing of Clemens's books was of "paramount importance" to him; "he tended much of the time to look upon his travel books as merchandise." The publishing of subscription books was a world of cynical and dishonest practices; yet Hill found "not a single indication that Clemens disapproved of or deplored the methods his publishers used." As for the condemnation of materialism that appears in Clemens's fiction, "There was more than a hint of public confession in his portrayal of schemers, inventors, and entrepreneurs."[8]

Nor is Hill in any doubt that during the period in Clemens's life that he examined closely (the last decade) monetary interests dominated the writer's thinking. Clemens "looked on his manuscripts as many of us would on a portfolio of blue-chip stocks or well-located real estate. . . . Get-rich-schemes were never far from the forefront of his mind, and he was willing to drop all literary endeavors to scheme and plot an over-night fortune by speculation." His interests "seemed almost monomaniacally centered on the monetary aspects of his writing."[9] In short, he displayed a hypertrophied market mentality.

Brooks's supposition that Livy could be blamed for her husband's engrossment in money has no discoverable basis in fact. Clemens's childish fantasies about wealth came early. Calvin Higbie, a friend of his western years, writes that Clemens was determined "to have a marble mansion several stories high with ample grounds, fine horses and carriages, and a pack of hounds. He was very emphatic about the hounds, and a steam yacht he could steer himself."[10] Before Clemens began his courtship of Livy, when Elisha Bliss, Jr., of the American Publishing Company proposed that Clemens prepare what became *Innocents Abroad* for publication, Clemens called the question of how much money he might possibly make from the projected book one that had a degree of importance for him which was almost beyond his own comprehension. As he explained to his friend Frank Fuller, the matter boiled down to "*how much bucksheesh.*" He had no desire to touch another book (after *The Celebrated Jumping Frog of Calaveras County*, 1867) unless there was money in it.[11] And Fuller was only one of several to whom Clemens made such remarks.

Although before Clemens married Olivia her mother and father showed solicitude about his ability to provide for her, their chief concern was about his character and habits. And, so far as their expectations that he be "settled" and "financially responsible" went, Clemens did not take the least exception to their attitudes. He sounded very much like a Langdon, in fact, when he wrote later to Mrs. Fairbanks about the approaching marriage of her son: "A body can't marry too young, I judge, except he be under twenty. I mean, a body whose place, position, & vocation are settled, & a comfortable living *assured*. Without these things, I judge a body can't marry too late."[12]

In 1867 when young Charles Langdon on board the *Quaker City* first showed Clemens "a dainty miniature done on ivory in delicate tints" of his sweet-faced sister, Clemens, according to this particular item in his legend, promptly fell in love. The story has, at any rate, appropriate symbolic value: Clemens fell in love with an image of his own creation. The miniature was more than a representation of a girl; it was an icon that limned the things Clemens wanted: status, culture, a gentlewoman for wife, and money—the most bewitching possibilities in life. In 1866 Anson Burlingame, United States minister to China, gave the humorist-reporter when he met him in Honolulu a good deal of Polonian advice, such as, "Never affiliate with inferiors; always climb."[13] When Clemens sought a bride, he climbed.

It would probably be incorrect to say—as a few persons may have hinted at the time—that Clemens married Olivia for her money, certainly not in any banal sense of the phrase; but he very much wanted to be rich. Part of Livy's initial charm for Clemens was money—whether for merely vulgar and careerist reasons is questionable. He might have felt what Gatsby said of Daisy Buchanan's voice: it was full of money. Nick Carraway, agreeing, tried to define the richness of the statement's meaning: "That was the inexhaustible charm that rose and fell in it, the jingle of it, the cymbal's song of it." Money made Livy potently talismanic. Clemens left California with escape from a West that had come to bore him and with conquest of the East in mind: acquiring Livy and her money, especially when challenged by the opposition of her family, was a demonstration of several kinds of possession and dominance.

One of the falsest of many false notes that Clemens struck in his letters to the Langdons during the period of courtship came when he wrote (with characteristic uncertainty about grammar) to Mrs. Langdon of Olivia and himself: "Neither of us are afflicted with a mania for money-getting, I fancy." That Livy knew the value of money better than Clemens, as Paine believed, is literally correct; but Paine's judgment that she cared more for it "in her way" requires interpretation. Livy was much less intense about money than was Clemens. Having money and spending it or not having it and not spending it made relatively little difference to her.[14]

Livy was accustomed to being comfortably well-off; she was not ambitious to be superlatively rich; and she was not a gambler. She valued money in ordinary ways, and when need arose she tried to economize. As early as 1873, when Clemens took the family to Europe in order to save on living expenses, Livy was the one who worried about costs and the exchange rate. It is true that some of the Clemenses' household expenditures suggest that Livy had no more practical notion of how to go about economizing than would a princess of the blood. She and Clemens began their married life in debt. They also began with a cook, a maid, and a coachman, all hired for them by one of Langdon's employees but paid, apparently, by Clemens. The family in motion resembled a royal progress. In 1891, when greatly worried about money, they occupied a handsome apartment at the Hotel Royal, one of the best addresses in Berlin; and when practicing the most stringent of economies as they worked toward settling with creditors following bankruptcy proceedings, they established themselves with a retinue of servants in a splendid house in England. During the same period of austerity, they had two parlors, a study, and four bedrooms at the Hotel Metropole in Vienna, again with their own servants. A little later, they moved to the more expensive and more luxurious Hotel Kranz. The blame for such extravagances apparently fell more on Clemens than on Livy; he was unwilling to change his style of life.[15]

Livy not only handled money more sensibly than did Clemens; but insofar as her feeble lights permitted, she placed a greater value on literature, that is, on Clemens's writings and on his place in literature: she was a devotee of Art. She opposed his selling manuscripts to inferior magazines simply because they paid well, and she tried to hold him to what she conceived to be high literary standards. As a member of a capitalist-philanthropic family, she took conventionally responsible views of what constitutes financial integrity and of the obligations of the rich, God's stewards. (Philanthropy by capitalists is, of course, frequently explained as a device for suppressing feelings of guilt.) She enjoyed making gifts, and we may imagine that the gesture fed her ego. Her view of her role as the employer of servants followed self-congratulatory, Mandevillian lines. Writing to her mother from Munich, she expressed sorrow that George Griffin, who had been the Clemens's butler in Hartford, was out of work: "One of the great objections to our leaving home was the fact that we in that way threw three people out of work—however we keep some busy here so perhaps it is in a measure balanced."[16]

In 1871 Olivia drew from her brother the information that he could easily send her three to five hundred dollars a month from her share of the Langdon coal interests. With this much money regularly available, Livy could see no need for Clemens to give readings. In a loving, touching, not fully literate letter, she urged him to devote himself to his writing: if income from the estate were to prove inadequate, they would change entirely their mode of living. When the Clemenses built their mansion in Hartford to grandiose specifications, Livy was the one who fretted about expenditures; in the midst of visitors and ostentatious entertaining, she sighed in Horatian fashion for the peace of her sister's farm, near Elmira.[17]

The ostentation suited Clemens's swollen desires; but he was perfectly capable of blaming on his family what had been occasioned by his indiscretions. He took heavy, unnecessary business and gambling losses and at the same time said, and no doubt believed, that he was mercenary about his writings for the sake of his family. When H. O. Houghton, the publisher, invited him in 1875 to contribute a short novel to a proposed series, Clemens answered, "I like the whole plan except the money side of it. I do not believe there would be much money in it, and I find that trying to support a family is a thing which compels one to look at all ventures with a mercenary eye. I hope to see a day when I can publish in a way which shall please my fancy best and not mind what the banking result may be—but that time has not come yet." He wrote in the same vein to Howells explaining why he couldn't afford to print *The Adventures of Tom Sawyer* (1876) in the *Atlantic*: "You see I take a vile, mercenary view of things— but then my household expenses are something almost ghastly."[18]

High though household expenses were, they were not the cause of Clemens's chief difficulties. They had nothing to do with his eagerness for maximum profits when he first negotiated with the American Publishing Company or with the pressures for high pay that he exerted before his marriage on the owners of newspapers. It should also be noted that after

Livy's death, when Clemens selected a house to rent near New York City, it was in ultrafashionable Tuxedo Park, and that Stormfield, the mansion he built near Redding, Connecticut, had nineteen rooms and was ordinarily staffed by eight to ten servants or personal attendants.

At times Clemens could be relatively realistic. He wrote to his mother in 1878, "Life has come to be a very serious matter with me. I have a badgered, harassed feeling a good part of my time. It comes mainly from business responsibilities and annoyances."[19] He had sold at substantial losses his house in Buffalo and his interest in the Buffalo *Express,* was struggling to manipulate the troublesome but lucrative subscription publishing business to his advantage, had built the great house in Hartford, and was dabbling in speculations. The Langdons were in some ways a model for Clemens, but, overly ambitious child of liberal America that he was, the association in his mind of lady-wife, costly mansion, and yearned-for fortune was much more nearly autogenous than Langdon-inspired.

Brooks and others have made too much psychological capital of trivia and have given undue symbolic weight to single instances; yet Clemens's habits of thought are compellingly suggested by some of his phrasings and actions. The language of finance suffused his imagery. In his farewell statement (described below), made before he left Vancouver on August 23, 1895, for his around-the-world tour, he said, "I meant, when I began, to give my creditors all the benefits of this, but I begin to feel that I am gaining something from it, too, and that my dividends if not available for banking purposes, may be even more satisfactory than theirs."[20]

The threads connecting money, happiness, and love are visible, too, in the present Clemens made to Olivia on their wedding anniversary on February 2, 1895. Livy wrote to her sister, "As I was starting down the stairs for my breakfast this morning Mr. Clemens called me back and took a five-franc piece and gave it to me, saying: 'it is our silver-wedding day, and so I give you a present.'" Clemens was pleased enough with the symbolic resonances of the five-franc piece to open a letter to Henry Rogers, then engaged in working Clemens out of bankruptcy, with a mention of it.[21]

Money problems attendant upon speculations badgered Clemens for much of his life. The chief cause of his worries was the Paige typesetter, a never-perfected, never-marketed machine that he expected to revolutionize printing. Complete accuracy about his tangled affairs is impossible. S. C. Webster thought that money drained from Webster & Company to support the Paige machine was responsible for the failure of the company; but

Webster & Company went into bankruptcy mainly because of its own errors. The publishing house seems to have absorbed nearly all of Clemens's accrued dividends, his royalties, his working capital of $75,000, and more than $60,000 in loans from Livy. In a letter of February 5, 1894, Clemens informed his sister that Webster & Company owed him $110,000, but he did not specify what he included in this figure. The company in the end owed creditors $79,704.80 (exclusive of indebtedness to Livy); the assigned estate paid 27.7 percent of that figure, Clemens the rest.[22]

Precisely how much Clemens lost on the Paige typesetter is also in doubt. Paine set the figure at $190,000. Clemens began investing in the machine in 1880 or 1881 and may not have given up all hope for it until about January 2, 1895, when Rogers—who himself invested approximately $78,000 in it at Clemens's urging—wrote that the enterprise was dead.[23] If one adds to the costs of wildcat speculations the losses that Clemens suffered from the sales of his houses and of his interest in the Buffalo *Express,* he may well have dissipated $700,000 on investments.

In early 1887 Clemens felt the lack of cash so severely that he declared that he had put his family on very short commons. During the summer of 1890, while he was frantically feeding the voracious typesetter, Livy sought to lessen his worries by making special efforts to economize, and during the difficult years that followed she continued to attempt to sustain and comfort her husband. So far as the published record goes, her only intimation of unhappiness arose by way of expressions of relief when Clemens sent joyous letters mistakenly informing her that their troubles were behind them. She answered—with considerably more animation than was usual for her—that if money actually came in, she thought she would "jump around and spend money just for fun, and give away a little if we really get some." In another letter she wrote reassuringly, "You know we have an income of about $6000 a year and with what you can comfortably earn in addition, without taxing yourself we can live perfectly well for our requirements."[24]

Livy seems never to have offered the least reproach to Clemens for dissipating the major part of her fortune as well as his own large earnings. The bankruptcy of his publishing house (precipitated in April 1894, when notes were called) distressed her deeply; but this was because she conceived of bankruptcy as a loss of honor. Unburdening herself in a letter from Paris to Susan Crane, she wrote, "I cannot get away from the feeling that business failure means disgrace. . . . Sue, if you were to see me, you would see that I have grown old very fast during this last year."[25]

Livy had been under wracking tensions about money for more than a decade. A generalized anxiety dominated even the lives of the daughters. Given these years of active distress, so much the more extraordinary were Clemens's behavioral oxymorons, his expressions of anguished regret closely followed by evidences of immoderate pleasure at his immersal in new speculations. He was incapable of responding realistically to the effects of his speculations, and he was charmed out of regrets and guilt by manipulative activities. Following the declaration on April 18, 1894, of bankruptcy by his publishing company, he was ebullient as he and Rogers haggled with his creditors. At such moments of frivolous delight his bankruptcy and its consequences seemed no more than one of Tom Sawyer's entrancing games.

The ethical positions taken by Clemens and by the notoriously ruthless Rogers during these exciting, strenuous days appear to have been shifting, but Livy's position was lodestar constant: she repeatedly pressed Clemens to be scrupulously honest. When, following urgent pleas from her and protestations of probity from him, Clemens expressed admiration for Rogers's caustic way with creditors, Livy, model of rectitude, tried to bring him back to earth. "Oh my darling," she wrote, "we want those debts paid and we want to treat them all not only honestly but we want to help them in every possible way. It is money honestly owed and I cannot quite understand the tone which both you & Mr Rogers seem to take—in fact I cannot understand it at all. You say Mr Rogers has said some caustic and telling things to the creditors. (I do not know what your wording was) I should think it was the creditors place to say caustic things to us."[26]

Livy offered Rogers $30,000 that was coming to her from her brother to pay creditors, adding that she knew that neither Charlie nor Clemens would approve.[27] If *conscience* may be given the sociological definition of subscribing to social norms, probably Livy's standards were those to be expected of an idealistic woman of her class. They were not irrational, however, and the correspondence indicates that it took determination on her part to enforce them.

On his side, Clemens received and accepted public acclaim for paying the creditors sums beyond what was legally necessary. Although Paine, Clara, and others make it seem that full payment was Clemens's idea, this is inaccurate. Guided by Livy, who received some help from Rogers, Clemens did come to enjoy proclaiming the notion that he was morally superior.

While in Vancouver, about to start on his world tour, he published what has been called a sour, would-be comic statement in the San Francisco *Enquirer* for August 24, 1895. In addition, helped with the writing by Samuel Moffett, his nephew, he made a self-serving statement—Justin Kaplan accurately calls it a "gassy refrain"—to a correspondent for the *New York Times* (it appeared on August 17, 1895). The United Press promised him to broadcast this statement to the world. A merchant, Clemens said, can take advantage of the laws of insolvency and start again, "but I am not a business man, and honor is a harder master than the law. It cannot compromise for less than 100 cents on the dollar and its debts never outlaw."[28]

In all of his woes, Clemens characteristically vacillated between expressions of guilt and efforts to find scapegoats. After the death of Susy, he wrote Livy that he would never forgive himself for the troubles his mistakes had brought upon her. But he also blamed God for his bankruptcy, for his carbuncles, and for Susy's death. Possibly he was blaming Livy indirectly for certain of his sorrows: she was the authority-figure who forced him to satisfy his creditors: "Do you remember, Livy, the hellish struggle it was to settle on the lecture trip around the world? How we fought the idea, the horrible idea, the heart-torturing idea: I almost an old man, with ill-health, carbuncles, bronchitis and rheumatism. I, with patience worn to rags, I was to pack my bag and be jolted around the devil's universe, for what? To pay debts that were not even of my making." His jeremiad continued, "But once the idea of that infernal trip struck us we couldn't shake it. Oh, no! for it was packed with sense of honor—honor—honor—no rest, comfort, joy—but plenty of honor, plenty of ethical glory. And as a reward for our self-castigation and faithfulness to ideals of nobility we were robbed of our greatest treasure, our lovely Susy in the midst of her blooming talents and personal graces. You want me to believe it is a judicious, a charitable God that runs this world. Why, I could run it better myself."[29]

On November 1, 1896, Clemens wrote characteristically to Rogers, "I am thinking much more about creating an income for my family than I am about paying creditors." During the same year he explained, contradictorily, in a letter to E. C. Stedman that he was resigning from the Author's Club "solely because I am in debt and must economise even in trifles when I am spending other people's money." He permitted Rogers to have his typesetter stock assigned to Livy as a preferred creditor and had Rogers remove the Hartford mansion from the list of his leviable assets on the claim that it was paid for entirely with Livy's money.[30]

He was quite willing to enter into a scheme for obtaining gifts from friends and admirers in order to pay off his debts. When the New York *Herald,* seeking publicity, devised this project, he gave an interview intended to get it started, saying, as he frequently did, that his bankruptcy occurred "not by any fault of mine." At first he concealed the plan from Livy because, as he wrote to Rogers, she "would have forbidden me to touch it." Livy was, in fact, strongly opposed. Rogers cabled that all friends thought it a mistake, and Frank Bliss, the publisher, wrote that the *Herald* was hurting Clemens's reputation. Clemens then put a stop to it, declaring that he spurned letting others share the load "while my health is good and my ability to work remains."³¹

This subscription plan took in relatively little money before it was canceled, and in the end the press and the public took Clemens pretty much at face value, that is, as a hero of capitalism. In March of 1898 newspapers announced that he had paid off his debts. The feat was described as "a fine example of the very chivalry of probity," comparable to the case of Sir Walter Scott. Later, Howells wrote, somewhat wryly, "He had behaved like Walter Scott, as millions rejoiced to know, who had not known how Walter Scott behaved till they knew it was like Clemens."³²

Clemens's willingness to accept donations from friends and strangers does not mean that he did not indulge in charitable gestures himself. He took pleasure in making gifts and did not always publicize them, but his particular delight was in dramatically generous gestures. He also delighted in doing well by himself. Beginning as early as his piloting days when he went ashore in New Orleans and later during his western period, especially when he was in San Francisco, he treated himself to expensive foods and wines. When staying in San Francisco at the opulent Occidental, he described it as "Heaven on the half shell." Although he was in debt throughout much of his stay in Nevada, as a newspaper man he could be influential, and he was often presented with small interests in mines or was given drinks and dinners. He wrote to his mother, "I lead an easy life. . . . I fare like a prince wherever I go."³³

There were times after his marriage when Clemens expressed nostalgia for the carefree life of a bachelor-printer, and occasionally he pictured himself as a plain westerner; but in fact, once his moderately impoverished childhood and the sometimes rough living of his western years were behind him, his sentiments in favor of the simple life and a boardinghouse ease were dreamily reminiscent, not meant as plans for action. Instead, he made pompous his Hartford and Redding mansions. He associated himself with *le gratin*—with European nobility and American families of substance. His taste was keen for the costly dinners offered by Henry Rogers and by other men of wealth; and it was his habit during much of his life to attend those long-drawn banquets popular in Boston, New York, and London at which rich foods and mutually congratulatory toasts and speeches were featured.

According to Paine, Clemens's prodigality was accompanied by a few penny-pinching habits, such as trying to make sure that he was not over-charged for cabs and turning down gas jets when he left a room. He regularly called for cheese-paring by his business associates, and he under-paid certain of his employees; but there is little evidence of effective efforts toward retrenchment on his part when money was short. He did issue dark warnings to Livy and his daughters that they might all end in the poor-house.

Material comforts and sensuous pleasures were only a small part of what money meant to Clemens: its meanings were complex and intensely numi-nous. It was a sign of success, a proof of worth. It established him among the upper bourgeoisie and was a factor in self-definition.

Freud stresses the anal character of money and equates money and feces: it means power, vitality, potency. To throw money away may be indicative of a strong feeling of guilt. Money may be dispensed in place of libido. It may assuage guilt or win approval. It may be equated with love, or it may be used to buy love. Gaston Bachelard, in *The Psychoanalysis of Fire,* tries to show that all alchemy was penetrated by a revery of sex, power, wealth, and rejuvenation. Quite possibly all of these were present in Clemens's fan-tasies.

Altogether different ideas may also be associated with money. It carries a burden of meanings related to venality, guilt, remorse, and sin. If one rejects as naive Freud's theory of money, of anal eroticism, of anal character, and of anal neurosis, and if one also rejects the association of anality with the death wish, one may still argue that money was for Clemens, in Shake-speare's words, "the invisible god," in Luther's, "the God of this world," and that Clemens vexedly needed to defend himself for his choice of divinities. While he was composing *A Connecticut Yankee in King Arthur's Court* (1889) and his difficulties related to the Paige typesetter were mount-ing, he reassured himself with entries in his notebooks attacking the En-glish nobility: if "we Americans worship the Almighty Dollar . . . it is a worthier god than Hereditary Privilege."[34]

There are moments when, agreeing with Howells, nearly any critic would be pleased to attribute to Clemens—enveloped in his fantasies of easy, sudden affluence—a Gatsby-like innocence in the midst of corruption, to view him as childishly sportive, untouched by the atmosphere of money-lust in which he moved. In one way Paine was right: there was frequently an element of game-playing about Clemens's drive for money; but his speculating was deadly, like the Mayan ball-playing. The full truth shows darker tones than Howells and Paine—given the complaisant disposition and admiration of the one and the discipular piety of the other—seem ever to have imagined. Dreams and neuroses lie close together. Clemens named the febrile postwar period the Gilded Age, identified monetary corruption as a national curse, and published moralistically tinged tracts and stories on the subject; but he fantasized bonanzas, and he repeatedly acted out in speculative enterprises his obsession with the idea of opulence.

Clara gave a flatteringly jejune explanation for Clemens's high-risk ventures, proposing that Clemens invested largely because he found it "difficult to refuse aid to any man so enthusiastic as the inventor of a new device." Paine wrote lightly that Clemens's "tendency to speculative investment" was acquired during his "restless mining days." Clemens (and his brother, Orion) did indeed speculate in mines. In October 1861, he tried unsuccessfully to induce his Uncle Jim Lambton to come from Missouri to Nevada, bringing money to be used in working mines—finding mines was not the problem—and he expressed excitement at the prospect of becoming wealthy. Although he is supposed to have lost money speculating in mining shares, it is also supposed—probably incorrectly—that when he became a reporter for the Virginia City *Enterprise* he was able to be "simply an enchanted spectator of the mining boom." What the West with its hectic atmosphere actually had to do with Clemens's later speculations is impossible to say; but to think of him as the boyishly venturing forty-niner is misleading: he was the Dostoievskian gamester. One should also note that he was speculating in commodities while he was a pilot on the Mississippi.[35]

Personality disorders make themselves known by a variety of signs, not by one alone, and in the case of Clemens other signs have been noted, although they have not been assembled, evaluated to weed out the inauthentic, or woven into a pattern. Biographers—both the worshipping and the selectively critical—from Paine, Brooks, DeVoto, and Wecter to Kaplan and Hill have been struck by odd verbal aggressions, paranoid displays, manic-depressive tendencies, psychic masochism, hyperbolic expressions of guilt feelings, suicidal inclinations, exhibitionism, extraordinary efforts to make his daughters inaccessible to men, evidences of prurience and prudery, occasional drunkenness, and a strong attachment to prenubile girls. What are supposed to be evidences of abnormality have been found in his writings as well as in his life.

One of Clemens's oddities—and one which relates quite obviously to neurotic gambling—was his fantasizing the possession of unusual power. This begins at the level of the physical and runs through the spiritual. Like his sometime friend the tiny George W. Cable, Clemens (who was only five feet eight) identified with small but quick and mettlesome men: "All his life he liked to elaborate fantasies about small men with unsuspected giant strength who were always surprising people with it."[36] On the immaterial side, the idea that Clemens was a person of profound insight who looked deep into the heart of things was not uncommon during his life and has been developed since. (Maxwell Geismar probably took to its most improbable extreme the notion of Clemens as a daring guide to life.) The scattered references to him in the correspondence as St. Mark may all be read as at least faintly jesting; yet a vein of seriousness runs through Clemens's own remarks on the awful truths contained in such works as "What Is Man?" and the Autobiographical Dictation. A certain solemnity may possibly show itself in the unfinished Eddipus manuscripts. In that story of an age one thousand years after ours, Mark Twain is remembered as a bishop, and his work "Old Comrades" (the Autobiographical Dictation) is seen as a sacred book.[37]

Clemens's speculating—a key and readily accessible issue—like neurotic gambling, had an obsessional character. Paradigms of abnormality make clear that Clemens's speculations went beyond what was normal in his culture. In the paradigms there appear a number of elements resembling the constellation of traits to be found in him. Aggressiveness, manic-depressive tendencies, psychic masochism, and paranoia make themselves obvious in Clemens. (No attempt is made here to trace the origins of his neuroticisms.)

Anna Freud is reported to have said of gambling, "I knew nothing about the subject, so I did what we all do—looked it up in Fenichel."[38] Fenichel regards a passion for gambling as a displaced expression of conflicts around infantile sexuality, especially those centered on masturbation. The conflicts are aroused by the fear of losing reassurances regarding feelings of guilt. The excitement of gambling corresponds to sexual excitement, that of winning to orgasm and killing (patricide), that of losing to castration and being killed. To gamble is to force fate to make a decision for or against one. Losing is preferable to a continuation of unbearable pressure by the superego. Winning represents a successful rebellion; losing, an ingratiation, a satisfying punishment. Like manic-depressive states, impulse neuroses present an alternation between periods of guilt and periods when the superego is apparently inoperative. Both gambling and masturbation may be a kind of play intended to relieve tensions by the active repetition or anticipation of them in self-chosen dosages and at self-chosen times. Under the pressure of inner tensions, however, the play element may be lost; the ego may not be able to control what it has initiated.[39]

Edmund Bergler's discussion of gambling includes a review of the salient features of the chief theories that have been proposed. One theory stresses anal-sadistic regressions, equates gambling with forepleasure, winning with orgasm, losing with ejaculation, defecation, and castration, and holds that gambling satisfies the bisexual ideal which the Narcissus finds in himself. According to another theory, the gambler acts out his unsatisfiable plea for love to surrogate figures, of the mother most likely but of the father also. Yet other theories emphasize the gambler's (unconscious) attempts to regain the lost feeling of infantile omnipotence, his manifestations of homosexual drives, and his wish to lose. (The wish to lose may be interpreted as relieving the gambler of guilt for the Oedipal father's death.) It is generally agreed that money may be the token of gambling but not the aim.

Bergler himself observes in gamblers psychic masochism, pseudoaggression, and fantasies of grandeur. The megalomaniacal attitude of the gambler is, Bergler thinks, an act of aggression against the parent or against others who have forced him to recognize that he is not omnipotent. He endlessly reenacts a drama in three scenes: he generates situations that lead to his defeat; he strikes out against the world's cruelty and injustice; and he pities himself because Fate has been unfair to him. The painful pleasure that accompanies gambling arises from the tension generated by the conflict between a conscious wish to win and an unconscious wish to lose. Punishment may be sexualized, of course, by the psychic masochist.[40]

Gambling on a large scale charmed Clemens. He dreamed of cornering markets, establishing hegemony over great industries; but the devotion he gave to his speculations was not always a function of the amounts he hoped to gain. He was infatuated with inventions that linked him to technological progress and to the mystery of creativity. His was, of course, an age devoted to the idea of progress, proud of its inventions as furthering the advance of mankind. It is not surprising that Clemens, from his early years until the end of his life, should interest himself in inventions, but the intensity of his involvement indicates abnormality.

Various passages in Clemens's life, particularly his life in Hartford, beginning in 1871, brought him close to technology. Hartford as a whole was commercial, industrial, and technological in orientation, as any reader of *A Connecticut Yankee in King Arthur's Court* (1889) might surmise. Of special interest is his relationship with General Joseph R. Hawley. Clemens introduced Hawley at political gatherings in Hartford in 1876 and in Elmira in 1886; and in March 1888, he and Livy were invited to visit the Hawleys (Hawley was then senator from Connecticut) in Washington. In addition to being a brevetted major-general and a senator, Hawley was at various times the editor of the Hartford *Evening Press,* editor and part owner of the Hartford *Courant,* a governor of Connecticut, a United States representative, and president of the Centennial Commission that supervised America's first International Exhibition, held in Philadelphia from May 10 to November 10, 1876. When Hawley closed the exhibition, he mentioned a total attendance of ten million, a paid attendance of eight million—greater numbers than had seen the Paris Exhibition of 1867. In a "snapper" to his speech introducing Hawley in Hartford, Clemens alluded to the general's having "taken in gate-money amounting to as much as $121,000 a day—'and never stolen a cent of it!'"[41]

Compelling though the exhibition was to the American imagination, Clemens vacillated about visiting it. He ended by spending an entire day in attendance and decided that it would have taken him two or three days "to examine such an array of articles with anything like just care & deliberation."[42] Among the most impressive displays was that of Pratt & Whitney, of Hartford, "America's foremost manufacturer of machine tools." These tools permit high-speed mass production—"the American System of Manufacture." The exhibition displayed (among a thousand other evidences of American talent) lathes, printing presses, cotton presses, power looms, steam hammers, milling machines, pumps, wire cables, sewing machines, a typewriter, locomotives, air brakes, and rubber boots. Also exhibited were a calculating machine (an American version of Charles Babbage's calculator), Thomas Edison's "multiplex" telegraph, Alexander Graham Bell's telephone, the world's first machine gun, the Gatling gun, and the heavy breech-loading Parrott gun. Clemens mentioned most of these machines either before or after he visited the exhibition.

As early as 1870 Clemens wrote his sister Pamela an idealizing appreciation of inventions, which incidentally flattered their brother Orion, whom Clemens usually considered to be miraculously fatuous. Orion's version of a drilling machine had received some passing attention. Clemens was enthusiastic: "An inventor is a poet—a true poet—and nothing in any degree less than a high order of poet—therefore his noblest pleasure died [*sic*] with the stroke that completes the creature of his genius . . . little minds being able to get no higher than a vulgar moneyed success."[43] In January 1889, at a moment when he thought the Paige typesetter had been perfected, he set down a series of memorial notes and wrote several eulogia, including a letter to Orion in which he said, "All the other wonderful inventions of the human brain sink pretty nearly into commonplaces contrasted with this awful mechanical miracle. Telephones, telegraphs, locomotives, cotton-gins, sewing-machines, Babbage calculators, Jacquard looms, perfecting presses, all mere toys, simplicities! The Paige Compositor marches alone and far in the land of human inventions."[44] And in 1907 he entered in his Autobiographical Dictation a reference to his pleasure at having seen and talked with Marconi, Morse, Bell, "and others among the men who have added the top story to the majestic edifice of the world's modern material civilization."[45]

Money was usually a factor in the appeal that inventions had for Clemens, no matter how he might rhapsodize about inventors being poets and superior to cash rewards. In a letter of 1879 he gave Pamela a glimpse of his more habitual attitude: "I got up a kind of marvellous invention the other day & I could make a mighty fortune out of it but for the fact that anybody can infringe the patent that wants & I shan't be able to catch them at it." And in 1883 he was outraged at the premature publicity that his good friend, the Reverend Joseph Twichell, gave to "a history game" that Clemens, nevertheless, continued to try to perfect and market.[46]

Among Clemens's own inventions were a notebook with corner tabs, a pregummed scrapbook (devised in 1872 and, for a time, a money maker), the history game, other games, bed clamps intended to keep a child from throwing off his covers, and a perpetual calendar. He devised presumptive cures for piles and chilblains. He backed a few of Orion's inventions; but the scissors for harvesting grapes that he financed, had manufactured, and lost money on were invented by William Cooper Howells, father of William Dean Howells.

Certain of Clemens's large losses unrelated to inventions may be attributed to commonplace errors in judgment and to bad luck, not to an infatuation with technological progress. In most of his speculations, however, he showed carelessness and possibly a megalomaniacal self-confidence. He took large losses when he sold his interest in the Buffalo *Express,* his house in Buffalo, and his mansion in Hartford. The house in Hartford cost him about $131,000 or, including more than $16,000 in upkeep while it was vacant, as much as $150,000 (although that total may include $21,000 for furnishings). He and Livy could not bring themselves to live in it again after the death of Susy; and eventually he sold it for $28,000.[47]

Some of Clemens's speculations were actually profitable; some, if taken out of context, would appear to have been instances of normal risk taking; in total, they are pathological manifestations of psychoneurosis, not to be explained by poor judgment and bad luck. Even Paine did not altogether gloss over Clemens's disregard for ordinary prudence. In 1881, for example, Clemens expended more than $100,000. Out of $46,000 that he put into investments that year, $41,000 was a loss. Clemens was, Paine explained, a child in practical business matters; he had "no moral right" to engage in business. He became excited, worried, impatient, alternately suspicious and overtrusting, rash, and frenzied. Yet he could not stop speculating, Paine noted, "until the end of his days." And shortly before Clemens died, Paine requested Clemens's hosts in Bermuda to guard him against "schemes, plans, investments, and the like."[48]

When everything is considered, Clemens must be classed as a compulsive gambler. That a few of his speculations made money or did not lose money does not alter their psychoneurotic character, nor does the fact that he at times went through rational procedures of investigation and evaluation similar to those that nonneurotic investors follow.

The Paige typesetting machine and his own publishing house were the most immoderate in monetary terms and the most emotionally wasting of his many enterprises. Taken alone, establishing the publishing house could be considered a standard venture, but the emotional extremes to which he went when backing the typesetter and his heterogeneous minor speculative enterprises, in view of the spirit which animated him when he engaged in them, indicate a pathological condition. He speculated in mines when he was in Nevada; he was in debt while he was courting Livy. In explaining his original investment of $2,000 in the Paige compositor, he wrote, "I was always taking little chances like that, and almost always losing by it, too." His speculations, all told, constituted an almost unbelievable drain on his time, energy, and income.[49]

An unequivocal indication of the obsessive nature of Clemens's habit is the feverish way in which he entered into new schemes as soon as he recovered, with the help of Rogers, from pressing monetary and emotional burdens following the bankruptcy of Webster & Company.[50] For years his letters had contained renunciations, some of them exclamatory. Although he may have been simply offering an excuse for not sending Mrs. Fairbanks money, as early as 1879 he wrote her when her husband was in financial straits, "Confound speculation, anyway! It nips us all sooner or later; but it won't nip me any more—nor Mr. F. I judge." He asked Fred Hall, when Hall was managing his publishing house, to get him out of business, declaring himself to be by nature and disposition unfit for it. As he tried to save the publishing house, he wrote to Livy, "The billows of hell have been rolling over me." And again to Livy he wrote, "Farewell—a long farewell—to *business*! I will *never* touch it again! . . . I will live in literature, I will wallow in it, revel in it, I will swim in ink!"[51]

Such protestations meant nothing. After the bankruptcy, as Clemens's financial situation improved, he recovered from being Atlas bearing the unbearable. Anxieties, remorse, and a family kept on short commons were forgotten. Rogers had built up capital by using Clemens's surplus income for successful speculations on the New York stock exchange. Rogers's successes probably helped incite Clemens to speculate on his own. He turned ebullient after months of depression and once more fantasized that he would be a magnate. This was expectable recidivism, a reinvigoration of the psychomasochist's drive toward the pleasures of measured pain.

The remarkable story of Clemens's fresh ventures during 1898 is most fully told in Notebook 32 and in letters (beginning March 17–20) that he sent to Rogers from Vienna.[52] He had, he wrote Rogers, landed a big fish. Having heard by accident that the American patents on "an ingenious and capable Designing Machine" for carpet (and other textile) patterns had not yet left the hands of Jan Szczepanik, a young inventor, and his financial backer, a banker named Ludwig Kleinberg, Clemens hastily invited them to talk with him. Two days after that first meeting, Clemens secured an option (the sum he paid is not revealed) on the American rights for the manufacture and sale of the machine at a price of $1,500,000. In preparation for making this bid, Clemens exploded into action. He gathered sketchy information, made rapid notes, and projected extensive, Sellersian calculations on such things as the probable number of Jacquard carpet factories in America, the probable number of designers employed, their wages, and the savings that could be effected by replacing the workers with Szczepanik's machine. "Had a very good time indeed," Clemens wrote.

"Good time" understates the rapture with which Clemens whirled about. The euphoria of the pathological gambler marks the tone of his first letters; it was drink after long abstinence. He wished to share his wealth to come with Rogers, his benefactor. He repeatedly urged Rogers to drop everything and come to Vienna; and he issued instructions to him on setting up a company to build and market the machines, giving Clemens one-tenth of the shares: "I can get along without cash, but I can't live without that stock." He reported with semihumorous complacence that the Viennese banker admired his acumen and that the entire Jacquard industry in America would be "in the hands" of the company he formed. His chief worry was that he might not be able to avoid letting a representative of American carpet interests who was then in Vienna make him an offer for his option that he could not afford to refuse: "I was born with the speculative instinct and I did not want that temptation put in my way." Before the end of March he was proposing that a world patent be placed "in the grip of a single corporation"; he wanted for himself a supplementary option that would cover the globe. Kleinberg was impressed: "Ach, America—it is the country of the big! Let me get my breath—then we will talk."

By April 21 Rogers had forwarded a report that disclosed some of the reasons why the wonderful design machine using its remarkable photographic process would be worthless in America. Strangely enough (that is, if a neurosis were not involved) Clemens's disappointment was not particularly keen. His attention had begun to shift to other devices by Szczepanik and to an exciting invention by "a Dutchman" that was supposed to permit the economical spinning of yarns for blankets and other textile goods out of peat fiber mixed with cotton or wool. Head over heels in his dreams of entrepreneurial profits, Clemens made plans to go for a holiday in England in order to market in that country the proposed machine for spinning peat fibres. During this same period he was adapting and translating three Austrian plays for the American or the English market. Royalties on every performance—that was the bait the translations held out; the theater offered a way to make money while one sleeps. Nothing came of any of these enterprises.

Always the gambler, however, in 1898 and early 1899 Clemens considered mortgaging his house in Hartford to buy shares of stock in Federal Steel. Holdings of Livy's that had for years been presumed worthless came alive again by March 1900 and were valued at $175,000. The thought of so much fresh money in the offing stimulated Clemens to write to Rogers asking for $12,500 to be used as first payment on a $25,000 block of shares in the English company established to market Plasmon, a health food made, Clemens said, very cheaply of "the milk that is usually given to pigs." A little later he bought into the newly formed American Plasmon company, and the two companies occupied a considerable part of his energy over the next eight years. He could not persuade Rogers to invest in the health food; but he tried it on his family (even though Livy, whose main sustenance Plasmon was during some weeks of illness, detested it) and urged it upon ailing friends. For a time his faith in the English company remained unshaken, but by February 1904 he considered the chief officer of the American company to be a scoundrel and the investment to be one of those he would like to forget.

Plasmon and the carpet design machine are only two of the better documented of Clemens's speculations following his recovery from bankruptcy. He invested $16,000 or more in a "mechanical cashier" that never reached effective production, bought stock in a company that financed the "Booklovers Library," in the Formaline Company, in the Koy-lo Company, in a company that made patented spiral hatpins, and in an organ manufacturing company—all losers. During the last dozen years of Clemens's life his speculations did diminish somewhat, and his passion for buying into companies that promised enormous profits slackened to manageable proportions. This was, to be sure, a period when his energies were declining; and Rogers or Paine or both were watching over him.

Livy was in no obvious way responsible for Clemens's preoccupation with money. She did not share her husband's enthusiasm for his speculations: "She did not oppose them, at least not strenuously, but she did not encourage them. She did not see their need."[53] Apparently Clemens did not consult Livy about his ventures. Her role would seem to have been to supply money, if needed, and sympathy.

Whether art and money are natural enemies is a suggestive but unanswerable question, one shrouded in social thought, economic doctrine, and metaphysical theory. It would not be possible to demonstrate that all writers who have chosen to engage in business or to write for large audiences have been the worse for the choice. Most writers are interested in their royalties, and excellent artists have been men of affairs. Nevertheless, Clemens's obsession with money and his speculating went beyond the normal even in a lively money economy. He wasted himself on business matters, and it may hardly be doubted that his writing would have profited if he had been more devoted to art, less to speculation. Livy, Howells, and even Rogers, in his way, were more concerned about the entailed misuse of Clemens's talent than he was. A passage in young Susy's biography of her father says, "Mama and I have been much troubled of late because papa, since he has been publishing General Grant's books, has seemed to forget his own books and works entirely."[54]

One of the extraordinary things about Clemens as a writer is not that he wrote hundreds of worthless pages but that, given the attention he paid to money matters, he could produce any literature so fully achieved and so compact of American ideals and anxieties as to hold our attention and compel our admiration. One must point out, however, that what he learned from adventures in business added social complexity and emotional depth to his work, put him intimately in touch with American ideologies and *mentalités,* and presented him with themes, mainly intractable, on which he repeatedly tried to elaborate.

Marx, Freud, Georg Simmel, and others have presented ideas about economic and psychological alienation that relate closely to questions about art and money. It is now a commonplace to hold that in an industrialized society, the division of labor alienates the producer from his work. The product is meaningful to the producer only in terms of other products or in terms of money, the purest form of interchangeability. As a kind of universal solvent, money may be taken to be a device for converting chaos into order; indeed, Ernst Troeltsch, R. H. Tawney, Werner Sombart, Max Weber, and Erich Fromm take the psychological nexus between Protestantism and capitalism to be an image of God as the God of order.[55]

Marx's notions of what he called commodity fetishism are particularly useful in explicating the positions on art and money that are exemplified by Clemens's career. From the publication by a blatantly sales-oriented subscription firm of his first travel account, *Innocents Abroad* (1869), most of Clemens's books were, as nearly as he could make them so, abstract commodities, items in the exchange system. Through that great equalizer, dollar value, they were equated with other commodities. Clemens himself was the habitual bookkeeper, totting up the number of pages he had written, the number of books his publisher had sold, the number of dollars he had received. His calculations could involve subscription book requirements or his price per word to magazines. No matter that he said, very late, in "The Turning Point of My Life" (1910), that he was essentially a writer: that was for public consumption and personal encouragement. Few men have written more; yet over the years he had liked to think of himself as an inventor, businessman, or investor. He set literature aside if what seemed to be better prospects for getting rich presented themselves. Editors of Clemens's notebooks point out that so little was he dedicated to art that he looked forward to being freed from the burden of writing by success in business.[56] He was, of course, a writer but in some senses not essentially a writer: he wrote from habit, or he wrote to make money when other sources of revenue failed him.

Putting his footloose, slightly disreputable past behind him, Clemens was never before or afterward so nearly the contentedly enwombed bourgeois gentleman as he was from the time he went to Hartford in 1871 to the time of his desperate troubles in the 1890s. He remarked during the halcyon days, "whatever I touch turns to gold." His books sold remarkably well, and he could always force more through the production line. His readings and lectures brought him money and reputation. He was perpetually on the verge of making millions by speculative investments, and he was almost always short of cash. The mansion that he completed in 1873 gratified his exhibitionistic tendencies. Within the mansion his wife, daughters, and—as he saw it—tastefully displayed possessions combined to place him in an appropriately lavish setting and to suggest a firmly corporeal, stable personality.

Looking backward after bankruptcy and family tragedy, Clemens could not decide whether this period of happiness was real or a dream. Regardless of his monetary and psychological circumstances, however, his status as a hero developed and persisted. He satisfied conflicting national needs. He was a devotee of nostalgia and a worshiper of progress; and America luxuriated in the belief that he, under the guise of his metaphoric pseudonym, both embodied the myth of a bygone West and presented the industrial present in an acceptable guise.

In actuality, by the Marxist formula, Clemens, as writer, busily transformed himself into as nearly perfect an example as may be of capitalism at work to dehumanize the artist. He had used several impermanent pen names when he first contributed to newspapers, and in 1863 he chose what proved to be a lasting pseudonym: Mark Twain. This was not to conceal identity (as it often was in eighteenth-century England, for example) but followed a popular custom, authorized a humorous tone in his letters and reports, and gave them a special cachet. As he gained in reputation, letters signed with the pseudonym were paid for at a higher rate than were letters left unsigned. At the time of his bankruptcy in 1894, he took a highly symbolic step that further alienated him from his creations. Allegedly in payment for Livy's loans but in truth more to protect future royalties from creditors, he assigned copyrights to his wife. After that, "Mark Twain" and the books belonged to Livy; and Mark Twain's money value was presumably guarded against the indiscretions of Samuel Clemens. Toward the end of his life, as a final masterstroke, he incorporated himself as the Mark Twain Company and made "Mark Twain" into a legal trade mark intended to perpetuate the exchange value of his products. As the *New York Times* put it, the intention was to keep the earnings of his books "continually in the family, even after the copyright on the books themselves expires." In the forthrightness of its details, this metamorphosis of self and works into commodities has never, I think, been matched. It is, nonetheless, the potentially representative by-product of the capitalist paradigm, the model for others to approximate. The historical materialist could read it as prophetic, as a social enthymeme which included the tacit assumption, or unstated premise, that under capitalism all artists are en route to being Mark Twains, engendering objectified capital from what under different circumstances would have been uniquely expressive artistic creations.

That Clemens should make his pseudonym into a trademark may be taken as a strong indication that to him his writings very much resembled manufactured goods. Two related episodes speak eloquently of his attitude. Shortly after the publication of *Innocents Abroad*, a book that proved to be a big money-maker, Charles Langdon was being sent around the world with a "local savant" named Darius R. Ford assigned to instruct and watch over him. Clemens wanted Ford to write travel letters that Clemens would rewrite and publish. This scheme fell flat, but Clemens remained enamored of the basic conception. In 1870–71 he made enthusiastic plans to subsidize a journey by James Henry Riley, a journalist friend, to the diamond fields of South Africa, then excitingly in the news. Riley was to make notes, return, and let Clemens pump him dry in order to construct a book. Riley would then move on to another in a series of "quaint" countries, and a stream of sequels would ensue. Although Riley actually made the excursion to South Africa, he died before Clemens got around to pumping him dry.[57]

In these cooperative enterprises, Clemens's function as a writer would have been to arrange and adorn for a popular audience materials that were presented to him as on a production line. He would clip, screw, or bolt on picturesque descriptions or salient facts from the notes or works of others and color the whole assemblage with his own brand of humor. The product would be the saleable article that "Mark Twain" had come to stand for.

Even though the book on the diamond mines was never written, other travel books were; and they more or less followed the projected model. The writer's seal was placed on assorted materials that often had little or nothing to do with him. As Simmel points out, under conditions of this kind the artist becomes acutely subjective and dissociates himself from the object he makes. Not all of Clemens's work fits into the category described—particularly not his few mysteriously individualized achievements—but this tendency to standardize the product (and to alienate the artist from his writings) continued throughout his career. To put the idea of money before everything else became a kind of reflex; and the standardization of the product was matched by a dehumanization of the writer. The dollar awards that he passed out in his writings—as to Tom, Huck, and Jim—are paralleled at points in his life, as in his deathbed bid for Clara's love when he informed her of how responsibly he had tried to care for her financial future. His lasting monument was not—like that of Captain Isaiah Sellers, a Mississippi River pilot whom Clemens wrongly alleged to have preceded him as "Mark Twain"—an easily eroded sandstone image of himself standing at a pilot's wheel but a lasting, financially rewarding trademark.

Ferdinand Tönnies considered land to be the primary value in a gemeinschaft, money in a gesellschaft. In accordance with the Tönnies formula, Clemens was a quintessentially modern man, the representative American capitalist, for whom art—like technology and politics—is simply a form of business: in this light conflict between art and money is not possible.

If Clemens's critics frequently have been wide of reality in the attributes which they have assigned him as a representative American, this does not mean that he was not in important ways representative, most of all, perhaps, in the impoverishment and distortion of his personality by his absorption in money. His imagination was thoroughly monetized. He was authentically a man of the Gilded Age in his greed, in his reification of money as something more than abstract economic value, in making money what Simmel calls a very distinctive extension of the self, in his lavish symbolizing of money, and in tacitly accepting money, especially in its displayed forms, as the final definition of reality. The mansion that he built at Redding contained, it is said, nineteen rooms. There in the master's orbit circled

Paine, Isabel Lyon, and—at times—his daughters. There were, in addition, numerous visiting sycophants, both adults and children. His great house in Hartford and the mansion at Redding reflected his *folie des grandeurs* and gave expression to the power and wealth that he gloried in. They also bolstered his ego; he reassured himself with luxurious living. To the psychoanalytic view, however, the acquiring of money and the spending of money were ultimately diversionary tactics that cloaked the fundamental theme of guilt and punishment that is spelled out more clearly in his speculations.

Clemens's speculating may appropriately be seen as an obsessive manifestation and a symptom of more than marginal psychic masochism. Many of the elements that are emphasized in the theories of gambling are in his case pressingly heuristic; and the more we know of him, the more exigent are the formulations of the analysts. He did possess, however, a kind of double vision; he was not always lacking in self-perception. After the failure of the Paige typesetter, he managed to write with wry humor of inventors, speculating on inventions, and speculating in general. When the author of a book calculated to assist inventors and patentees wrote asking for his endorsement, Clemens answered, "I have, as you say, been interested in patents and patentees. If your books tell how to exterminate inventors send me nine editions. Send them by express." He devised maxims against speculation: "October. This is one of the peculiarly dangerous months to speculate in stocks in. The others are July, January, September, April, November, May, March, June, December, August, and February." More succinctly: "There are two times in a man's life when he should not speculate: when he can afford it, & when he can't."[58]

In a letter of March 24, 1898, Clemens told Henry Rogers, "I feel like Col. Sellers." At times he was as nearly as could be the ludicrously aberrant colonel of *The Gilded Age* (1873) with most of the comedy stripped away and the pathology showing. He took little interest in his reasonably safe investments. He preferred to back long shots which he, in his superior wisdom, knew to be nearly sure things. The Paige machine exactly suited his tumescent fancy: it was a complicated apparatus in a field in which Clemens considered himself to be an expert. During euphoric periods he could believe that the machine would make him rich beyond measure, a prince among capitalists, admired for the genius he had displayed in backing the invention and capturing financial control.

In his role as the lord-to-be of men and machines, Clemens would reachieve something like the infant's assumption of omnipotence. When the typesetter proved to be a failure, he suffered from poignant remorse; but, following his customary pattern, he was soon exculpating himself and castigating scapegoats. The addiction remained: he was, no matter how irrationally, a speculator still. In his recidivism the depriving parents had their answer; he was in the end defiant, unconquerable. And yet, deep anxieties remained.

As Clemens wondered in his late fictions whether life was or was not a fully determined dream, he was presenting a variant on a defensive explanation often given to psychoanalysts by speculators: all life is a gamble in which one is fated to lose and therefore may not be blamed for losing. In fact, as the psychoanalysts add, the patient clearly hopes to expiate his guilt by losing.[59] But expiation through losing brought, of course, only the most transient of satisfactions to Clemens. The conception of a divine order became an abomination to him. His clamorous outcries were likely to be puzzled, indignant, and self-pitying, as when bankruptcy followed by the loss of Susy (who died horribly of meningitis on August 18, 1896) brought all of his anxieties to a temporary focus. His confused mingling of love, happiness, money, and their loss permeates a letter to Joseph Twichell, his minister friend: "To me she was but treasure in the bank; the amount known, the need to look at it daily, handle it, weigh it, count it, *realize* it, not necessary; and now that I would do it, it is too late; they tell me it is not here, has vanished away in a night, the bank is broken, my fortune gone, I am a pauper. . . . Why am I robbed, and who is benefited?"[60]

Clemens's pseudoaggressions against Authority are compressed even more positively into a tribute to Susy written on the first anniversary of her death. At Weggis, by Lake Lucerne, he composed a brief memorial in wooden verses and, probably on the same day, a few lines in prose entitled "In My Bitterness." In the prose he fell with a seeming inevitability into the language of gaming. Susy's death becomes the culminating event in a long feud conducted by the Ultimate Authority, a God in whom Clemens thought he did not believe, against a suffering, courageous, enduring, victorious Samuel Clemens. God plotted Susy's death as a torment to Clemens, but his final punishing machination was a wicked blunder and a failure: "No, He gives you riches, merely as a trap; it is to quadruple the bitterness of the poverty which He had planned for you. . . . Ah, yes, you are at peace, my pride, my joy, my solace. He has played the last and highest stake in His sorry game, and is defeated: for your sake, I will be glad—and am glad. You are out of His reach forever; and I too; He can never hurt me any more."[61]

1. *Samuel L. Clemens, 1851 or 1852*   2. *Olivia L. Langdon, 1872*

3. Mark Twain in his study at Quarry Farm

4. *The Clemens family on a porch of their Hartford house in* 1885

5. *East facade of the Hartford house as restored*

6. *Mark Twain and George W. Cable,* 1884

7. *Samuel L. Clemens and Olivia L. Clemens in front of their house at 14 West Tenth Street, New York, in 1900 or 1901*

8. Mark Twain at Stormfield about 1908 in his Oxford cap and gown

9. *Mark Twain and William D. Howells at Stormfield, 1909*

10. *Mark Twain and Dorothy Quick, one of the Angel Fish*

OLIVIA,

GENDER,

AND

TASTE

▲ ▲ ▲ ▲ ▲ ▲ ▲ ▲ ▲

Olivia Clemens has often been considered a kind of nonperson who, nonetheless, either corrupted Mark Twain as an artist or failed to corrupt him only because in their lovingly bitter psychomachia, their war between the spirit of the East and the spirit of the West, Twain's primitive, masculine strength was too much for her debilitating powers. Van Wyck Brooks thought that she existed only as a reflex of upper-crust Elmira, New York, the home of her solidly bourgeois parents and that Elmira was but a dim reflection of a mawkish, traditionalist Boston. He held that Clemens was the pawn of social and psychological forces, that Olivia won the struggle for his artistic soul and bore the major responsibility for his ruin. Although, as we have seen, Bernard DeVoto opposed Brooks on nearly everything, he, too, thought that Twain confronted the dessicated remains of a once-vital eastern culture—DeVoto wrote of it, intending to insult, under the heading "Cryptorchism"—but did not succumb to it; instead, he won his battle.[1]

That both Brooks and DeVoto scorned the literary culture of the East made it easy for others to agree with this judgment even though they might disagree about the effect of the East on Twain. DeLancey Ferguson, like DeVoto, praised him as the supreme American man of letters, more representative than Emerson or Whitman. In a tone of bluff, Johnsonian punditry—a tone favored by DeVoto, also—he asserted that although Livy rightly deleted small bits of the macabre and gruesome from her husband's manuscripts, Twain was his own man. He dominated Livy in all important ways: his books were frank and socially courageous; there was nothing unusual about his commercialism; and his love of luxurious living simply reflected the need of a sensitive nature for shelter.[2]

Ferguson's positions are orthodox among academic Twainians. Those of James M. Cox are more extreme. Cox has portrayed Olivia's existence not as a reflex of Elmira but as entirely dependent on Clemens: she was his invention. Apart from him, she had no personality, no essential individuality. A play element controlled their relationship, with Clemens acting out his part as a humorist. He played at doing obeisance, played at endorsing sexual taboos, pretended to respect women—and all of this "impersonating" was a way of gaining approval "for whatever subversions his humor would enact." This totally insubstantial Olivia occupied a niche within the Freudian scheme of the mind. Like the superego (but does this interpretation falsify the endopsychic nature of the superego?), she offered a necessary friction. By setting free Clemens's memory and humor, she enabled him to write.[3]

That Livy's opposition enabled Clemens to write would seem to be sheer fancy—he wrote before he met Livy—but suppositions of Livy's lack of individuality or of her essential nullity have a limited validity at least for the period of Clemens's courtship and for the early years of his marriage. The young Olivia tended to be a congeries of pallid conventions; later she became more self-willed and more of a person, not at all a ventriloquist's dummy, speaking the part given her in a comic dialogue of Clemens's anarchic arrangement.

At the heart of the mystery and importance of Olivia to the critics is her editing, bowdlerizing, and otherwise exercising influence on the writings of Clemens from the time their courtship began in the autumn of 1868 until her death in 1904. In the beginning, particularly, her incapacity for ordinary editorial duties was beyond dispute. She had almost no formal education; she had read little; her taste was insipid; her spelling was atrocious; her punctuation uncertain; and her actual editing concerned itself for the most part with minor matters. Nevertheless, Samuel Clemens—a rising writer and lecturer—implored this incompetent young woman to reform his western habits and attitudes and to purify his works.

In "The Young American" (1844) Emerson followed a set of recognized favorable conventions in associating the West with the production of American genius. Nine years later (drawing on Carlyle?) he made the sobering observation that societies, like individuals, develop, mature, and die: the flowering time is the end, and "we ought to be thankful that no hero or poet hastens to be born." The imagery here would seem to have been grounded in a belief that the Kantian Reason, nurtured by the wilderness, is destroyed by cities; and in hitting upon his trope, Emerson may have been remembering Pope's melancholy comment to Swift: "The flowers are gone, when the fruits begin to ripen." Sad fruition or not, influential critics saw Clemens as the frontier hero for whom America had been waiting. Clemens, however, had a rather different role in mind for himself.

Clemens's utter self-abasement before Livy did not have its origins in the deceptions of romantic love. He felt great anxiety about his westernness and was disposed to subject himself to sympathetic representatives of high culture before he left California. If he entered the East famous by reason of his associations with frontier, Garden, and authorship, Livy was to him aural by reason of being rich, eastern, and a woman. To Brooks, Livy represented an America that was profoundly hostile to art; to Clemens, allowing for a certain ambiguity, she represented civilization at its zenith. He asserted repeatedly that she deserved all the credit for his serious work. She was for him a principal symbol of cultural status and an inhibiting, protecting amulet.

Psychological as well as social explanations may be offered for Clemens's exaggerated conceptions of Livy's editorial usefulness. As one chain of reasoning runs, Clemens, affected with more than marginal psychic masochism, sought controlled rebukes, failures, and punishments. As wife and as censor, Livy "dusted him off," was a surrogate for the lovingly punishing parent or parents. Other approaches would tend to identify Livy as an external sexualization of the idealized mother imago or as the narcissistically cathected self-object which supplies a confidence otherwise lacking in Clemens, who inadequately idealized his superego.[4] My intention, however, is not to pursue psychological explanations but to review biographical-historical elements that relate to Livy's authority: Livy's identity, the geography of taste, and the role of women as connoisseurs.

The early emphasis by Clemens and by others on Livy's exceptional refinement and fragility consorted with a stereotype. Howells called her "the flower and perfume of ladylikeness." Annie Fields, wife of James T. Fields, the Boston publisher, described her as an exquisite lily, "so white and delicate and tender!"[5] A lily in danger of being crushed, one supposes, in the embrace of a wild man from Washoe. Reality was different. Livy was never physically strong, but she held enormous powers from the start of Clemens's courtship. After her marriage, she was not a domestic tyrant; but she was mistress of the house, and when she had children, she governed them. In Heidelberg in 1878, Clemens set down a snatch of conversation between Susy, then six, and their landlord at the Schloss-Hotel: "Why your papa would let you have wein," said Mr. Albert. "Yes," replied Susy, "but we do as mamma says." A few years later, Susy remarked acutely in her biography of her father, "Although papa usually holds to his own opinions and intents with outsiders, when mama realy desires anything and says that it must be, papa allways gives up his plans (at least so far) and does as she says is right (and she is usually right, if she disagrees with him at all)." After Livy's death, Clemens moaned, "She who is gone was our head, she was our hands. We are trying to make plans—*we*; we who have never made a plan before, nor ever needed to."[6]

Wives are in some ways the inventions of their husbands, husbands of their wives; but, however derived, Livy had a personality, a will, and a conscience. It was a Victorian notion that women possess reality chiefly as they relate to their fathers, husbands, employers, and other dominant male persons. This conceit is, of course, to a large degree a manifestation of phallocentrism. Brooks not only projected this idea about Livy's essential nullity but associated her (and other women who supposedly assisted in emasculating Clemens) with debased Puritanism and social conformity.

Insofar as Clemens's possibilities as an artist were cankered, he was responsible for the blight. Olivia and the East did, however, have an enormous effect on him, for ill as well as for good, and not only when he supposedly threw them such sops as *The Prince and the Pauper* (1882) and

Joan of Arc (1896). His humorous stance may have been largely set when he left the West, but his prose style, social attitudes, themes, and subjects were not entirely fixed. Although ambivalent about East and West, he believed in the general superiority of eastern culture to western culture. Bret Harte and others had refined him in the West; in New York he was quite ready to adapt his sketches and his lectures to eastern taste. Moreover, he tended to accept as privileged the judgment on cultural matters of eastern gentlewomen. His need for eastern editing was not, however, as acute as he feared: his ethos and the ethos of the dominant culture were in most ways the same.

Critical opinion about the origin and the extent of the influence on Clemens's prose of the cultivated East has long been mixed. Albert Bigelow Paine, an active exponent of good taste who silently bowdlerized letters and journals as he published them, argued for a rapid improvement in Clemens's writing beginning in 1867 when he sailed from New York on the *Quaker City*. Without question, Clemens was under genteel pressures, both friendly and hostile, on board the ship. Paine believed that chapters 8 and 9 of *The Innocents Abroad* (1869) "reveal a remarkable and rather sudden development in Mark Twain's literary style," and he explained that the new cultural milieu, which included Europe and the Middle East, had something to do with it: "His imagination responded readily to the picturesque, and to the poetic association that clings to crumbling historic landmarks."[7]

A few modern critics have agreed that Mark Twain in 1867 needed civilizing influences and benefited from them. Dixon Wecter calls the period between 1867 and 1871 decisive years in Mark Twain's development and credits Mary Mason Fairbanks (Mrs. Abel W. Fairbanks) with considerable influence. Walter Blair thinks that Mrs. Fairbanks pounced on Clemens at the start of the voyage, lectured him, and informed him when his copy lacked refinement. Justin Kaplan believes that by the time the *Quaker City* was in the Mediterranean, she had become Clemens's mentor in morals and in writing.[8]

Dewey Ganzel, in his book on the voyage of the *Quaker City*, sees no important influence by fellow passengers. He points out that Mrs. Fairbanks probably did not become friendly with Clemens until the ship left Alexandria, homeward bound, the trip more than half over, and that the later letters, which he thinks she copyread rather than edited, were generally inferior, written in haste. Nor, he thinks, was Mrs. Fairbanks, who wrote letters home for her husband's paper, the Cleveland *Herald*, capable of improving Clemens.[9] In these judgments, Ganzel is, I think, only partly correct. Mother Fairbanks, as Clemens called her, did write dull, conventional letters, loading her pedestrian prose with cliché allusions; but she wrote correctly, and she did more than copyread. During the early stages of their friendship, Clemens seems genuinely to have valued her advice on such matters as grammar, vulgarity, impiety, and the lampooning of fellow passengers.

Most critics have directly opposed Paine, considering the West to be the true America and the decisive influence on Clemens. The East was a simple polishing agent or, at worst, was injurious. William Dean Howells identified Clemens's style as "the American Western." Bernard DeVoto insisted on Clemens's essential westernness. Edward Wagenknecht asked rhetorically what the difference is between Clemens and other authors: "The answer may be given in a single word: the Frontier." DeLancey Ferguson identified as a commonplace the opinion that Clemens's mature style was first established fully in *The Innocents Abroad*; but he himself thought that Clemens's style was almost equally advanced in the *Alta* letters, from which the book was, for the most part, compiled. Franklin Walker wrote that when Twain left San Francisco, "The Western frontier had given him all that he could use." Edgar M. Branch stressed that Clemens learned what he needed to know in the West; his letters from the Sandwich Islands rounded out his formative training. Henry Nash Smith summed up dominant opinion before Van Wyck Brooks questioned it as holding Clemens to be "the typical Westerner, a spokesman for the frontier in literature."[10]

Stephen Fender has discredited extravagant positions taken by western chauvinists but believes that the West made a difference in Clemens's writing beyond that attributable to practice and normal maturation. In the West Clemens began his search for a style of living and a style of writing. To Clemens, the West was wild, without standards, the East normative, more central to American culture, possessed of the true values of a stable society. Although the contrast between eastern gentility and western savagery provided him and other Washoe wits with material for humor, yet Clemens could not stand firmly either inside or outside so ill-defined a society. As a result, he took the position now of the East, now of the West.[11]

Protagonists of both the East and the West have tended to neglect traditions and myths. Advocates of eastern influences have seen Clemens's imagination blossoming as it responded to Europe, to history made manifest; western chauvinists reply that the democratic West was inspirational, its newspapers an adequate school for writing. They oppose the deep, instinctual impulses of Washoe and the invigoratingly original, masculine speech and attitudes of its people to the standardizing, falsely rhetorical voices of the East.

As expressed by champions of the West, this opposition resembles a struggle between an inspirational id and a cramping superego, with the ego at peril in the middle. Where virtue lies is not in doubt. Deep in the background are images of the Garden; closer to the surface is Romanticism. Society, as Rousseau said, corrupts. And this is the lesson, as partisans of a vernacular West usually see it, taught by the literary career of Samuel Clemens and by his masterpiece, *Adventures of Huckleberry Finn* (1885). The West made Mark Twain: it gave him a mode and an orientation. When he departed from the western scene and from the western tone—from the Great Valley, the heartland, the frontier—barren codes of a culturally debased East enfeebled him.

Most of the westerners whom Clemens knew were, of course, transplanted easterners or middle westerners who were undergoing cultural change. Like Bret Harte, he made the conflict between cultures the subject of sketches; but for him the radical opposition of symbolic systems came later. Before he left the West, his assignment to "write up" the sugar industry of the Sandwich Islands put him in the position of being "a spokesman for respectable opinion," that is, for business interests and genteel society.[12] But what is sometimes thought of with some justice as a Great Divide does seem to have been made emphatic when he came under the influence of the passengers on board the *Quaker City*. Something of his openness to new experiences and opinions is suggested by the intensity of his feelings about those whom he liked or disliked.

Starting from New York on June 8, 1867, the paddle-wheel steamer journeyed to Europe, along the northern shores of the Mediterranean to the Black Sea, and arrived back in New York on November 19. This luxury cruise, the first of its kind, immersed Clemens in a pious, upper-middle-class atmosphere at a time when his life and career had reached a major turning point. He was prepared to adapt to eastern culture; but he was not prepared for the hostile treatment that some of his fellow passengers accorded him, and he ended by detesting most of "the Quakers." Letters to family and friends make clear that he did not despise the Quakers because they (or some of them) were wealthy and genteel. It seems to have been in part because they thought him boorish that he decided that they were dull, grasping, and sanctimonious; and he took pleasure in portraying them as such in letters to newspapers. At the same time, he worked to make himself invulnerable: he would be famous, rich, and correct; perhaps the East would be his oyster.

The letters about his travels that Clemens contracted to write were supposed to be amusingly suffused with his own literary persona. The *Alta* wanted comments on the Old World from the standpoint of a frontiersman with a sense of western humor: "You will continue to write . . . in the same style that heretofore secured you the favor of the readers of the *Alta California*."13

The irreverence, vulgarity, and buffoonery that were expected of Clemens by the *Alta* were part of his stock-in-trade, but they disturbed some western readers and were distressing to a good many readers and reviewers in the East. His problems with easterners were, nevertheless, more a matter of manners than of substance. As his correspondence with Livy and with Mrs. Fairbanks makes plain, if his values were not already identical with theirs, he would learn to conform. The pressures he felt while on board the *Quaker City* and the adverse comments that he received on *The Innocents Abroad* reinforced his belief that eastern taste and western taste were drastically different and that eastern taste was, on the whole, to be preferred.

Mrs. Fairbanks, originally an Ohioan but educated in the East, considered Clemens to be a brilliant young man who needed to have his rough edges smoothed, and Clemens received her chiding with sincere if sometimes playfully exaggerated gratitude. Solon Severance and young Emma Beach, two passengers whom he liked, are said to have recollected that Clemens discarded pages of which Mrs. Fairbanks disapproved.14

When Mrs. Solon Severance, another of Clemens's favorites on the *Quaker City,* expressed to Clemens her pleasure in *The Innocents Abroad* but added that she found in it things that should have been omitted—probably meaning impieties and the caricaturing of fellow passengers—Clemens agreed that he, too, wished that he had weeded out more of the things that now grieved him: "But for you & Mrs. Fairbanks it would have been a very sorry affair. I shall always remember both of you gratefully for the training you gave me—you in your mild, persuasive way, & she in her efficient tyrannical, overbearing fashion." Clemens's sincerity in such statements is attested by his telling his publisher earlier that "the irreverence of the volume appears to be a tip-top feature of it ⟨financially⟩ diplomatically speaking, though I wish with all my heart there wasn't an irreverent passage in it."15

Three weeks after the end of the cruise, Clemens wrote a letter to his family that reflects his desire to conform to the East. Mrs. Fairbanks, he said, "was the most refined, intelligent, & cultivated lady in the ship." She sewed his buttons on, fed him on Egyptian jam when he behaved, and lectured him on moonlit promenading evenings. She "cured me," he added, "of several bad habits. I am under lasting obligations to her."[16]

Clemens retained, to be sure, a good opinion of himself and of his prose style. Western humor had opened up both the West and the East to him; he could regret yielding to its excesses, but he could not renounce it. And later, when adverse British criticism of *A Connecticut Yankee* (1890) stung him, he could, for self-protection, claim never to write for the thin top crust of humanity but only for "the mighty mass of the uncultivated who are underneath."[17]

Clemens's efforts to please the Langdons by entirely reversing his irreligious inclinations lasted only briefly. His attacks, mainly private, on some of their dearest shibboleths were not, of course, a matter of an East-West polarity. During the 1870s and 1880s he wrote, but did not publish, such sketches as "The Holy Children," "The Second Advent," "The Lost Ear-Ring," and "The Emperor-God Satire." These skeptical jottings ridicule self-satisfied moralism, literal readings of the Bible, the merit of established churches, notions of special providences, and the idea of the virgin birth.

Most of Clemens's writings of this kind were begun, set aside, reworked, and left unfinished. Olivia found those sketches that she read to be objectionable, and Clemens seems almost always to have yielded to her opinion when she opposed publication. He did, nevertheless, incorporate excerpts from a few sketches into other writings and sent at least two completed pieces to editors, only to have them rejected. After Livy's death he continued to suppress most of these manuscripts, usually by failing to complete them.[18] Although Clemens refused to give up certain of his intellectual convictions, he found no problem with trying to make the bulk of his work attractive to genteel readers; and the impressive sales of *The Innocents Abroad* established that, with a little care, he could pass the inspection of eastern critics and appeal to a national audience.

Even earlier, as Clemens began to rework contributions to the *Alta* for use in *The Innocents Abroad*, he wrote from Washington to Mrs. Fairbanks that he didn't like "any of those letters that have reached me from California so far. I may think better of those you weeded of slang, though."[19] Writing from California, where he had gone to gain control of the letters that he sent to the *Alta*, he reported that "the most straight-laced" of the San Francisco preachers were blasting him for what he wrote about the Holy Land (yet what in that "was so peculiarly lacerating?"), but that ministers of high rank and real influence "have complained of nothing save the rudeness & coarseness of those Holy Land letters which you did not revise."

In another letter Clemens mentioned the demanding standards of eastern lecture audiences as contrasted with western and reassured Mrs. Fairbanks that he had benefited from her instructions. Although he had pleased his large, fashionable audiences in San Francisco, he did not forget that he was among friends and that he "would be pretty roughly criticized" if he were to deliver the same lecture in an eastern town. He knew one thing, however: "There is no slang, & no inelegancies in it—& I never swore once, never once was guilty of profanity." (This distaste for elements that he lumped together as slang was not new. In a letter of May 23, 1867, to the *Alta*, he had protested its use.) Again, writing to Jervis Langdon, he confessed that his conduct while he lived on the Pacific Coast was not of a character to recommend him "to the respectful regard of a high eastern civilization, but it was not considered blameworthy there, perhaps."[20]

During this period of attempted self-transformation, Clemens resented unauthorized advertising that his brother, Orion, and his publisher, Elisha Bliss, gave to humorous contributions that they assumed he would make to a proposed periodical. "I lay awake all night," he wrote to Orion, "aggravating myself with this prospect of seeing my hated nom de plume (for I loathe the very sight of it) in print again *every* month."[21] He hated the pseudonym because it was associated with western comedy: Livy considered comedy to be a debased form of literature.

Clemens's expressions of revulsion at what he had been when he arrived in the East were repeated from time to time. In 1874 he praised the *Atlantic* audience because it did not require a humorist "to paint himself stripèd & stand on his head every fifteen minutes." The following year when Howells, reviewing *Sketches, New and Old* (1875), found "a growing seriousness of meaning in the apparently unmoralized drolling," Clemens wrote that Livy was grateful for this utterance of a truth that others lacked the courage to speak: "You see, the thing that gravels her is that I am so persistently glorified as a mere buffoon, as if that entirely covered my case—which she denies with venom." In 1884 he groaned to George W. Cable, with whom he was giving readings, "Oh, Cable, I am demeaning myself. I am allowing myself to be a mere buffoon. It's ghastly. I can't endure it any longer."[22]

When Clemens published such works as "Mental Telegraphy," *The Prince and the Pauper,* and *Joan of Arc* he dissociated them from his pseudonym and the expectations of comedy that accompanied its use. The more important of these works were forthright bids to join eastern society on its own terms, to separate himself from the primitive, and to compose serious literature.

The attitudes of Livy and of the Clemens children toward Clemens's humor and his westernness were similar to but more extreme than those of Clemens. They could be proud of his wit and his fame, but they were embarrassed by his personal crudities and by his reputation as a punchinello. Grace King, a well-bred young woman from New Orleans who won a name for herself with her feeble stories, visited the Clemenses in Hartford and at the Villa Viviani in Florence. On first acquaintance in 1888, she declared that Livy's "taste in literature was impeccable" and that the censoring of Clemens's irreverencies was a good thing. Susy, Miss King reported, could be extremely bitter about the categorization of her father as a comedian. In Florence, Susy spoke of how she felt about a ball she attended in Berlin: "She loathed the memory of it and hated her pretty dress. She had received no attention save as the daughter of Mark Twain." Susy elaborated: "How I hate that name! I should like never to hear it again! My father should not be satisfied with it! He should show himself the great writer that he is, not merely a funny man! Funny! That's all the people see in him—a maker of funny speeches!"23

Clemens eagerly pursued the remarkable sales that his comedy brought him, but he wanted in addition the praise of the sophisticated. He was sensitive to the scandal that he generated in Elmira, Hartford, and Boston with his unfashionable overcoat, his slippers, his string ties, his whiskey, his drawl, and his oaths. Perhaps his most characteristic response to suggestions that he was personally uncouth was to exaggerate his mannerisms. Being a humorous westerner was his profession, his livelihood, an important part of his public self, and an ineradicable part of his private self.

The editor of the Springfield, Massachusetts, *Republican* joined those, including Livy and Howells, who thought Clemens's humorous speech at the dinner party honoring Whittier's seventieth birthday (1877) to have been in bad taste; and he called the speaker a "wild Californian bull." In this instance Clemens was, at least initially, contrite about his blunder, but there were other occasions, early and late, on which he showed resentment at adverse attention. As a reporter for the Virginia City, Nevada, *Territorial Enterprise,* he protested that a compositor was "too rotten particular" in changing *devil* to *d—l*. He would if he chose "use the language of the vulgar, the low-flung and the sinful, and such as will shock the ears of the highly civilized." Contrasting the inert language of a *Territorial* representative with his own, he wrote, "My language may be unrefined, but it has the virtue of being uncommonly strong."24

Western ways and southern and western audiences always had a strong appeal for Clemens, but as a writer he did not rely on uninterpreted recollections. Eastern associations and wide reading formed the basis for much of his work. While he was in the West he felt himself to be at ease but superior; once he left it, he returned only briefly and with no intention of remaining. The West became a shadowy memory of bohemian experiences that could never be repeated.

His status in the East was more complex. There he often felt himself to be an alien catechumen and possibly inferior. He also inclined to believe that he was superior to the East because he was western, natural, and an exponent of rational morality. Moreover, a generalized attitude of superiority accompanied his particular comic perspective: more than most humorists, he was the transcendent stranger and truth-teller, a gentile in any tribe.

Olivia Clemens, daughter of the first family of Elmira, epitomized to Clemens the best aspects of eastern society. When he pressed her to civilize him and amend his writings, what he wanted was to be brought into conformity with the linguistic and social norms of the upper class. That he gave up smoking, drinking, and profanity only temporarily has helped to enable critics to preserve a mistaken image of him as an independent man of the frontier. It is true that he powerfully influenced Livy, as in shaking her religious convictions; nevertheless, as woman, wife, and symbol Livy had exceptional power to enforce the restrictions that Clemens implored her to impose.

Dominant conceptions of women during the period in question may be said to fall into two rough, overlapping categories. There were more or less conscious responses to demands for women's rights; and there were inherited, often covert or unconscious attitudes. Clemens was fully aware of the ongoing debate on "the Woman Question." Not long before his marriage, he wrote to Livy that he had intended to mark and take to her S. R. Wells, *Wedlock; or the Right Relation of the Sexes* (1869) but found it a mass of platitudes and maudlin advice. William Dean Howells took an interest in rights for women. The Nook Farm neighborhood of Hartford in which the

Clemenses lived for twenty years was in some respects a seedbed for advanced thought. And as a constant reader of newspapers and magazines, Clemens was exposed to a flood of topical articles.

Sketches that Clemens wrote for the *Territorial Enterprise* in 1863 indicate that he was then as patronizing toward women as he was offensively superior to blacks. His attitudes were, of course, commonplace and existed even at the top of intellectual society. In February 1851, Emerson wrote in his Journal, "Women carry sail, and men rudders. Women look very grave sometimes, and effect [*sic*] to steer, but their pretended rudder is only a masked sail. The rudder of the rudder is not there."

In the early tales, sketches, and letters that treat women, Clemens inclined to a bantering tone and represented their occupations, interests, and practical capacities as being trivial. This attitude is fully exposed in three newspaper articles on suffrage for women published in March and April of 1867—before Clemens met any of the Langdons—when he visited his family in St. Louis.[25] During a brief stay in New York immediately prior to this, he had heard Anna Dickinson, who gave popular lectures on feminism, speak on the meager work possibilities open to women. He thought that she commanded respect, although personal liking for Miss Dickinson may have been responsible for this favorable opinion. Now, writing in St. Louis, he declared that, given the vote, every woman would run for State Milliner. His own family (he had none, of course, in the sense intended) would go to destruction, for he was not qualified to be a wet nurse. The second article was his own bogus reply to his first, written as though by three irritated feminists, one of them named Mrs. Mark Twain. The third article portrayed an imaginary legislature dominated by women, the male members trampled upon, the discussions centering on style and on restrictive measures for husbands.

Justice, Clemens admitted, called for female suffrage; but his explanation smacked of Know-Nothingism: an educated woman would have better judgment than could "the stupid, illiterate newcomers from foreign lands"; and "first-rate female talent" would be superior to the usual incompetent male legislator. Despite the possible injustice, however, women should not be given the vote: to do so would increase mediocrity in government. The female rascals would work, bribe, and vote with all their might; the better women would cling to the home and refuse to cast ballots.

In a letter to the *Alta* of May 19, 1867, Clemens repeated his opposition to suffrage for women. The letter was a topical olio on riverboats, river traffic, government, public schools, his lectures, his articles, and changes in the St. Louis he had known years earlier. The women of Missouri have, he explained, "started a sensation on their own hook" by petitioning the state legislature for the privilege of voting "(along with us and nigs., you know)." To his amazement, some of the best-known ladies of St. Louis signed the petition, and thirty-nine members of the legislature declared themselves to be for it. The proposed innovation is of colossal dimensions: "It is time for all good men to tremble for their country." Although he had attacked "the monster" in the public prints, he feared that "it might get uncommon warm for one poor devil against all that crinoline," so he had "antied up and passed out." He did not want to say much about it in the *Alta*, "because the ladies may take it up on the Pacific next, and I don't want to get myself into trouble there also."

The arguments that Clemens marshaled against suffrage for women were both hoary and pseudochivalric. He found distasteful the very notion of women "voting, and gabbling about politics, and electioneering." Voting and all it entailed would be degrading to the sex. He did not wish to take "the High Priestess we reverence at the sacred fireside and send her forth to electioneer for votes among a mangy mob who are unworthy to touch the hem of her garment." Universal suffrage would reduce women "to the level with negroes and men!"

In 1869 the subject of women's rights was brought very closely home to Clemens when he became acquainted with Isabella Beecher Hooker, a nationally prominent, doubtfully sane Nook Farm resident, said to have believed intermittently in her destiny—under God and her "adorable brother, Jesus"—to be grand matriarch of the world in a new apocalypse. Upon hearing from Livy in 1872 of Isabella's announced subsidence into private life, Clemens wrote home from London gibbeting her in one of his more remarkable impromptu invectives. Mrs. Hooker's solemn retirement from public life was, he said, news as grateful as humorous, but the tremendousness of her reason for retiring "(because 'her work is done' & her great end accomplished)" surpasses the merely humanly humorous, is the awful humor of the gods. Under the impression that she was helping a great and good cause, Isabella had been "blandly pulling down the temple of Woman's Emancipation," was a very "Spirit of Calamity," and "after all these long months, wherein she never rested from making enemies to her cause save when she was asleep, she retires serenely from her slaughter-house & says, in effect, Let the nations sing hosannah, let the spinning spheres applaud—my work is done!"[26]

Also in 1872, in a strikingly nativist essay, Clemens satirized the methods used by women crusaders for shutting down saloons. Their actions might be considered justifiable, however, because women were voiceless in the making of laws and in the election of officials. In 1891 Clemens's notebook observations on the defeat by a close vote of a woman suffrage bill in Illinois repeats his disparaging ideas of 1867: it was a narrow escape; the ballot is useful only when it is in the hands of the intelligent, and it would have gone to the wrong women.[27]

Probably few literate men of Clemens's generation went through life without altering in some degree their opinions on rights for women— certainly, late in life, after his more important writings were completed, Clemens gave evidence of revising his thinking. Apparently in utopian situations, suffrage for women is appropriate. Women vote in "The Curious Republic of Gondour" (1875) and in the republic planned by Hank Morgan in *The Connecticut Yankee in King Arthur's Court* (1889). In a notebook jotting set down while in New Zealand in 1895, he took a Condorcettian view of progressive stages in man's development: "We easily perceive that the peoples furtherest from civilization are the ones where equality between men and women are furthest apart—and we consider this one of the signs of savagery." Our stupidity, he added, prevents us from pursuing the argument and realizing "that no civilization can be perfect until exact equality between man and woman is included."[28] The unpublished "An Imaginary Interview" (1898) is supportive of women; and in 1901, arguing from the generally accepted premise that women are more moral than men, he assured his audience at the Hebrew Technical School for Girls, New York, that he would like to see women help make the laws, sweep away corruption in the city, and vote against unjust wars.[29] Between 1905 and 1910 he made several statements to the press that were favorable to women's rights.

As we shall see, to be set against this shift in Clemens's public expressions of opinion from the formulaic condescension of his earlier statements are the gynophobia and misogyny revealed in the erotic jokes that he was entering during these same years in his notebooks.

Clemens's belief that women were in certain ways superior to men was part of an ancient vision of complementarity that distinguished characteristics natural to the sexes. Medieval religious writers, for example, divided personality traits between men and women, fathers being associated with authority, mothers with affectivity. Although the frontier was in rare instances thought of as feminine and nurturing, this complementarity of the sexes paralleled the oppositions that were standard when the myth of the East was opposed to the myth of the West—discrimination against grossness; decorum against the boorish. It had some bearing on Clemens's acceptance of a complex dogma—one accepted by imitators of the Leatherstocking novels—grounded in beliefs about region, class, and gender: eastern gentlewomen possessed superior taste. George W. Cable, a reconstructed Confederate, sent the heroine of *John March, Southerner* (1894) to the North to acquire tact and taste from New England ladies. The vivacious conversation of Elinor Howells, who originated in Brattleboro, Vermont, was for no easily discernible reason thought to be fascinating by Clemens; and Livy considered Mrs. Howells to be *exceedingly* bright—very intellectual. It was in this context of gender, class, and place that Clemens invited Olivia to edit him. According to the dogma, she possessed an intuitive knowledge of aesthetic, social, and moral truth.

Livy's allegorical status was supported by more than a simple fiction about the genders: classic, neoclassic, and Romantic notions about art and taste lay behind it. Most authorities agreed that taste, whether innate or not, is educable; yet they tended to stress its spontaneous nature. Thus an epistemological opposition underlies much of the poetics of the eighteenth and nineteenth centuries. Taste was, generally, a separate faculty, an inner sense, one which acts without reflection. Any inference of anarchy could be countered by appealing to the uniformity of human nature, the verdict of the ages, and the universal principles of association.

Ideas of this kind were validated by the authority of writers like Père Bouhours, Vico, Lord Kames, Jean Paul, Novalis, and Blake. The extent to which the idea of spontaneity was popularized may be judged by turning to definitions in Larousse and Littré. Taste belonged, first, to the learned humanist, then to the cultivated gentleman, and finally to the gentlewoman. This chronological progression involved received ideologies about art and morality, taste and sensibility, and the special capacities of women, all matters that were debated endlessly in the periodicals of Europe, Britain, and America.

A connection between art and morality was generally taken for granted. (Kant would be an exception.) Plato, Shaftesbury, and Berkeley considered virtue and beauty to be twin sisters. Voltaire believed that good taste involved the moral and social sanctions of society; and Alexander Gerard made virtue one of the several components of taste. Ruskin, an extremist, wrote (in "Traffic") that a moral society and good art are necessary companions and that good taste is "not only a part and an index of morality; it is the *only* morality." In Clemens's society, religionists, publishers, editors, and general readers agreed that good art is moral and that good taste involves distinguishing the moral from the immoral.

This assumed relationship between art and morality when added to the notion that women are more moral than men fortified the assumption that women by nature possess good taste. John Stuart Mill, arguing in *The Subjection of Women* (1869) for the equality of the sexes, noted that women are more given than men to rapid insights into facts and are also superior in morality. These two conceptions—women are more spontaneous than men and the heart is their natural domain—relate to the earlier division of knowing into two kinds, one through the understanding, the other through *ingenium,* Kames's sense which acts without reflection, Novalis's postulation of an alogical sense in the critic.

John Gregory's enormously popular *A Father's Legacy to His Daughters* (it went through sixty-one editions between 1774 and 1869) asserts that women are inclined to delicacy, sensibility, elegance, and heart. Hannah More, Mary Wollstonecraft, Albertine Adrienne de Saussure Necker, and George Eliot argued that women are peculiarly endowed with taste. Coventry Patmore discoursed in insufferably candied tones of Victorian concerns about the disordered strivings of men and the calm, orderly world of women.[30]

Hugh Blair, much studied in America, offered a practical reason for supposing that women, more than men, possess good taste. Each sex possesses the rudiments of taste, but these rudiments may be developed. Because we must fill the vacant spaces in our lives and because gentlewomen have more vacant spaces to fill than do gentlemen, they are better able than are men to develop their potentialities. Furthermore, although good taste and morality are not the same, "the exercise of taste is, in its native tendency, moral and purifying."[31] This postulated conjunction of taste and morality had wide effects. Writers asked, for example, whether museums should be comprehensive or selective, that is, whether they should simply illustrate what exists, or should they discriminate in order to inculcate good taste and, at the same time, good morals.

Dixon Wecter asserted that Clemens "enjoyed a touch of feminine domination all his life—believing, with a faith characteristic of Victorian and western America, that woman with her finer sensibilities was the true arbiter of taste, manners, and morals." Wecter also held that Clemens was in love with ideal womanhood, which tradition exalted as a mystery "transcending the moral quality of the male."[32]

The superiority of women in taste and morals could be believed and disbelieved at the same time. Clemens was deeply ambivalent about women and their powers, but he never stopped talking and writing about Livy's good sense and her unerring literary judgment. His heroine in an unfinished novel of 1898 or 1899 was modeled on his idealized conception of Livy: "She had a sound, practical business head, and in the next compartment of her skull a large group of brain-cells that had a vivid appreciation of the beautiful in nature, art and literature, and an abiding love of it."[33]

In the American version of the hypothesis that women possess special capacities, eastern gentlewomen were sometimes given privileged status, thus associating the basic hypothesis with notions of frontier crudity versus eastern decorum. Even the South—locked in furious cultural combat with New England, Cavalier against Puritan, from about 1820 on—acknowledged during Reconstruction that its antebellum denigration of New England had in some respects been a perversion of the truth: New England was superior in education, publishing, and the arts. George Cable specified in *John March, Southerner* that Boston ladies were possessed by breeding, training, and intuition of something like perfect social tact. Howells accepted flattering conventions concerning eastern gentlewomen. Mildred Howells, writing almost as though she were drawing upon eighteenth-century theories of taste, speaks of her mother's "wonderfully true sense of proportion" in art and literature: although "she could never argue them out, her intuitive criticisms of books or pictures were almost unerring." One biographer, implicitly accepting East-West stereotypes, relates Elinor Howells's alleged capacities to her social and regional background, explaining that she "had the sharp intelligence, the intuitiveness, and the good taste tending toward hyperesthesia which was cropping out in that last true generation of the Brahmins."[34]

Remarks about Elinor Howells's intuitive judgments may be compared with what Clara Clemens wrote about her mother, whom she called an inspiring appreciator and critic, one "who had a pure instinct for the correct balance of values in literature as well as in life, and one whose adverse criticism proved invariably to be a just criticism because her intuition—born of a large heart and mind—hit the target plumb in the center." Though tallying with her father's judgment, this amiable characterization may be modified in the light of what Susy once wrote to Clara about their mother. At the time Clara wished to stay on in Berlin, where she was studying the piano and enjoying her social life, rather than return to Florence. Clara's letters about her "perfect time" in Berlin made Livy cry, Susy reported, because Livy thought that Clara didn't care any more for her "or any of us." Nor did Livy understand Clara's love for music: "She never has had any great artistic interest and she can't understand why it should make you *want* to stay away from her."[35]

When Howells was composing his elegiac "My Mark Twain" in the spring of 1910, he vaguely remembered that in 1875 Clemens may have been doubtful about the propriety of publishing *Tom Sawyer* and, at Livy's insistence, brought him the manuscript. This recollection appears to have been decidedly inexact, but what Howells writes of Livy's misgivings about her husband's work is both characteristic of her sentiments and indicative of the kind of West that Howells felt that Clemens should represent. Livy wished Clemens to be known not only for his wild and boundless humor but for beauty, tenderness, and natural piety. She would not have him "judged by a too close fidelity to the rude conditions of Tom Sawyer's life." In other words, Clemens's Mississippi Valley should be pleasingly pastoral, the barbarisms filed away.[36]

Clemens assured Livy that the taste with which she furnished and decorated their mansion in Hartford made it superior to anything that he had seen in Europe. After editorials condemned his comic speech at Whittier's birthday dinner, he sent an almost groveling letter of apology to Emerson, Longfellow, and Holmes. His blunder was not unlike having profaned a shrine, but it was, he protested, an innocent error, committed out of ignorance, because he didn't have "a fine nature." Then he interposed Olivia, who did have a fine nature, between himself and the men he had burlesqued. Her distress was "not to be measured; for she is of finer stuff than I; and yours were sacred names to her."[37]

Looking back in 1897, Clemens spoke typically of Olivia: he could do the spelling and grammar alone, "but I don't always know just where to draw the line in matters of taste." Also late in his life he explained to a biographer, "I never wrote a serious word until after I married Mrs. Clemens. She is solely responsible—to her should go the credit—for any deeply serious or moral influence my subsequent work may exert."[38]

From the beginning Livy did more than copyread and delete stray words and phrases from manuscripts. She was a bourgeois, churchly conscience; she influenced planning, writing, and publishing. At first she was modestly uneasy in her role, pleased and proud that a woman of letters like Mary Mason Fairbanks could think her capable of helping her famous fiancé; but modesty was quickly replaced by serene self-confidence. And why not? Clemens assured her that her supervision was invaluable, and the genteel public, including editors, would have agreed with him. Men are the movers and shakers; women possess culture and taste.

Olivia had not enjoyed Mrs. Fairbanks's advantages, but she kept a commonplace book and browsed in devotional literature: she was serious. She undoubtedly improved Clemens's writings by screening minor improprieties and inelegancies from them; more questionably, she impelled Clemens away from comedy toward sentiment, earnestness, morality, and elevated rhetoric. Even before he felt her pressure, however, Clemens was inclined to strive toward what Hugh Blair called "the sublime parts of eloquence."

That Livy was pleased when Clemens was lofty reinforced his tendency to vacillate between burlesquing the shoddy, popular "grand style" and trying himself to achieve elevation. The set descriptive passage, especially when given grandiose historical associations, what Mrs. Fairbanks in the Cleveland *Herald* called Clemens's "gorgeous word painting"—landscape, forestscape, seascape, riverscape, cloudscape—was his favorite device for attempting grandeur.

Clemens was sufficiently aware of the dangers inherent in the ornamented style to append to some of his own efforts joking disclaimers meant to bring the reader back to earth and to create a comic effect that would appeal to the common sense of plain men. One explanation of this unmasking of the inauthentic and showy is that Clemens, in his vernacular wisdom, was always self-consciously superior to genteel forms. It would be possible, however, to assemble some hundreds of examples of Clemens's ornamental prose ranging from the successful to the incompetent that were all offered seriously. His notebooks and his letters are also corroborative: he diligently tried his hand at decorative set pieces.[39]

Clemens's assertions that Olivia enabled him to transcend his past, to rise above his pseudonym, have a certain truth about them. When he entered the East, accomplished though he was in short journalistic forms, he was in his new environment an apprentice without a master. Instead of fixing upon a writer or a school of writers to follow, he subjected himself and his old modes to the mastership of upper-class culture. Livy, a concretion of that culture, was Agape; she was his Uranian muse—she led him to the heights.

Mother Fairbanks, Livy's predecessor, was quickly superseded and eventually became what she represented herself to be, a pathetic, managing old woman who was in the end very much down on her luck: "I know that I am only a kind of Mrs. Partington, but you are not Ike, and my apron string is no check to you."[40] Clemens partly outgrew Livy, too. He warned her in two or more instances that what he had written must not be changed; he came to omit her from the greater part of his sometimes manically active social life; and during the last half-dozen or more years of her life he wrote much that was displeasing to her. His relatively complete mastery of the East was established early. Hostile reviewers might call *Huckleberry Finn* vulgar, but beginning in 1874 the *Atlantic* begged him for contributions; and later he put William Dean Howells on his payroll to do hack work for him. He became a hero in Vienna, Berlin, and London—in the East's own East.

Successful though Clemens's books were, his generalized anxieties mounted during his later years. If Olivia lost some of her powers as literal censor, she may have gained strength as a personal guardian angel. Clemens's darkening mood has often been attributed to such definite causes as bankruptcy, the death of Susy, and the death of Livy, but these events may have been no more than possibly precipitating and reinforcing factors. Other explanations point to his inability to arrive at a satisfactory definition of his own selfhood and to his wrestling with determinisms that implied for him that all men are helpless creatures adrift in an absurd universe.

We may well believe that Clemens was burdened by his popular reputation, his public status, his personal and business losses, and by irresolvable philosophical issues. His contempt for aspects of the society to which he belonged and his distaste for various popular religious dogmas increased. His comedy had always made sport of the ridiculous, the pretentious, and the illogical. Now he was less quick to arouse laughter as a release from socially provoked tensions, more inclined to daydream of a society built to his own specifications, to dwell on the horrors that he thought were unreasonably visited upon him, to declare his hatred for a malevolent God, and to fantasize catastrophic voyages on uncharted seas.

It was contrary to Livy's wishes that he devoted himself to strivings toward pessimistically august intellectual achievements. For approximately fifteen years before his death he worried about the dangerous responsibility involved in setting down audacious, Olympian truths that would be unveiled eventually for the instruction of posterity. The attempt to reveal truths destructive of religious and, in some limited ways, of social orthodoxy became central to his writing. He began to insist that he would compose only to please himself. In 1896 he told a reporter for the Bombay *Gazette* that he enjoyed literary work for its own sake—he should like to have half a dozen works going "just for the pleasure of writing them." The following year he explained to a British civil servant that two of the books he was working on were not for publication in his lifetime.[41]

Some critics believe that Clemens, the western sky-hawk, through sibylline utterances avoided sinking without canonical trace into a comfortably bourgeois haven in the midst of the scientific, social, and philosophic American vortex; but late compositions do not justify any such optimistic interpretation. They have great psychological interest but, except for bits of autobiographical writings and, possibly, "The Mysterious Stranger," little literary importance.

The faith in progress through technological innovation and free enterprise that Clemens clung to for most of his life may be seen as a standard expression of a desire to bring order back into the disorderly late-nineteenth-century world. He was fascinated by ridiculous fads—by health foods, mind cures, and mental telepathy. He took a pessimistic view of "the damned human race," of God, and of nature. Perhaps as a way of escaping responsibility, he argued in favor of biological-mechanistic and environmental determinisms. He wrote privately and naively on aspects of sexuality. He made superficial, largely unpublished attacks on illogicalities in Christian belief, inconsistencies in the Bible, the institutionalized missionary business, and the murderous nature of imperialism, whether American or European. He intended to bare his soul in his autobiographical writings, but he did not—the more interesting sections are mainly gossip or diatribe.

By opposing him or by praising him, a conventional Livy, the equally conventional Joe Twichell, and the sycophantic nonentities with whom he surrounded himself after Livy's death encouraged him in his assumption that he was dealing with philosophic profundities and explosive truths. In actuality there was nothing original or masterful about most of his efforts: he followed the leadership of others even in his highly successful brief satires on missionaries and imperialism.

Clemens's numerous explanations of his reasons for suppressing most of his later writings, especially in view of their innocuousness, may be indicative of timidity in the face of bourgeois society, a general satisfaction with bourgeois society, and most especially of an excessive esteem for his own powers as an iconoclastic thinker.

What Is Man?—loathed by Livy, written under her ban, and published anonymously after her death—was "not offered for sale." Parts of the autobiography were to be withheld from publication for up to five hundred years. His view of man was such, he told Howells, that he would not in the future print much, for he didn't "wish to be scalped, any more than another." In 1895 he declared in a notebook entry that, because he had a family, he couldn't tell the truth about the useless universe and the contemptible human race. The epigraph and preface for the *Autobiography* as edited by Paine states that Clemens is "writing from the grave" because "on these terms only can a man be approximately frank." In the afterword Clemens wrote, "The human race is a race of cowards; and I am not only marching in that procession but carrying a banner."[42] Such observations may be perceived only as pretentious.

Biographers usually portray Livy as a loving wife and doting mother, Clemens as a worshiping husband and tender father. The life of the family is told as a whimsical success story exhibiting almost unparalleled mutual admiration and affection, poignantly shadowed in the end by death and financial disaster. Heavy shadings must be added to that account.

We have arrived at a point where East and West, gender, and taste come together. As we have seen, when Clemens married Olivia, she existed as a reflex of Elmira, that is, was a relatively ordinary, unindividualized young woman—as Jane Austen remarked of Catherine Morland in *Northanger Abbey,* "about as ignorant and unformed as the female at seventeen usually is," except that Olivia was an exceptionally inexperienced twenty-five. To Clemens she became at once an accordant eye, a trusted extension of the self, a touchstone for identifying bad taste.

He could elevate her as muse and depreciate himself because as an eastern gentlewoman she possessed an averred exact, intuitive literary sensitivity; also because the aspects of his writing over which she exercised control had little to do with such matters as spelling, punctuation, grammar, structure, character, and images, much to do with taboo words, decorum, morals, and religion; and finally because Clemens believed in general in the values which she espoused. As he saw it, Olivia's sanitizing presence ensured the assimilation of his western comedy to High Literature.

Olivia's limited, literal censorship removed a few obviously objectionable elements from his prose and helped him to bridge the gap between the low style in which he had perfected himself and a higher style to which he had long aspired. She esteemed the overblown set pieces that Clemens scattered throughout his works; like Clemens, she saw them as patches of the sublime. She commended the dim sentiments and cheap effects of writings like *The Prince and the Pauper*; they, too, accorded with her notions of the serious in art. In all larger matters her influence, which did not as a rule run counter to what Clemens thought good public taste should be, was to our present view stifling.

The death of Livy in 1904 made it necessary for Clemens to replace the fiction that she imposed her censorship on his works with the parallel semifiction that society forbade: society was not ready for his lately discovered, terrifying truths. Uninhibited publication would deprive him of readers, status, and money. This shift in his explanation for suppressing heterodox thoughts was, of course, more apparent than real: Clemens was always his own censor. Society was a depersonalized copy of Livy, and Livy and Clemens were much alike.

An explanation for this censorship from the Freudian standpoint would be that the entire process of writing and suppressing, both before and after Livy's death, was an aborted or controlled precipitation of punishment by surrogates for the parents—by Livy or by the genteel culture. Clemens was notably insecure and masochistic, but his late megalomaniacal trend is not contrary to expectations. His proposals that his vatic insights went beyond the capacity of his society to understand or to absorb is not unlike earlier aggressive and defensive maneuvers.

Olivia represented the eastern moneyed class directly; indirectly she symbolized all of the ego-gratifications that may be fantasized as correlative with gold hoards, including psychic security. In a not unusual Romantic way, Clemens conceived of himself as a unique personality possessing a unique sense of taste; yet he was insecure, and Livy became a second, better self that enabled him to polish away differences between his taste and standard good taste.

Correctly performed ritual observances ensure the achievement of a desired object. As a fetishized reminder of what Clemens took to be his highest goals, Olivia brooded over the routines of composition and publication. She was a shield against the hazards of the East, a haven from free-floating angst, a mother guarding his vulnerable psyche.

Social anthropology offers explanations for the more than normal powers that Clemens attributed to Olivia when he alluded to her as his angel, muse, and savior. The relationship resembled that of the individual, or the clan, with created sacred beings. Ideas of impersonal forces are, Durkheim tells us, social in their origins, and a complementary argument from a Marxist perspective is that the unity and survival of the community depend on the existence and actions of an imaginary being: man's relationship with his conditions of existence is both a real and a fantasmal one.[43]

We can now hypothesize that Clemens's cult of Olivia must be associated with the collective cult of the gentlewoman. Clemens set a fetishistic valuation on virginity; and his insistence on the separation of the sacred and the profane (during courtship he specified that Livy was the purest woman he had ever known and must remain so) may relate to her efficacy in purifying his works. Her oversight becomes an instance of the myth of the preeminent good taste of the gentlewoman made performative, turned into a rite.

As primitive man devises a god, so in a sense did Clemens. After transforming Livy into a protective divinity, he suppressed his awareness of his generative act. Olivia became a Presence at the same time that she remained real, studied German, and supervised the Clemens ménage. The physically infirm creature whom Clemens made his own by something resembling the abduction-acquisition method became a numinous paraclete who imposed the bonds of the sacred. By exercising her talismanic authority, she warded off the dangers of the alien culture; her domesticated mana was more potent than the demonic mana of the external world.[44]

Clemens himself proclaimed the legend of Livy as necessary editor, adored and flawless wife. Under scrutiny, Livy as the helper of peerless taste simply vanishes; and if the legend of a marriage that matched male and female in perfect unity does not vanish, it certainly must be questioned. Clemens's neuroses, tantrums, and misanthropy may not be treated as humorous eccentricities, and they did not habitually appear as such to Livy. There were destructive intrafamily tensions, especially during Livy's later years and after her death.[45] The relation between worshiper and protective spirit is not necessarily an unchanging one. Gods may chide or reject their devotees; and devotees may tease, neglect, and defy their gods. Perhaps Clemens's complex attitude toward Olivia roughly paralleled his sometimes troubled relationship with the East. To satisfy his material and psychic needs, he had to appropriate a new culture, to woo an East that was partly real, partly an aspect of an imagined pastoral: he had to dominate both the real East and the mythical East. At times Olivia and the East seem to have functioned as similitudes, even as twinned identities.

SEXUALITY

AND THE

CLEMENSES

6

▲ ▲ ▲ ▲ ▲ ▲ ▲ ▲ ▲

Although sexuality is crucial in the Freudian analysis of neuroses and although Clemens gave evidence of being more than a little neurotic, our present knowledge of his sexual nature from unambiguous sources is far from secure. Some speculations have proved to be altogether wrong. Van Wyck Brooks, for example, erred by attempting to establish as the causes of Twain's neuroses events supposed to have taken place during the writer's early youth, events which proved to be imaginary. Standard scholarship, on the other hand, generally errs in taking for granted that Mark Twain, western eidolon, had no psychic problems.

My intention here is to assemble pertinent information on selected aspects of sexuality among the Clemenses and to comment on symptoms rather than on originating causes. An important general article by Alexander E. Jones on Clemens's sexuality, although very much out of date, is helpful in introducing the subject.[1] Jones's article gathers the significant material that was available to him and points cautiously to hypothecated causes of Clemens's neuroses. He notes that a sense of guilt is one of the bases of Clemens's mind, and he explores in conventionally Freudian fashion ways in which that sense of guilt is linked with sexuality.[2] Clemens's often remarked recoil from sex, he reasons, may be attributed to an unresolved Oedipal conflict: a clinical history of the Clemens family during Sam's boyhood would have all the well-rounded symmetry of a textbook case. Citing evidence, Jones sees an unstable child who suffers from nightmares, convulsions, and somnambulism; an eccentric but warmhearted mother trapped in a loveless marriage, turning to her children for emotional responses; a stern father (eminently qualified to produce a castration complex in his son) whose early death prevented the proper development of Sam's superego and ego ideal. Today, additional biographical details could be adduced to support Jones's belief that he had a textbook case in hand.[3]

Otherwise puzzling aspects of Clemens's adult behavior are interpreted by Jones as regressions or continuations of phallic sexuality occasioned by a psychic trauma during the phallic stage of psychosexual development. Jones also supposes that if we remove Clemens's history from this Freudian context, we may still believe that in a loveless home the boy would have developed the idea that nice people must repress erotic tendencies. He chose Olivia Langdon as a wife because he wished to be mothered and correctly sensed that she would make an effective substitute mother. Although possessed of an active carnal appetite, he entered upon marriage awed by an ideal of purity and inclined to look upon sex as coarse. Because he thought of sex as polluting, he may have believed that he was corrupting Livy. His marriage was not an unhappy one; yet his masochistic feelings of guilt erupted with increased violence after marriage; and he engaged in actions vis-à-vis Livy that, even though they might be carried out semi-humorously, had mildly sadistic overtones.

One effect of Clemens's feelings of guilt, according to Jones, was to exclude sex—tabooed by genteel society and by his superego—from his writings. (This virtual exclusion of mature sexuality and of its problems from Clemens's writings has been noted often. Bernard DeVoto, for example, concluded that Clemens suffered from a castration complex and surmised that the thrust of death was joined in Clemens's fantasy with the fear of women's sex.)[4] Clemens's basic fantasy, Jones continued, could well have been that sexually aroused, mature women may unsex a lover. In accord with the conventional opinion of psychiatrists, Clemens's strong interest in obscene stories is to be considered a form of exhibitionism and is to be related to phallic sexuality. Because pornography, unlike sex, may be interpreted as having its existence outside the limits of conventional society, it is amoral; and under certain circumstances men, if not women, are free to enjoy it. In this connection, Jones notes, Eden before the Fall was masculine to Clemens: many passages in his works describe male nudity; except in early writings, his unclothed females are not women but little girls.

Clemens's phallic sexuality, on which Jones places great emphasis, derives from Freud's final scheme of phases in the development of the libido. In this scheme autoeroticism is followed by narcissism, orality, the analsadistic, the phallic (not introduced by Freud until 1923), and the genital.[5] The phallic stage represents an advance beyond the pregenital but is not fully genital in the adult sense; it takes only the male genital into account and represents a primacy not of the genitals but of the phallus. It is during this phase that the castration complex is presumed to have its origin.

Jones did not take Clemens's compulsive speculating into account in deciding that his sexuality was arrested, but, as we have seen, psychoanalysts who have treated neurotic gamblers hold that their sexuality is never fully matured, though not always arrested at the phallic stage. Indeed, anyone who follows Freud in this theory of neuroses, shifting though it was, and who believes in addition that Clemens was a moral masochist would necessarily agree to this.

Jones also touches, though briefly, on a series of related topics: scopophilia; evasions of reality; nudity, both male and female; pornography; purity; masturbation; loss of virginity; and pedophilia. I shall discuss here and in the following chapter topics that have probably been least considered by other students of Clemens yet are, in their interrelatedness, exceptionally important. In order of initial presentation, these are: purity in several of its aspects; masturbation; impotence; and pedophilia.

Rousseau was heterodox in *Julie, ou la nouvelle Héloise* (1760) when he deprived virginity of its status as a synecdoche for virtue.[6] Although in the American culture of the nineteenth century the value set on purity in women was high, Clemens's valuation was abnormally so. He tended to divide women, as they had been divided by many men for centuries, into two antinomical categories, saints and whores. Among his most extreme expressions of devotion to purity as an ideal are those in letters to Livy during the period of his courtship. He pictured her as a saint, telling her that she was "so pure, so great, so good, so beautiful" that he could not keep from worshiping her; and he wrote to Joseph Twichell that she was "a messenger-angel out of upper Heaven."[7] He intended to shield her, while she would reform him. He would censor her reading carefully, because vulgar language (though found in the classics) could stain her innocence: to read of sexual matters is to be victimized by an insidious form of seduction. He himself was reading *Gulliver's Travels,* much more charmed with it than when as a boy he gloated over its prodigies and marvels; but he would "mark it & tear it" first if Livy wished to read it, for portions are "very coarse & indelicate." It pained him that she had started on *Don Quixote* without first letting him censor the book. If she had not finished the book, he adjured her not to:

> You are as pure as snow, & I would have you always so—untainted, untouched even by the impure thoughts of others. You are the purest woman that ever I knew—& your purity is your most uncommon & most precious ornament. Preserve it, Livy.—Read nothing that is not *perfectly* pure. I had rather you read fifty "Jumping Frogs" than one Don Quixote. Don Quixote is one of the most exquisite books that was ever written, & to lose it from the world's literature would be as the wresting of a constellation from the symmetry & perfection of the firmament—but neither it nor Shakespeare are proper books for virgins to read until some hand has culled them of their grossness. No gross speech is ever harmless.[8]

Although Clemens saw no need to have his own reading censored, male virgin though some have thought him to have been at the time of his marriage, he did expect Livy to exert a purifying influence on his speech, his writings, his manners, and his habits. Some idea of what she was to do about his language may be gleaned from his first letter to her. In it he enjoins her to scold and upbraid him when he neglects the proprieties. If Livy gives him a command, he says, he will obey it or break his loyal neck trying. Upon reconsidering, he canceled the phrase "break my loyal neck" and substituted the presumably less vulgar "exhaust my energies."[9]

In addition to protecting him from genteel critics, Livy would shelter him in other ways, as by making a home that would be untroubled. Clemens described his home-to-be in terms marked by the religiosity that pervades his correspondence during the courtship period.[10] To him, as to many others, home should be a womblike place, a haven from the trials and temptations of the world of trade, politics, greed, and corruption. Women presided over the haven because the home was where they belonged by nature, also, paradoxically, because they could not be trusted to maintain their integrity in the outside world.[11] An inveterate escapist in fact and in literary fancy—in fancy by way of doubles, rafts, balloons, dreams, child-hood—Clemens liked to retreat in actual life to a protective, admiring home circle after having made exciting forays into the dangerous, tense world of men and affairs.

Clemens's insistence to Livy on the importance of purity above all other virtues foreshadows the restrictions that he placed on the conduct of his daughters as the girls reached nubility. Livy was conventionally strict and at the same time extravagantly loving.[12] Clemens, usually affectionate, was at times temperishly rigorous; and it seems likely that his extreme protective-ness was one of the causes of the serious psychic imbalances that afflicted each of his daughters. (Among other possible causes would be his displays of choler, his depressions, and anxieties brought on by his speculating.) The problems of the daughters—which included Oedipal conflicts, roman-tic love, sexual frustration, and the desire to establish a separate home— may not be easily dismissed as no more than the upsets that have, until recently, been considered normal to adolescence.[13]

Susy, born on March 19, 1872, received her father's most concentrated attention and suffered severely from it as she matured sexually and socially. During her childhood she seems to have been unequivocally devoted to her father, even if, like the other daughters, frightened by his tantrums. At thirteen she opened her biography of Clemens by writing, "We are a very happy family! we consisted of papa, mamma, Jean, Clara, & me."[14] But during the year she was twenty-one Susy expressed bitter distaste for the general dullness of her life in Florence; and she could scarcely endure the tensions generated by her father at the Villa Viviani. She found it necessary, for example, to absent herself from the breakfast table. At this same time she declared herself to Clara to be "really smitten" with the Count de Cabry, a married Italian whom she seems to have pursued with indecorous zeal. She had "queer times of feeling faint" and decided after having reestablished some self-control that "up to this time I have been pretty much the same as crazy." Only if she were granted "the emotional excitement that a lasting life long love would bring," could she imagine a satisfactory existence for herself.[15]

By 1895, as Clemens, accompanied by Livy and Clara, started his tour of the world, Susy had quieted. She wrote Clara that she was a fool to have stayed in the United States: "We *are* such a congenial family. It seems to me no one understands us as we understand each other. We *do* belong together." She adds, more pathetically, "I do not really love anybody but you dear three, and of course nobody else loves me."[16] One notes that Susy omits her sister Jean from her roster of loved ones. Apparently Jean was often little regarded by other members of the family, perhaps least of all by Clemens himself.

Clara (born June 8, 1874), though better balanced than Susy and more adept at handling or avoiding her father, endured a full complement of tensions. During Susy's winter of misery in Florence (1892–93), Clara escaped to study in Berlin. She was then a gay, vivid eighteen; and the Clemenses bombarded her with sharply anxious instructions and warnings about her social behavior. The allegedly infamous Moritz Moskowski, with whom she studied the piano, is said to have attempted to seduce her; and the Clemenses found other reasons to be anxious.[17] At a moment when she was not enjoying herself and thought of returning to Florence, Susy fended her off: "You seem to *forget* the life of the Villa Viviani. What *are* you thinking of?"[18]

As Clara approached thirty and was trying to establish herself as a concert singer, Clemens strove to make sure that she always had an escort or a guardian. Clara, for whatever reasons, became hypochondriacal and emotionally unpredictable. She spent approximately a year in a nursing home after the death of her mother in 1904, acted oddly at other times, and repeatedly went into retirement or secluded herself in sanitaria. During the latter years of her father's life, she sometimes found drugs and alcohol to be essential supports. On one occasion she screamed at Isabel Lyon for whiskey and then had to write an apology.

Clara drew heavily on her father for money both before and after her marriage to Ossip Gabrilowitsch and tended to bully him when she was at home. In sanitaria she might be well enough to receive friends but unable to endure the presence of her father. Miss Lyon, who thought it terrible that Clara and Jean could not come, as she did, under the spell of Clemens's glories, subtleties, and sweetnesses, quoted Clemens as saying in 1907 that he got very little good out of Clara and that when he went to her rooms he felt like a stranger making an untimely and unwelcome visit. The surmise is inescapable that he went to Clara not so much to display affection as to seek love and admiration. Clara must, in any event, be considered the most successful of the daughters in living her own life. She was attractive to men and married twice.[19]

The case of Jean, born on July 26, 1880, six years younger than Clara, is in many ways more distressing than that of Susy. Jean was apparently too young to be particularly close to her sisters and had a rather plain and bony countenance. In her diary she declared her jealousy of Clara when Clara was, to Jean's mind, overpraised for her beauty and talents. Although Jean was not diagnosed as an epileptic until 1896, she may have developed the disease as early as November 1890. Her family first thought that they observed a striking change in the stability of her personality in 1892.[20] Later her passionate outbreaks included striking in the face and attempting to kill Katie Leary, a longtime servant of the family. Hamlin Hill, the most explicit writer on the troubled relationships between Jean and Clara and their father, suggests a common cause for their difficulties; he connects Jean's epilepsy and the "neurasthenic" illnesses of Clara (one could also say of Susy, when she was alive) to the demanding roles they had to play as members of Mark Twain's family.[21]

Prolonged anxiety is frequently assumed to be one of the possible precipitating factors in bringing on epilepsy; but it seems probable that Oedipal conflicts, rather than general tensions, were at the root of many of the family's problems. Jean, who is thought to have been the daughter who most resembled her father in appearance and in personality, may on that account have suffered most.[22] After the death of Livy, Clemens often found Jean's presence to be irritating. A device for remedying the situation was to send Jean off for extended periods to caretaking establishments "in spite of her pathetic requests to be allowed to return to live with him at Redding, Connecticut."[23] Jean could hardly have been easy to live with. To control her emotional disorders, she was put on medications, some of them said to be potent. Bromides (taken also by Miss Lyon and by Clara) were probably administered to her on a regular basis. Clemens's treatment of her was at times, Jean wrote in her diary, "unfriendly," "unaffectionate," or "horrid"; yet she regretted deeply that "Clara's love for Father is not what it should be"; and when Clemens shunted her off, her stratagems to secure his attention were, it is said, transparent.

Passages in Jean's diary for 1907 are reminiscent of Susy's despair of ever finding a man she could love and live with. Jean found it necessary to restrain her love for Gerry Thayer, a man much too young for her, and later she longed to excite the emotional interest of a physician at the sanitarium she was then in. "I don't in the least hope to win him," she wrote; "that desperate hunger for love does not leave me. . . . No one will ever care for me and I shall have to drag my useless, empty life out by itself. Oh! is there no hope whatsoever for me? What can I do! I feel that I must find some means to prove attractive to a person that I can also learn to love." Clearly Jean's was an emotionally deprived life.

Clemens's responses to indiscretions on the part of Clara or to attentions paid her by men were absurdly restrictive. When his daughters were alone with men, written to by men, or stared at by men, Clemens apparently perceived this as a species of defloration or as a prelude to defloration. In October of 1891, Livy and Susan Crane went to Berlin apartment-hunting while Clemens stayed with Clara, who was then seventeen, in Marienbad. Because a young German officer and Clara seemed to Clemens to be too much interested in each other, Clemens locked Clara in her room.[24] Although Livy repeatedly expressed concern that Clara be prudent and respect conventions, it is unlikely that she would have sanctioned paternal actions of this kind.

Much later, in 1903, Clemens responded even more surprisingly when he, Clara, and Miss Lyon were together at a tearoom in Florence and a group of young Italians stared at Clara. They stared in part, or so Clemens thought, because Clara was wearing a pretty hat adorned with artificial fruits. Once back at the Villa di Quarto, Clemens hunted up "a pair of scissors and sheared off every piece of fruit from her hat."[25] This snipping off of the fruit has inescapably symbolic overtones. The "phallic eye," known in Andalucia as the *mirada fuerte*—the deliberately insulting inspection whereby a woman is visually stripped and raped—is notoriously common in Italy. Clemens's action obviously meant that he was depriving Clara of those sexual attractions that invited symbolic defloration. It may also have carried the implication that he was unsexing the Italians who had committed ocular rape.

An essay by Clemens bears witness to the horror that he sometimes expressed at the idea of premarital sex relations or of rape. It may have been written because he suspected Clara of having affairs with Charles E. Wark, an accompanist, and with Gabrilowitsch before her marriage to him.

Whether with Clara in mind or not, he published in 1902 what has been described as a "hysterical article" entitled "Why Not Abolish It?" "It" is the age of consent. The essay argues that as premarital sex relations not only sully the purity of the woman but injure her relatives, there should be no age at which a woman may legally assist a criminal in destroying the honor of her family.[26] "Why Not Abolish It?" is not, however, an isolated instance of moral rigidity. Long before, in *Innocents Abroad* (1869), Clemens approved of the murder of Abelard, calling the lover of Héloise "unmanly" and a villain of "degraded instinct."

While in Florence in 1892, Clemens composed "In Defence of Harriet Shelley" (published 1894), a bludgeoning attack on Edward Dowden's *Life of Shelley* for soiling the reputation of Harriet. He turns to invective when characterizing Shelley, Cornelia Turner, and Mary Godwin. A more puritanically moralistic polemic would be difficult to imagine. A kind of Watch-and-Ward-Society jealousy of sexual liberation (or profligacy), especially of guilt-free sexuality, would appear to be involved. Clemens writes as though Cornelia Turner's and Mary Godwin's sexual offences or suspected sexual offences were injuries to him personally. He lards his text with terms like "degraded," "depravity," "fetid fascinations," "the Boinville menagerie," "sty," and "odorous paradise." Cornelia's interest in Shelley, he specifies, occurred in those "sweet early times" when she was her warm-blooded self, "before antiquity had cooled her off and mossed her back."

During his later years, what Clemens took to be inadequate compliments and displays of affection from Clara and Jean aroused his resentment. He felt free to be inattentive to his daughters, but he was piqued when they were inattentive to him. In letters to the pretty and charming Mary Rogers, daughter-in-law of Henry Rogers, he humorously demanded "butter" of her and complained about Clara and Jean. He mentions, for example, what became a running controversy between Clara and himself as to whether he should "lead her on" when she gave concerts. Probably because Clara knew her father's fondness for usurping the center of the stage, she at first refused him but wavered while en route to the station for her initial concert and sent word back of a change of heart; she would like to be led out by him. Clemens wrote joyously to Mary, "Mariechen, it's butter from the butterless! and very gratifying. Next there'll be butter from Jean—yes, and even from you; I am not despairing."[27]

In July of 1906 Clara seems to have made up for previous neglect by writing her father an immoderately flattering letter about an essay on

Howells that he had just published. Clemens sent the letter on to Howells. Much later, Isabel Lyon remembered Clemens's saying in his covering letter, "That miracle has happened again which happened months ago, one of his children has complimented her father." Clemens must have written something of the sort, for Howells answered soothingly, "Thank you for letting me see Clara's just tribute to you! It is a great thing to have one's children not rise up and knock one's head off after reading one's writings, but it seems that it happens in your family some times as it does in mine."[28]

Clemens's championing of the ideal of premarital chastity and marital fidelity for women may be seen not just in his letters to Livy and in his governance of his daughters but scattered throughout his letters, his notebooks, and his major books. He despised the French for their supposed immorality; he resented the droit du seigneur; he raged at the libertinage of English aristocrats. In their different ways, *The Gilded Age* (1873) and *Personal Recollections of Joan of Arc* (1896) constitute primary examples of his attitudes.

Dixon Wecter believed that "the known facts" suggest that Clemens entered into marriage as a virgin of thirty-four.[29] Relevant "known facts" drawn from the life appear not to exist; but it is generally agreed that in America during the entire nineteenth century the Puritan tradition, reinforced by the Evangelical Movement, dominated genteel society. Presumably informed observers held that chastity among young males was by no means unusual. When Emerson attended a dinner with John Forster, Dickens, Carlyle, and a Mr. Pringle in Lincoln Inn's Fields, he argued the case for American virtue by contrast with that of England, especially by contrast with the shameful lewdness of London: "I assured them that it was not so with us; that, for the most part, young men of good standing and good education, with us, go virgins to their nuptial bed, as truly as their brides."[30] Emerson intended no irony.

A few scholars, disagreeing with Wecter, are apparently as distressed at the idea of premarital sexual continence in Clemens as Emerson was at the incontinence of the gilded youths of London or as Emma Willard, founder of Miss Willard's seminary in Troy, New York, was by the nude male statues in the Tuileries garden. (Mary Fairbanks attended Miss Willard's seminary.) To contradict Wecter, Bernard DeVoto, Jones, and others point to the years that Clemens spent on vice-ridden Mississippi packets, in wide-open mining camps, in prostitute-infested San Francisco, and as a newspaperman among companions who were certainly not models of propriety. One may also point to the lively interest that Clemens displayed during his youth in a number of young women and to the emphasis that he places in late writings (published only posthumously) on sexual intercourse as supreme among all delights available to man. The question of Clemens's premarital chastity as such has very limited significance, however; much more important are his views on virginity and purity as ideals for women.

It is possible to infer from Freud's ideas of the censor, totem, taboo, and the interchange of opposites that "the tabooed object is always an indication of the society that forbids." George Bernard Shaw considered decency to be indecency's conspiracy of silence. Gaston Bachelard declares without reservation, "Psychoanalytically speaking, cleanliness is really a form of uncleanliness."[31] This application of reasoning by paradox is commonplace even in popular writing: "Such prudery actually draws attention to the vice it is supposed to suppress. The very act that forbids speech or prohibits sight dramatizes what is hidden."[32] On these terms, Clemens's stress on purity may be interpreted as indicating a preoccupation with impurity; yet the automatic translation of a professed aspiration in one direction as a telltale sign of a genuine devotion to the concealed opposite may be incautious, may become "a closed and self-confirming system."[33] Probably the grounds for Clemens's identifying virginity and virtue, for his fascination by the pornographic, and for his displays of prurience are too complicated to be altogether explained by the application of any formula, whether sophisticated or naive, but we may attempt to work toward answers in a historical-analytical way.

Clemens repeatedly evidenced an exceptional drive toward sexual intercourse countered by great discomfort in contemplating strong sexual impulses on the part of gentlewomen. He feared sex, and he delighted in it. He sired four children and referred with considerable directness in letters to Livy to the eagerness with which, after an absence, he looked forward to lovemaking. Published letters indicate no feelings of guilt or pollution attached to marital intercourse: "I love to picture myself ringing the bell, at midnight—then a pause of a second or two—then the turning of the bolt & 'who is it?'—then ever so many kisses—then you & I in the bathroom, I drinking my cocktail & undressing & you standing by—then to bed, and— everything happy & jolly as it should be. I *do* love & honor you, my darling."[34]

For a late, ambiguous, but possibly revelatory example of Clemens's expressed interest in sex we may consider his diatribe (429 unpublished pages) aimed at Isabel Lyon (Ashcroft), a valued member of the Clemens establishment from November 1902 until near the time of her dismissal in March 1909. Clara, who thought that Miss Lyon was seeking control over Clemens's money, convinced her father of this, and Clemens joined Clara in showing envenomed hostility. He suggested that Miss Lyon wished to marry him and attempted to seduce him. She was not, he testified coarsely, to his taste—he would rather marry a waxwork: she was "an old, old virgin, and juiceless, whereas my passion was for the other kind."[35]

The intended intimations here contain elements of what seems to be patent misrepresentation. Clemens was lustful as well as fearful, but no evidence has ever been adduced to support the bragging suggestion that he enjoyed numerous sexual conquests. He liked pretty young women, but the hint that he aggressively sought excitingly sexual females runs contrary to what we know of his inclination to attach himself to mother-figures and to prepubescent girls. As for the possibility that he might have yielded to Miss Lyon's seductive approaches had she been more youthful and desirable, Clemens, as the following chapter indicates, may have been impotent years before Miss Lyon—when she was in fact a handsome thirty-eight—first came into the Clemens household. His chief purpose in this "geyser of bias, vindictiveness, and innuendo" is, of course, not to set the record straight but to degrade Miss Lyon. As an unworthy gentlewoman, she deserved to be dishonored.

Clemens's alleged passion for "the other kind" of woman, not the juiceless sort, was one that he could write of lightly or could relate to explicit feelings of guilt and terror. He gives full-bodied sexuality a comic treatment appropriate to readers of the *Alta California* in his description of "raven-haired, splendid-eyed Nicaraguan damsels . . . singularly full in the bust" whom he saw as he made his way from the Pacific coast to the Atlantic coast in 1867. "Two of these picturesque native girls were exceedingly beautiful—such liquid, languishing eyes! such pouting lips! . . . such ravishing, incendiary expressions! . . . such voluptuous forms." Like Clemens's allusion to "the other kind," this invocation of the tropical-erotic may be only a stock, musical comedy version of a male fantasy of female lubricity and a dream of perpetual orgasm; but Clemens characteristically matches desire with a kind of loathing by having his other self, the vulgarly realistic Brown, interrupt with, "But you just prospect one of them heifers with a fine-tooth—." Although the suggestion is said to have procured Brown's banishment at once, in truth, the Mr. Brown within seems rarely to have accepted banishment: ugliness, animality, illness, and horror lie close beneath the surface when Clemens dwells on beauty, especially on sexual beauty.[36]

The animality and horror are fully present in a recurrent dream that had troubled Clemens for a long time before he set it down in January 1897.[37] In the dream Clemens encountered "a negro wench." This "good-natured & not at all bad looking" young woman sold him a mushy apple pie. She also made "a disgusting proposition" to him. Clemens answered with "a chaffy remark," at which the woman made "an awkward pretence" of his having misunderstood her. In the dream Clemens commented sarcastically on the pretense and requested a spoon with which to eat his pie. The Negress, who had but one, took her tin spoon from her mouth and offered it. "My stomach rose—there every thing vanished." Clemens explains that his dream self does things his waking self would never do; but this is not helpful, for if the dream is considered nonsymbolically the dream self does nothing but reject some kind of sexual offer.

Arthur Pettit gives the most extended interpretation of the dream. His interpretation is, however, contradictory at important points. He alludes to the extensiveness of Negro concubinage in the Old South; yet he supposes that Clemens remained in bondage to white social and sexual values. The obvious contradiction here is that white southern values are said at once to permit extramarital sex relations with black women and at the same time to interdict them. Pettit also observes that late in life, when in India, Clemens acknowledged an attraction to persons of dark skin. But what Clemens actually says about the dark skins of Indians and Africans as contrasted with the white skins of Europeans has to do with aesthetics, not sexuality. Exactly why the dream woman's blackness is supposed to make her at once sexually available and desirable but taboo remains, then, unclear. Pettit is, I think, correct in holding that Clemens, by insisting that his rational, waking self bore no relationship to his dream self, is intimating that he may not be held accountable for the actions or thoughts of his dream self. He is certainly correct in noting that Clemens found it easier to make open remarks about sexuality in black women than in genteel white ones. There should be nothing surprising about this, for it only corresponds to a general social taboo and takes advantage of a socially acceptable way of relaxing the taboo.

Ambivalence among males about female sexuality has been made obvious since antiquity and is currently a common theme. Susan Harris observes that Clemens's dream reveals "male Victorian schizophrenia about female sexuality" and, further, that "if the white woman cannot provide a focus for sexual desires, the black woman must take her place." This argument is questionable in that white women did provide a focus for Clemens's desires, even though those desires were quelled by fears. Clemens is clearly telling us that he views with special distaste the invitation of the "negro wench." Harris is pretty much correct in holding that the dream exposes "how superficial Twain's racial liberation was—his response to sharing a utensil with a black woman reveals how little his subconscious was in tandem with his conscious struggle to have 'enlightened' concepts of race." The problem, of course, is not simply one of eating with a spoon after it has been in a black mouth; that spoon has symbolic significances.

If the dream is taken literally, there is no need for Clemens to have been defensive about it. When considered factually, the dream self engages in no bold sexual activity but draws back from a proffered tin spoon and from some form of carnality. Only in permitting such a dream to occur may the dream self be said to dare, and if the commonplace nature of black-white sex relations in the South may be taken as a given, then the dream self's disgust and possible terror were idiosyncratic, having to do with Clemens's general fear of sexuality and with his particular feeling about the sexuality of black women.

During Clemens's earlier years he considered blacks to be simple, fetid, loud, carnal, and presumptuous. Late in life, in *Following the Equator* (1897), he noted that nearly all brown and black skins are beautiful, whereas a beautiful white skin is rare. But this, as I have said, is an aesthetic preference recently and perhaps not very seriously arrived at and is not necessarily to be equated with a sexual one. The old prejudices were muted, but they were not abolished.

Any serious attempt to interpret the dream of the black wench—which promises to become a locus classicus in the criticism—is likely to lead one to a more general consideration of Clemens's life and writings. Pettit, remarking on the jokes about sexuality in black females that Clemens set down in his notebooks, comments that he may have been sexually troubled in his late years and adds that race came into it as an expression of his repression. Pettit also believes that Clemens "had a private, more or less conscious craving to find a credible sexual being in that most incongruous and puzzling of all places in the nineteenth century, namely a *white* woman." This emphasis on the supposed privacy of Clemens's sexual longing for a white woman goes hand in hand with the too facile explanation that in creating Roxana in *Pudd'nhead Wilson* (1894) he accepted the "Victorian" convention that white women are nonsexual and at the same time evaded the convention by portraying a provocative mulattress who was white to the eye if not to the ear. Among difficulties here is the dubious conception of the asexuality of white Victorian women, the equally doubtful belief that Clemens treats Roxana as a provocative woman, and the untenable assumption that Clemens could not concentrate his desires on a woman, or a girl, who was not made sexual by at least a few drops of black blood.

So far as one can tell, full-bodied sexuality had its terrifying aspects for Clemens whether associated with white women or black. The extent to which his southern (though they were not universally southern) attitudes toward black women were overlaid by a northern upper-middle-class respect for womanhood as such is not clear; but the reason for his terror would seem to be simple: in accord with folk belief on the subject, black women are more profoundly sexual, which is to say impure and, therefore, to Clemens, more dangerous than are white women. Although he may have seen some dark women as sexually desirable, others—like Moorish women, women in Palestine, and the Portuguese women of Fayal—he saw as dirty, animallike, and untouchable. The hot, mushy pie and the tin spoon that the black wench offers have high emotional values and would appear to be insistently symbolic. Sexuality is urgently involved, but wench, spoon, and pie do not signify a happy sexual association of any kind. Emphasis in the recurrent dream is unequivocally on the dreamer's feelings of anxiety and repulsion.

The Christian-fabular explanation which Clemens offers in one of his "Letters from the Earth" of the guilt that may accompany sexual acts cuts two ways. The guilt, he seems to say, is unwarranted but authentic. When Adam and Eve ate of the forbidden fruit and were expelled from the Garden, they lost many good things; but they gained one pleasure worth all the rest: "they knew the Supreme Art. . . . They practiced it diligently and were filled with contentment." The art and mystery of sexual intercourse was to them "a magnificent discovery, and they stopped idling around and turned their entire attention to it, poor exultant young things!" Nudity was, however, no longer innocent; they were made to be aware that they were naked. And since that time, although everyone has entered into the universe naked and unashamed and clean in mind, not everyone is permitted to stay that way. Although the convention miscalled modesty is opposed to nature and reason, "a Christian mother's first duty is to soil her child's mind, and she does not neglect it."[38]

Prominent among sexual activities that have entailed feelings of guilt is masturbation. In one place Freud holds that masturbation is the primal addiction for which all later addictions are substitutes and writes that "we find no cases of severe neuroses in which the autoerotic satisfaction of early childhood and of puberty has not played a part; and the relation between efforts to suppress it and fear of the father are too well-known to need more than a mention." In the Freudian paradigm a child masturbates and is threatened with castration (usually by the mother, who says that the father will perform the act). The child does not take the threat seriously until he gets a sight of female genitals. He then fears the loss of his penis, feels guilty about masturbation, and may think that unworthy women have lost their penises.[39]

Feelings of shame and guilt associated with masturbation were often reinforced by assumptions, common even among doctors, that the practice could lead to impotence or insanity. In one of Clemens's letters he seems to accept masturbation as natural and harmless to youth, but when he is discussing Rousseau, he takes the act to be shameful.[40] In addition, he finds what he seems to take to be the representation in art of masturbation by a woman to be unspeakably abhorrent. As notebook entries indicate he was altogether serious in expressing his disgust at the position of the left hand of Titian's *Venus of Urbino* (in the Uffizi) as it rests lightly on her pudenda.

The neurotically puritanical side of Clemens's ambivalence toward sexuality—his combination of prudishness and lust—and his minimal knowledge of art and of art history are well illustrated by his comments on this nude, made in the last chapter of *A Tramp Abroad* (1880). An irony is involved, he says, in leaving warm-blooded nakedness exposed in paintings while placing fig leaves on cold marble statues and curtailing such privileges of literature as were exercised by Fielding and Smollett. Anyone may look his fill on "the foulest, the vilest, the obscenest picture" in the world, Titian's Venus. "It isn't that she is naked and stretched out on a bed—no, it is the attitude of one of her arms and hands. . . . How I would like to describe her—just to see what a holy indignation I could stir up in the world. . . . Without question it was painted for a bagnio and it was probably refused because it was a trifle too strong."[41]

Material for this passage was furnished by a notebook entry made in June 1879, while Clemens was in Paris. In this entry he compares "Titian's Venus in the Tribune" unfavorably with a nude "pure in her thoughts" that he saw at the Salon. Clemens's pure nude would have been like the insipid, conventionalized nudes that were purchased by the state from the Salon of 1865. As T. J. Clark points out, those paintings were "derided even at the time as academic, empty, timid, prurient, and bourgeois." The Venus, Clemens writes—and we should keep in mind that this came at the time when he was attending meetings of the Stomach Club and trying his hand at pornography—is "grossly obscene—it is wholly sensual—the face, the expression, the attitude . . . she is purely the Goddess of the Beastly. . . . She inflames & disgusts at the same moment . . . . Young girls can be defiled" by looking at her.[42]

By modern critical standards, Clemens was nearly as wrong as is possible in what he wrote about the Venus. Far from being an isolated image, as Clemens intimates, Titian's nude is only one example, though a superbly fleshly one, in a multitudinously populated category of similar representations, both sacred and secular. One could begin with fertility figures and include Greek statues exhibiting the so-called modesty gesture, but Italian paintings comparable to the Venus are more to the point. Images of beautiful women—whether dressed, provocatively half-dressed, or naked—were a feature of sixteenth-century art. Reclining nudes are sometimes treated by art historians as allegorical figures, and iconographic readings are important to the understanding of a number of the paintings; but most of the figures were erotically intended representations of an ideal beauty, improvements on nature as demanded by contemporary aesthetic theory.

The *Venus of Urbino* belongs to that popular type known as the *Venus pudica* and though definitely a Venus Naturalis (contrasted by Plato with the Venus Coelestis) was closely modeled after Giorgione's magnificent, almost asexual Venus (Dresden). Raphael's influential *Fornarina*, transparently veiled, places one hand below her breasts and the other between her legs. Some historians think the gestures characterize her as a classical Venus and endow her with the qualities of a wife. They also think that the pose regularly denotes a relatively chaste or modest woman, but an opposed view holds that "it was not employed in this sense in Renaissance texts." Probably the pose should be seen more simply "as a device which allowed artists to draw attention to the very part of the female body which convention did not normally allow them to represent at all."[43]

In one way, then, Clemens was probably accurate: in this painting and in a number of others, Titian satisfied a taste for the erotic, though for the idealized erotic. The problem for those who would like to think of Clemens as always sexually bold is that Titian's Venus is not idealized enough, sentimentalized enough, undangerous enough to suit his taste in morals. If he had seen Edouard Manet's *Olympia,* which hung in the Salon of 1865, with what anathemas he might have blighted it! The *Olympia,* of course, aped Titian's Venus but left no doubt about its social and sexual meanings. By the logic of contraries Clemens's quasi-hysterical protest should spring from a secret libidinousness; and in fact the juxtaposition of his protest with the pornography that he was composing at just this time suggests that this is the case.

If sexual activities may be delightful, repellent, or injurious, they may also be comic. Two bungling pieces of Clemens's pornography treat masturbation by males in a vein appropriate to a particular kind of all-male audience. In "The Mammoth Cod" he offers thanks for the bull, the ram, and the boar that give us meat by the workings of their mighty cods; and in the last of four stanzas—the least metrically competent and verbally ingenious of the lot—he notes that man is the only beast created by God who purposefully and for amusement plays with his mammoth cod, that is, masturbates.

Although this stanza has been read as autobiographically meaningful, the reading is not easy to maintain. Clemens's playful accompanying letter is not helpful. He wrote this little poem, he says, for the instruction of children, to show them that animals do better by instinct than man does by reason, unless properly guided. The last of a series of mock objections (addressed to the Mammoth Cod Club) that Clemens appends to the poem may possibly have bearing. Here he says that he has devoted his life to pious study and meditation and doesn't know whether he has such a thing as a cod about him. Although he has heard of what men of the world call pleasure, his recollection of it is that it was so transitory that it was not worth his while to repeat it.

On the surface, at least, poem, letter, and objections appear to be no more than instances of the comedy (including, one would surmise from Clemens's Notebook 38, dirty jokes) that Clemens produced in part to entertain Henry H. Rogers and his circle. The final stanza reads:

> Of beasts, man is the only one
> Created by God,
> Who purposely, and for mere fun,
> Plays with his mammoth cod.[44]

A second piece of comic bawdry called "Address to the Stomach Club" or "Some Thoughts on the Science of Onanism" is in dreary prose, runs to approximately eight hundred words, and is no more fruitful in demonstrating Clemens's possible feelings of guilt over masturbating than is "The Mammoth Cod."[45] It begins with burlesque maxims and aphorisms misattributed to such alleged apologists for "self-abuse" as Homer, Caesar, and Queen Elizabeth, then shifts to opposing remarks by detractors. Desirable signs of indulgence are said to include a disposition by men to eat, drink, smoke, and meet together convivially. Echoing what sometimes passed at the time for medical knowledge, Clemens mentions the unfortunate results of onanism as including the losses of memory, virility, cheerfulness, character, and progeny. He concludes by enjoining his listeners not to play a lone hand too much, to get their Vendôme columns down some other way.

If these lamely pornographic items seem to be autobiographically unindicative, other writings show that Clemens gave serious thought to the subject of masturbation and expressed feelings of shame and guilt. In "Letters from the Earth," he associates Protestantism (some manifestations of which moved him to fury) with masturbating.[46] Protestant children, he says, study passages in the Bible forbidding pissing against the wall "more than they study any others, except those which incite to masturbation. *Those* they hunt out and study in private. No Protestant child exists who does not masturbate. That art is the earliest accomplishment his religion confers upon him. Also the earliest *her* religion confers upon *her*."[47]

These remarks, which are mingled with other exaggerated assertions intended to ridicule the Bible and conventionally Christian attitudes, provoke the conjecture that Clemens's charge of the universality of masturbating among Protestant children could be a way of shuffling off his own deep-seated feeling of guilt, just as his many arguments in favor of determinism may be interpreted as self-exculpatory. At any rate, impotence, a topic to which we now turn, is what Clemens may have believed masturbation most regrettably led to.

IMPOTENCE

AND

PEDOPHILIA

The idea of impotence excited Clemens's anxious interest: apparently he suffered from erectile dysfunction at about the age of fifty. Psychoanalysts have noted many cases in which diminished sexual capacity or dysfunction has been related to a constellation of psychic problems like those which affected Clemens. Evidence that he became impotent ranges from the filmy to the relatively firm.[1] Likelihood is high that diminished capacity may be inferred from his masochistically compulsive gambling, his comments on masturbation, the unusual attention he paid to prepubescent girls, his unfavorable contrast of the sexual capacities of men with those of women, and, most directly, his verses lamenting impotence.

In 1867 Mary Mason Fairbanks reported that Clemens said to her as they walked the deck of the *Quaker City,* "I am like an old burned-out crater; the fires of my life are all dead within me"; and in 1881 he wrote her, "Physically, I am an old man at 45—older than some men are at 80."[2] The first statement came before he was married and, enticing though the imagery is, must be dismissed. The second may carry some weight, though Clemens was strongly inclined to hyperbole and to self-pity. Also of doubtful value as evidence are comments such as that made by Livy in a letter written in 1895 during their trip around the world: "Mr. Clemens has not as much courage as I wish he had, but, poor old darling, he has been pursued with colds and inabilities of various sorts. Then he is so impressed with the fact that he is sixty years old."[3]

That Clemens found himself to be impotent—or so much reduced in sexual vigor as to think of himself as impotent—at about the age of fifty is powerfully intimated in "Letters from the Earth," composed at a time (1909) when he was writing mainly to please himself by setting down what he considered to be dangerous truths for posterity (but not for his contemporaries) to take to heart; and he seems to generalize about men by arguing from his own lack of sexual capacity. At one point he gives us—with striking inaccuracy—a description of the difference in sexual capacity of men and of women. By the necessities of temperament, he writes, no limits shall be put on sexual intercourse on the part of women at any time of life, whereas men are under inflexible limits and restrictions. Woman is competent day and night, as the candlestick is to receive the candle:

"Also she *wants* that candle—yearns for it, longs for it, hankers after it, as commanded by the law of God in her heart.

"But man is only briefly competent; and only then in the moderate measure applicable to the word in *his* sex's case. He is competent from the age of sixteen or seventeen thenceforward for thirty-five years. After 50 his performance is of poor quality, the intervals between are wide, and its satisfactions of no great value to either party; whereas his great-grandmother is as good as new."[4]

If Clemens's argument (and the development he gave it) may be read as autobiographically derived, it means that Clemens became more or less inactive sexually at about fifty and, less reasonably, that Livy was nymphomaniacal until the day of her death. Whether interpreted as autobiographical or not, the passage suggests that Clemens either had naive, distorted notions of sexuality or was, for his own personal or rhetorical purposes, grossly exaggerating the sexual powers of women and excessively depreciating those of men.

There may be little doubt that Clemens is expressing envy of and hostility toward women—and white women at that. His insistence on women's voracious appetites echoes innumerable jokes that directly or covertly aggress against women. His envy and resentment may have included Livy, for he held that all women could enjoy what he, after the age of fifty, could enjoy very rarely or not at all. Of four passages cited by Gershon Legman (who finds autobiographical significances everywhere) as proof that Clemens was impotent at fifty-one, three are in fact diaphanous.[5] Clemens, Legman says, "made impotence the closing point of '1601,'" tells a "symbolic" story of a turkey-gobbler that hatched a porcelain egg into a teapot without a spout, and refers in "At the Appetite Cure" to Oedipal conflicts and impotence.[6] But "1601," the most famous of Clemens's bawdy works, was written it seems when Clemens was only forty-one and presumably sexually active.[7] Absolutely nothing that is personal may be made of the teapot without a spout,[8] and "At the Appetite Cure"[9] is of consummate irrelevance for the demonstration of Oedipal conflicts and impotence.

Whereas these three passages assume confessional significance only when that significance is arbitrarily assigned to them, reinforcement for the supposition that Clemens became impotent and was continuingly disturbed by his condition may be found in Legman's fourth item, two stanzas (eight lines) of doggerel.[10] The verses apparently belonged originally to an extended imitation of Edward FitzGerald's *The Rubáiyát of Omar Khayyám* in which Clemens recites the infirmities of old age. He composed the verses in September 1899 at Sanna, Sweden, and retouched them in 1906. In one stanza Clemens writes that "the Penis mightier than the sword" is now calm and "dreams unmoved of ancient Conquests scored." The other melancholy stanza runs:

> A Weaver's Beam—or Handle of a Hoe—
> Or Bowsprit, then—now Thing of Dough:
> A sorry Change, lamented oft with Tears
> At Midnight by the Master of the Show.

Evidence of this kind does not prove that Clemens was impotent at fifty or at any other age. No witnesses have appeared, no medical testimony exists. Yet the cumulative weight of his repeated references to impotence does merit some credence. His psychomasochism also leads us to suspect impotence, for studies of the symptoms of psychomasochism attest to impotence as frequently concurrent. And Clemens's intense anxieties about guilt, age, and impotence do, by a permissible circularity, reinforce what is known about his psychomasochism. Guilt and impotence are, of course, strange traits to be associated with an American hero; and their bearing on his later writings has yet to be adequately assessed.

One of the consequences (and signs) of Clemens's moral masochism was his pedophilia. As has often been remarked, his inclination was to attach himself to mother figures or to little girls. At least as early as 1877 he started forming clubs consisting of himself and one or more girls. During his prime he took delight in lecturing to, talking with, dancing with, and tobogganing with somewhat older girls as at Vassar, Bryn Mawr, and a girl's school in Canada. In 1906 after a talk before Vassar alumnae in New York, he encouraged the younger women to kiss him. Where histrionics and comedy leave off and serious eroticism begins is impossible to say; but it was, in all probability, only after constraints were placed upon his speculating and after the death of Livy (in 1904) that his fondness for girls—but especially for prenubile girls—became an obsession. That it was indeed an obsession was either concealed or went unrecognized until recently.

Clemens himself dropped clues—possibly disingenuous ones—intended to explain his penchant either to mothers of the girls concerned or to the world at large. To the mother of Margaret Blackmer he must have said that he was attracted to Margaret because she reminded him of Susy, for Mrs. Blackmer wrote, "I'm sure you will think that she resembles more than ever your dear Susy." To Mary Rogers he wrote that he had reached the grandfather stage of life without grandchildren, "so I began to collect them."[11]

According to Paine, Clara was troubled by Clemens's attentions to girls. When Elizabeth Wallace was completing her bland, idealized sketch (1913) telling of Mark Twain's association with several of the girls whom he met in Bermuda and inducted into his "Aquarium" as "Angel Fish," Paine wrote to request that she not publish any photographs showing Clemens being affectionate with young girls, because Clara "feels pretty strongly about that."[12] Most of the published photographs of Clemens with girl companions display the girls in suitably subordinate though sometimes hovering poses. In 1961 Dorothy Quick did print snapshots exhibiting Clemens and herself in somewhat affectionate postures,[13] and John Seelye has published a number of similar photographs.[14]

That Clara protected her father's reputation by screening prospective publications, her own recollections, and the work of Paine has long been known, as has been Paine's practice of omitting or bowdlerizing. As late as 1926 Paine advised Harper and Brothers that for as long as he and they could control the matter no one other than he should be permitted to write about Clemens: "As soon as this is begun (writing about him at all, I mean) the Mark Twain that we have ('preserved')—the Mark Twain that we knew, the traditional Mark Twain—will begin to fade and change, and with that process the Harper Mark Twain property will depreciate."[15] Under the vigilant caretaking of Clara, Paine, and the Harpers, an idealized view of Clemens was perpetuated and the monetary value of his works zealously maintained.

Clara reported obliquely on the question of "children," writing that her father "loved almost all children and had a charming way with them that quickly won their affection in return. He liked to go driving or paying calls with some little child as companion and this feeling increased as he grew older."[16] Paine is careful to give the impression that even during Clemens's last years the zeal with which he sought out little girls was the genial idiosyncracy of a lovable old man of letters, "just another of the harmless and happy diversions of his gentler side."[17] In Paine's preface to Miss Wallace's book, he masked the possibilities, saying that Miss Wallace shows Clemens full of life and health (it was mainly ill-health) "and of that gracious sympathy with childhood which was always one of his chief characteristics and added comfort to his later years."

Miss Wallace, a dean of women at the University of Chicago, speaks of Clemens's "sweet affection for children" and remarks of Clemens in Bermuda that "if a child of ten or twelve happens to be anywhere within the radius of his glance he is inevitably sure of seeing her," and a delightful flirtation would begin.[18] Isabel Lyon, protective of Clemens though she was, is more provocative, remarking in her diary that Clemens's first interest in a new place was "to find little girls," and "off he goes in a flash when he sees a new pair of slim little legs appear; and if the little girl wears butterfly bows of ribbon on the back of her head, then his delirium is complete."[19]

Thus, in the more sheltering writers, Clemens's fondness for little girls is presented as natural, benevolent, endearing—a complement to his robust American humor—certainly not sexual in origin. Most often the girls are explained as a grieving father's surrogates for his dead Susy. Overwhelming objections arise, however, to this touching suggestion. Clemens's pedophilia began in a mild way many years before the death of Susy—in 1877 he founded the Saturday Morning Club of Hartford, intended for young girls. Susy was a woman, not a little girl, when she died; and Clemens's inclination apparently became an obvious obsession only after the death of Livy in 1904, not after the death of Susy in 1896.

Nor are explanations for Clemens's pedophilia offered by recent scholars altogether satisfactory. Hamlin Hill accepts the paternal nature of Clemens's interest but also associates it with Laura Wright, Clemens's boyhood sweetheart, whose memory haunted him until the end of his life. Laura, who was fifteen when she and Clemens met, is alluded to in Clemens's fiction and was persistently recurrent in his dreams.[20] Clemens's continuing absorption in memories of Laura constitutes an interesting sidelight but is not in itself an explanation of why Laura remained for him forever young, forever fair, forever to be sought in other little girls. (Alas, she is reported to have been neither young nor fair when he encountered her, late in life, in the flesh.)

John Seelye gives two main explanations: first, because Clemens's daughters were estranged and neglected him, he rebuked them by paying attention to children; and, second, because he was "a dirty old man," as is revealed by photographs and by passages in the notebooks. Actually, Clemens's fraternizing with little girls often took place in the absence of his daughters; and the explanation that Clemens was a dirty old man raises more questions than it answers. Although Seelye devotes most of his book to showing that Clemens was sexually motivated, at the end he retreats from the conclusion for which he has prepared the reader: "The little girls . . . are what you wish to make of them."[21]

Some truth must be associated with conventional explanations of Clemens's pursuit of girls. They may indeed have reminded him of Susy, of Laura, or have been surrogate grandchildren. Certainly they helped to keep him from being lonely or bored. They also fed his vanity, which was enormous. But a sexual explanation must be adduced as well. At periods in his life when he could not have been lonely, he was at least partly fixated on young, sexually inexperienced girls or on girlish-looking women. Girls probably filled his early fantasies as well as his old man's dreams; girls became highly cathected objects. By drawing on psychology, anthropology, and popular conceptions of childhood, and by adding details from what is known about Clemens's actual associations, it is possible to elaborate an outline descriptive of his pedophilia.

Psychoanalysts commonly observe that moral masochists tend to impotence and to substitute forms of sexuality, including pedophilia. Male pedophiles tend to have had incestuous desires, to have been checked in those desires, and to be, therefore, hostile toward or afraid of women who are of an age suitable to be sex partners. When mature sexuality is taken to be taboo, prohibitions lead to inhibitions; and inhibitions must be overcome before sexuality can be aroused.[22] Clinical studies of deviants who have offended against female children support the conclusion that the immature are a convenient substitute because they are neither feared nor hated. Freud said that children—rarely the exclusive objects of those who seek them out—are usually turned to "when someone who is cowardly or has become impotent adopts them as a substitute."[23]

Pedophiles undergoing treatment testify to having had less exposure to erotica than is reported by normal controls. As boys they heard little discussion of sex in their homes; they have had a low level of adult sexual experience; and they receive little satisfaction from sex. They tend to be strict in their attitudes with regard to premarital or extramarital sexual relations. The typically nonpermissive, moralistic patient responds positively to pornography, however, and masturbates relatively frequently. (His masturbation fantasies are not necessarily about children.)[24] When pornographic literature and pictures are readily available, offenses against children decrease, the lower incidence probably being attributable to the use of pornography as a stimulant to masturbation.[25]

A profile with applicability to Clemens may be abstracted from a discussion of group psychotherapy with male, heterosexual pedophiles.[26] All members of the group had experienced either a physical or psychological absence of the father. Their marriages could be regarded as continuations of childhood experiences: indeed, they often mixed up their mothers and their wives. In general, these patients were anxious, mildly depressed, dissatisfied with life, and defensive about their pedophilia. After several months of analysis they came to criticize their wives, complained of their own lack of aggressiveness, and acknowledged the sexual element in their interest in children. They were fearful of adult women, curious about the female genitalia, and apprehensive about the impairment of their masculinity. Although pedophilia was focal to the patients' problems, additional sexual deviations—including exhibitionism, fetishism, and voyeurism—came into the discussions, and patients expressed some confusion about their sexual identities. Some form of sexual contact with female children, though not necessarily intercourse, discharged their anxieties about rejection and impotence by providing feelings of mastery and masculinity.

Other recent observations on pedophiles have bearing. Pedophilia is related to purity and both are associated with impotence and exhibition-ism: "Possibly the choice of immature girls as sex objects represents an attempt to find sex partners who are innocent and free of the connotation of sin."[27] Exhibitionism is noted as one among the constellation of traits common to moral masochists. A man who is impotent (or situationally impotent with his former sexual partner) may develop a compulsive mas-turbatory-exhibitionistic behavior.[28] Exhibitionism—not always overtly sexual—intensified in Clemens during his later years together with his fondness for girls. Pedophilia, exhibitionism, and a preoccupation with erotic jokes may all be related to low or lost potency and to moral masoch-ism. All may have been surrogate activities heightened by the illness and death of Livy, who when in good health would have served as a restraining influence. Furthermore, under various constraints, Clemens had decreased his speculating, which may have been for him another and for a time extremely important substitute for normal sexuality.

Clemens's general narcissism and exhibitionism were notable. Critics have remarked on such manifestations as the crimson Oxford gown that he wore, the white suits, his scrupulously tended hair, his twin passions for being interviewed and photographed, his parading on shipboard and on Fifth Avenue, and his wishing to give the name Innocence at Home to the mansion that he built near Redding, Connecticut, because that would remind people of *him*. (He lost that fight to Clara and settled for Storm-field.) Early in 1906 Paine christened him the King. Both Clemens and his chief retainers liked that appellation.

Protectors of Clemens have presented his megalomaniacal, narcissistic, and exhibitionistic tendencies as though they were innocuous displays of panache or normal exercises in salesmanship. Dorothy Quick, who when a child snapped innumerable pictures of Clemens, quotes him as saying, "I like being the center of attraction. It's very pleasing, and no trouble!" He was never so happy, she added, "as when he had a number of congenial people around him, and he ruled his little household with a kindly despo-tism and accepted the homage he always inspired in his own gracious and lovable way."[29]

Little girls played a role in Clemens's public displays of himself and joined him in his pastimes. He rode side by side with his young companions in open carriages or, when in Bermuda, donkey carts. A child might go to a dinner party with him or stand with him at an afternoon tea where he went to be lionized. They joined him at billiards or cards, and they attended him on strolls. The great man, glorified by his crown of white hair, striking in his white suit, was to be seen as the gravely bending, graciously condescending, attentive cherisher of vulnerable innocence.

American ideas about children had behind them a thick network of Romantic and Victorian beliefs. Running through Clemens's own writings almost as consistently as through those of Rousseau is the idea that Nature is good. The child is natural, a kind of noble savage—although Clemens did not believe in *them*—or a pastoral type, standing for many things, including innocence and liberty. No matter how artificial Tom Sawyer may seem to a current critic, Clemens presents him as a natural boy. In his case *naughty* means *natural* and *good*, as in the case of Huck Finn *wicked* means *moral*. Tom rebels against a restricting society because society depraves and perverts. But when Clemens wrote *The Adventures of Tom Sawyer,* which is his *Emile,* he equivocated. The rebellion is a play rebellion, consisting mainly in throwing off conventional attire. Clemens amuses us with Tom's failure to understand the realities of an adult world: Tom will outlive this phase in his development and become a substantial citizen. It seems likely that critics will be permanently undecided as to whether the same equivocating holds good in the sequel of which Huck Finn is the eponymous hero.

As we have seen, in the minds of many who have written about Clemens, the natural order, which was once also God's order, is seriously to be equated with the spirit of the American West, which is to say with Mark Twain. But this same exaltation of the natural order, including the natural speech of ordinary men, marks the thinking of English Romantics; and Victorian writers for children stressed the importance of helping children to preserve their naturalness, their wildness, and their innocence. Catherine Sinclair was representative of those English storytellers who, writing before Clemens, were comparably influenced by Romantic doctrines. She informed parents that the minds of the children of her time were too closely regulated; nothing was left to nature, natural feeling, natural genius, and natural enthusiasm.[30] Her stories, however, were about the moderately well-disciplined children of the aristocracy.

The idea of children as innocents incorporated a variety of implicit ideas on virtue and vice. Youth, sexual inexperience, and virtue stand united on the one hand; on the other we find age, experience, and corruption. Clemens believed that to experience the world was to be debased by it: to live beyond childhood was to be corrupted; the only certain escape from experience—from the evil power of money, the dangers of sexuality, and the malignity of God—was in death.

The letters written by Clemens to Livy during their courtship make plain that he wanted an absolutely pure, tantalizingly virginal girl-bride *and* a sheltering, practical-minded, admonishing mother-figure. And although Livy was twenty-two when he first met her, the partly invalid, petted young woman—she spent two years in bed after a fall on ice when she was sixteen—was still in some ways remarkably childlike. After her death, Clemens asserted that for him, at least, "she remained both girl and woman to the last day of her life."[31]

Clemens seems to have been in earnest, not just playing a literary game, when in two stupefyingly sentimental letters he indicated that the prospect of the transition of Mollie Fairbanks (daughter of Mary Mason Fairbanks) from girlhood to womanhood was almost too painful for him to contemplate. After Mollie and her mother visited the Clemenses in 1874, he wrote to Mrs. Fairbanks that the girl, then seventeen, remained in his head "as the darlingest, daintiest, sweetest vision of this long, long time. She must come again, just as soon as possible, for time & sophistication will begin their hateful work by & by."[32] Then, early in 1876, Mrs. Fairbanks reported that Mollie had gone out to dine in "her first *long black* silk."

Clemens bewailed this devastating news in some twelve hundred insupportably saccharine words addressed to Mrs. Fairbanks. He mourned Mollie's loss of little-girlhood yet struggled to compliment her on becoming a "Woman." He learns "with a pang" that "the dearest bud of maidenhood in all the land" has "come out," that his "little dainty maid" has passed from under his caressing hands. Turning directly to Mollie, he tells her that she may, nevertheless, make her new rank outvalue the old: "The main thing is, to be as sweet, as a woman, as you were as a maiden; & as good & true, as honest & sincere, as loving, as pure, as genuine, as earnest, as untrivial, as sweetly graced with dignity, & as free from every taint or suggestion of shams, affectations of pretences, in your new estate as you were in the old." He would put her into the empty chamber of his heart where the Mollie was that is gone.

Even at this early date, a horror at maturity and reality is not uncharacteristic of Clemens. Mere maturity had transformed Mollie, it seems, into a kind of Hester Prynne. Only by the diligent practice of all the virtues might she find redemption. Later Clemens issued a succinct parallel injunction to Gertrude Natkin, who was fifteen: "Stay just as you are—youth is the golden time."[33]

To many writers and artists, prepubescent girls have seemed to be un-differentiated, at one with males. The immature bodies hint at a kind of physical apocatastasis, of a restoration to the refined, unthreatening de-lights of mythically androgynous love. They suggest that third kind of original being who, as postulated by Aristophanes in Plato's "Symposium," existed in a sexually conjoined state. Thomas Taylor, the Neoplatonist, declares Psyche to be "beautiful as every human *soul* is before it is 'defiled by matter.'" Joan M. Webber, who refers to "the mythic first parent as her-maphroditic" and to "a tradition that Adam was hermaphroditic before the creation of Eve," points also to a Christian acknowledgment that the nature of creation is to be fallen, to be divided, and to long for unity. Perhaps the unity may be with an androgynous figure who, like Patroclus to Achilles, is one's other self.[34] In Romantic art Eros and Psyche are sometimes shown as mirror images of one another—thus they set at a distance the differentiated indelicacies of male-female intercourse. As I have noted, the suavity of the immature has been supposed to attract frightened men, perhaps especially those who are bisexually oriented but fear sexual relations with either men or women.

To seek out girls is, by this view, one sort of fuguing, a flight from reality and responsibility into a world of fantasy: as in Pater, *flawless* and *clean* become operative words. Undifferentiated bodies have also been inter-preted, however, as masking an incipient or covert or unorthodox sexuality. A formulaic set of sentimental images in eighteenth-century art shows adolescent females in an excitingly uncertain state, trembling between smiling, sheltered innocence and grieving experience. As specified in paint-ing and in comparable topoi in the fiction, the experience that was about to arrive, or had just arrived, to vulnerable innocence was disturbingly sexual. The possibility of an intriguing heterodoxy is often emphasized: in Shelley and in Canova the androgynous is associated with an interest in her-maphroditism, incest, homoeroticism, and narcissism.[35]

Victorian attitudes toward youth were, as one would expect, mixed. It was possible to see children as pure, sexually quiescent beings who were nonetheless constantly open to stimulation and corruption, always in dan-ger of becoming little monsters of appetite.[36] Clemens, as we have seen, feared for the youthful Livy's purity if she read in an unexpurgated *Don Quixote*; and, as we also have seen, he went to extraordinary lengths to shield his daughters from the attentions of men.

It has been suggested that Clemens showed signs of latent homosexuality in *Huckleberry Finn* and in scattered references to nude males.[37] This is a possibility, of course, but the life and writings speak much more positively of an unfearful fondness for girls young enough to present an androgynous appearance. For Clemens their figures may have had the effect of de-materializing or derealizing the sexuality of the mature female body. To one who loves and fears women, a sexual relationship with a prenubile girl reduces the fleshly, frightening aspect of sexuality. A relationship restricted to hugs and kisses further idealizes and distances the perils of sexuality. Paradoxes abound with respect to this avoidance of the vulgarly normal in sex as contrasted with Clemens's often proud acceptance of literary or social realities and vulgarities. Critics recognize his voracious vitality, his use of incidents and themes that came from or could have come from newspaper headlines, his "authentic" language, "popular" images, and "vernacular" characters. What they tend to overlook are his reticences and anxieties.

The idea of adult sex may have a powerful appeal to the moral masochist, yet he may at the same time think of it as dirty, sinful, and prohibited. Masturbation is also proscribed (Clemens offers standard reasons in his "Address to the Stomach Club") though often practiced and so gives rise to apprehensions. Prenubile girls are not a danger: by convention, at least, they are pure.

At Oxford, friends and colleagues of Lewis Carroll permitted him, after suitable petitioning, to photograph their daughters—"innocent imps of God"—in the nude. American parents seem to have thrust their daughters upon Clemens, a famous, grieving, white-suited man. Little girls were not merely thought by genteel society to be taboo for sexual purposes, they were so definitively forbidden that it was difficult to conceive of them as sexual objects; they were safe from men and men were safe from them. Yet even genteel little girls do have sexual instincts; and children are frequently used for sexual purposes, most often by fathers, brothers, and friends of fathers and brothers. We are now keenly aware of the existence of nymphets and of how middle-aged Humberts work out their Oedipus-complex striv-ings through intercourse with Lolitas.[38]

Little girls were assumed, however, to be safe with Clemens; and they probably were. Although Clara and Paine were uneasy about these relationships, it probably did not occur to the mothers involved that the author of *Joan of Arc* might molest their daughters. Thus the girls offered what seems to have been a secure approach to some kind of idealized sexuality. They existed outside of the stresses and evils of the adult world; they could be confined to a universe of donkey carts and gentle splashings in translucent, sunlit waters. They could be set aside like dolls when Clemens wished to sleep or to write, and they were expected to hasten to devote themselves to him when he wished to play. (Only two little girls, Carlotta Welles and Helen Allen, are reported to have refused to let him monopolize them.)[39] In addition to being safe playthings, the girls helped Clemens to avoid the problems of living and dying, including the humiliating possible problem of being for perhaps a quarter of a century sexually impotent.

In these stainless young companions Clemens looked for good manners, a pleasing appearance, and a lively though unassertive intelligence. All of the girls seem to have belonged to families in easy circumstances, rich enough to take trips to Europe or to Bermuda—there were, most emphatically, no female Huck Finns among them. Their language probably showed little originality or high polish, but we may be sure that they spoke in reasonably cultivated voices, exhibiting no traces of nonstandard English in diction or intonation. When one of them used slang, which was for Clemens an inclusive word, he was seriously disturbed. Dorothy Quick meant to call a mounted moth a beauty, but in her excitement cried out, "It's a beaut!" Clemens walked away, and Miss Lyon whispered to Dorothy that "the one thing in the world Mr. Clemens actually detested was slang." Clemens himself corrected Mary Rogers, much as he admired her. She must avoid obvious remarks and commonplace phrasing. He was thankful that she had discarded slang: "You have goodness in abundance; you have native frankness and sincerity; you have high ideals—qualities these, of the clean mind and the clean heart: slang has no place in that regal company."[40] James Russell Lowell could not have issued a more Brahminical dictum.

It helped if the young companions could play billiards and hearts, take snapshots and dictation, and it was quintessentially necessary that they be affectionate and admiring. Clemens wrote of one of the girls who visited him at Stormfield, "She is a dear womanly child," and of another, "My Bermuda Angel-fish has been here. She has grown considerably, but is as sweet and innocent and unspoiled as ever she was."[41]

The innocence of little girls may be readily associated with the white suits that Clemens affected during his later years. The suits are usually explained as a harmless example of an amusing tendency to exhibitionism, and one might suspect a mild rupophobia; but in the autobiographical writings Clemens himself gives impetus to the finding of symbolic significance by relating the suits and the daily shampooing and fluffing of his white hair to cleanliness. His description of the treatment of his hair makes of it a kind of purification rite, one which could be interpreted as a reiterated absolution. Of his clothing he writes, "I am considered eccentric because I wear white clothes both winter and summer. I am eccentric, then, because I prefer to be clean in the matter of raiment—clean in a dirty world; absolutely the only cleanly-clothed human being in all Christendom north of the Tropics."[42]

Clemens's cleanliness and the purity of little girls are specifically connected in an incident on board the *Minnetonka,* where he met Dorothy Quick. He pointed out that in order for Dorothy to complement him she should wear white for the rest of the voyage, "because we're going to be together a lot, Dorothy, and we might as well match and present a perfect picture as we pace the decks."[43] This injunction, if at all accurately remembered, carries powerful connotations of exhibitionistic vanity, and more: a vision of ideality is realized when symbolic whiteness and girlish purity converge. Clemens is stage-managing the presentation to the shipboard microcosm of an image of a great author, a serenely wise old man, his moral purity accentuated by the virginal purity of his companion. Together they paraded, a spotless pair, set apart from the maculate, the gross, and the fleshly.

The insistent attribution by Clemens of shining innocence to Livy, Dorothy Quick, and a long list of others helps to explain the high valuation that he placed on his more insipid writings, most particularly on *Joan of Arc.* Joan's story had a powerful appeal to Clemens for a number of reasons. It contained, of course, mysteries and moments of high drama, offered opportunities for climactic scenes. Joan herself, however, was the chief attraction. Clemens liked the anticlerical strand in her legend and her status, at least in the nineteenth century, as a child of nature. More than any historical figure with whom he was familiar, she was an innocent who perceived truth. She was, moreover, sexually pure—it was reported that, as befit a medieval female cult figure, she never menstruated. Joan had, it seems, preeminently some of the qualities with which he endowed certain of his fictional heroines and which he demanded of his Angel Fish.

Clemens could say in perfect seriousness of his published works, "I often think that the thing that makes me happiest is that children read and love my books. I am proud that they can."[44] In the decline of his always uncertain critical powers he could take pride, too, in the good opinion of such women as Miss Wallace and the only slightly less banal Miss Lyon. This is another face of the pleasure he seems to have taken in the applause given by male audiences to his recitation of dirty jokes and bawdy verses.

At this remove in time, it would be difficult not to perceive in Clemens's relationships with young girls traces of the Lolita complex, undercurrents of teasing sexuality. The safe little girls were sometimes large for their ages, and they were not all either unisex in appearance or, strictly speaking, prepubescent. Dorothy Quick, for example, was a large child; and some playmates of ten or eleven had a way of maturing very quickly. Mollie Fairbanks was nineteen before she passed from under what Clemens called his "caressing hands." Helen Allen, with whose parents Clemens stayed in Bermuda shortly before his death, was at fifteen the last of the Angel Fish and much interested in a young man. Clemens relished sending an almost "improper kiss" to Gertrude Natkin when she was sixteen. Like Lewis Carroll, he seems to have delighted in caresses from his companions, in holding the girls on his lap, and in kissing them.

Certainly he liked to write about kissing, and he worked both kissing and caressing into one of his countless virtuoso landscape pieces. A long, mawkish passage in a letter to Elizabeth Wallace describes the autumnal splendors to be seen from the windows of Stormfield: "If you could look out at my bedroom window at this moment, you would choke up; and when you got your voice you would say this is not real, this is a dream. Such a singing together, and such a whispering together, and such a snuggling together of cosy soft colors, and such kissing and caressing, and such pretty blushing when the sun breaks out and catches these dainty weeds at it."[45] Perhaps more revealing than existing photographs is the fantasized hermaphroditic heroine, Hellfire Hotchkiss, in the preserved fragment of a novel that Clemens worked on (long before the death of Livy) during the summer and early autumn of 1897.[46]

If a few preserved photographs are suggestive, so are several anecdotes and allusions. After Miss Wallace explained to Margaret Blackmer in Bermuda that there was no Mrs. Clemens and that Clemens loved little girls because he had lost his own Susy, Margaret is said to have thought for a moment and then, with brown eyes full of tenderness, to have remarked, "I wish I was Mrs. Clemens, and then I would just care for him and care for him, and love him awfully!"[47] So far as is known, Clemens's was an unfulfilled Humbertism. Hamlin Hill does note, however, that an un-named informant refused to disclose for publication the story of an alleged incident in Bermuda in which Clemens may have proceeded so far as "improper comments or even actions."[48]

John Seelye thinks that four brief entries in Clemens's notebooks (July-August 1878) are thoroughly revealing of his sexual inclinations. Clemens mentions, for example, seeing several groups of naked girls bathing in the Neckar. One slender girl "snatched a leafy bow of a bush across her front & then stood satisfied gazing out upon us as we floated by—a very pretty picture." According to Seelye, the purifying transformation of this and similar passages in A Tramp Abroad (1880) strips Clemens himself naked and shows him in an act of wish fulfillment.[49] As I read the passages in question, nothing in the entries or in A Tramp Abroad supports so firm a conclusion; and the dates mark a separation from Clemens's period of obvious pedophilia. When everything that we know about his later life is taken into account, however, evidence of the latent sexuality in Clemens's relationships with little girls is persuasive.

Something of the covert sexuality that often lies hidden behind a show of innocence may be illustrated by an anecdote that Clemens tells of Margaret Illington, a popular young actress who was at the time the wife of Daniel Frohman, actor's agent and theater manager. Clemens made public and private capital of his whims and eccentricities; friends played up to him. By dressing herself as a little girl, Miss Illington dramatized a pretended desire to be admitted to Clemens's Aquarium along with his other juvenile Angel Fish. She appeared for dinner at Clemens's home in New York dressed "for twelve years and had pink ribbons at the back of her neck and looked about fourteen years old and so I admitted her as an angel fish and pinned a badge on her bosom. There are a lot of lady candidates but I guess we won't let any more in—unless perhaps Billie Burke."[50]

Not by the most arduous stretching of the imagination could Miss Illington and Miss Burke have been considered at the time to be prepubes-cent, sexually inexperienced Angel Fish. Nor could Mary Rogers, the vivacious, talented, and rich young wife of Harry Rogers, son of Henry H. Rogers. Beginning in 1900, Clemens became her Uncle Mark; she was his honorary niece and the recipient of honeyed letters that included many urgent invitations for her to visit him. As the daughter-in-law of Clemens's benefactor, Mary was presumably as safe as a church; and the moralistic nympholept could woo her with flattery as though she were a ten-year-old.

Perhaps the public positions of the Misses Illington and Burke made them, too, at once safe and attractive.

Although the general drift of the evidence is clear, most detailed conclusions about Clemens's sexuality must be taken tentatively. That Clemens felt guilt because he masturbated as a boy (and possibly as a man) would seem to be certain; and it is probable that he became more or less impotent at about the age of fifty, which, if true, may have heightened his guilt at having practiced masturbation. His fear of women's sexuality has seemed obvious to many; and it would relate to his stress on purity, his probable impotence, his pedophilia, his essentially misogynist tracts, and his fondness for jokes aggressing against women. He could and did shift quickly from sentimental assertions of desolation at the deaths of Susy and of Livy—two ethereal beings—to the tracts and jokes that reflect what I take to be his neuroses concerning women.

Clemens himself contributed to passages in his legend that are misleading, as in giving the impression that he was the ideal husband and father, the always chivalrous protector of women. Clara Clemens and Paine, guardian daemons at the entrance to the Mark Twain shrine, forbade or otherwise did what they could to prevent the publication of material that might damage the reputation of Clemens or that of his family. Books by Clara and by Paine expanded the legend as it came to them; and lesser celebrants like Elizabeth Wallace and Mary Lawton fell into line, as have more important biographers and critics.

A few additional points may deserve recapitulation. Problems of purity and pollution stimulated Clemens to charge women with being constantly, comically, and frighteningly lustful. The nude bodies of women—or more positively of girls—were to him forever tempting, but for him to seek the delights that mature sexuality offered could, if psychoanalytic theory holds true, provoke in him the fear of castration. Avoidance of women by way of masturbation was also forbidden: it was self-polluting and heightened the danger of impotence. Substitute gratifications for uninhibited sexuality are possible, however, and for Clemens prominent among these surrogates during his later years was the companionship of little girls. This association, apparently ripe with hugs and kisses, appears to have been both psychically and physically satisfying; one judges that it eliminated the possibility of pollution and restored feelings of masculinity and dominance. At any rate, he and his protective circle transformed his pedophilia into a culture-approved, circumspect affection for children.

An overview of salient aspects of Clemens's character structure from the perspective of a psychiatry that pays some attention to cultural factors helps to authenticate our profile of his sexual nature and tells us something of the extent to which his problems corresponded with conflicts frequently observed in his society, differing from the normal primarily in their intensity.[51] The consequent deformations of character are most observable late in his life, especially after his bankruptcy in 1894. From about that time forward his neuroticisms, his guilt, his suffering, and his protective aberrations increasingly manifested themselves.

The competitiveness that marks the American bourgeois spirit is noticeable in Clemens from an early age; it was heightened following his removal from the West to the East, his start on book publishing, and his marriage to a provincial heiress. During the period when he courted Olivia Langdon, her family (particularly her mother) was openly, persistently dubious about his character. The word *character* included, of course, ideas about his conformity to standard Protestant doctrines and his capacity to make money.

The demands made by the Langdons forced Clemens temporarily toward acceptance of churchliness and may have permanently reinforced the strong inclination to speculative investments that he had demonstrated as early as when he was on the Mississippi. Throughout his career he consecrated himself more to the pursuit of great wealth than to the pursuit of great literature. Following his bankruptcy, his fear of failure and his sense of guilt reached climactic heights. By that time he had dissipated much of Livy's fortune and was compelled to attempt to borrow from her brother, an all the more humiliating necessity because Charles Langdon had been his protégé on board the *Quaker City* a quarter-century earlier. Charles was now socially and financially secure, a man of judgment, and he attempted to guard what remained of his sister's money.

Clemens's excessive protestations of guilt developed together with the development of his neuroses. As a boy he reproached himself when he gave (or later said he gave) tobacco and matches to a drunken tramp in the Hannibal calaboose and the tramp burned the building down with himself in it. He experienced guilt when his brother Henry died as the result of a steamboat accident; at the death of his little son, Langdon; at the death of his daughter Susy; at his bankruptcy; and at a hundred other events. His protestations of guilt (like his suffering, they served as protective devices) alternated with efforts to blame others. Late in life he projected his hostilities on Clara and Jean. Earlier and much more obviously he formed the habit of projecting his money lust and his hostilities on colleagues. Those associated with him—with the notable exceptions of James Osgood, briefly his publisher, and Henry Rogers, his financial savior—he characterized in rancorous diatribes as rogues, cheats, and incompetents. He considered them to be responsible for his failures or to be blameworthy when his monetary successes were less glorious than he would have liked. (It is true that several of his associates deserved his censures.) When late stories like "Which Was It?" are given psychoanalytic readings, they may be reasonably interpreted as efforts to intellectualize his problems and so to wipe the slate clean of disapproval, anxiety, and guilt.

In the end human scapegoats alone would not serve. Determinisms— carrying implications that the individual is powerless and therefore not responsible—were of some protective value, as were fantasizing projections on a grand scale. In a number of unfinished stories, inexplicable forces turn happy lives upside down. Or, more in the tradition of rebels against the culture, Clemens attributed his own hostilities, magnified, to God: when victimized by God's malevolence, even the best and strongest individual must feel bewildered and infantile.

We do not know the intimate details of Clemens's life very well, particularly of his early life; but he often mentions his restlessness and unhappiness, and we can perceive that he frequently lived in a state of quiet or unquiet desperation. Moral masochism is evident throughout his career. He sought to master the world in order to protect himself from it; but escapism was also a dominant protective tendency. He was alienated in the Freudian as well as in the Marxist sense of the word: he felt himself to be emotionally alone, longed for affection and approval, yet increasingly disdained his friends.

His escapism began early and took divers forms. Society, social obligations, and the Self were afflictions. Within him he heard a confused parley of voices that at one or more times provoked him seriously to consider suicide and repeatedly led him to praise death as man's ultimate savior. He escaped from war in Missouri to the West, from complications in San Francisco to a cabin in the hills and to the Sandwich Islands. Repeatedly he yearned for the peace of life at sea. In *Roughing It* a stagecoach and western irresponsibility are his warm cocoons. He fled the pressures of New York on board the *Quaker City*, retreating to the open sea, Europe, the Middle East, and an unapprehended past that demanded interpretation by a new

Adam. He discovered idyllic boyhood in *Tom Sawyer*. *Huckleberry Finn* as a whole may be read as a great evasion, perhaps most significantly when Clemens, in the person of Huck, immerses himself in the godlike River and, shedding the Self, achieves a feeling of cosmic unity. In book after book, he sought refuge from the nineteenth-century society that he consciously praised for its progressive modernity. Childhood anxieties—linked in all probability to sibling rivalries and repressed Oedipal feelings—developed to include a lust for women concomitant with hostility toward them. He narcotized himself with teas, dinner parties, billiards, and alcohol. He replaced achievable objectives for himself as man and writer with grandiose dreams of plutocratic status, of himself as a bringer of culture and— perhaps not altogether playfully—as a religious leader. Most important in considering the topic of his sexuality, he suppressed anxieties occasioned by libidinal impulses through speculating, pedophilia, and, possibly, by masturbation.

The problems related to Clemens's sexuality appear to be common in modern Western societies. The complex social forces that played upon his fellows played upon Clemens. He was a man of his times, not altogether a rare victim of childhood traumas. He was aggressively competitive, repressed hostilities, experienced gnawing apprehensions, endured the sting of failure and the absence of love. He felt alienation and helplessness. In a sense—though not in the sense that has been promoted by heroizers—he was, to a degree, both an exceptional and a representative American.

TENDENTIOUS

JOKES

8

▲ ▲ ▲ ▲ ▲ ▲ ▲ ▲ ▲

Jokes and joking may be serious matters. William Dean Howells repeatedly stressed the moral rectitude that gave significance to Mark Twain's comedy, how unlike it was to the bumptious and vulgar jests of most western comedians. To counter the pejorative implications often attendant upon westernness, he stressed, too, the fastidious nature of his friend, his almost womanly tenderness, and the exceptional delicacy of his sentiments. Howells's remarks of this kind were received gratefully by Clemens.

Similar dubious compliments have been paid Clemens by other critics: he is benevolent, compassionate, an *amiable* humorist, and an innovative moralist. Wishing to place him in a favorable light, critics have obscured the aggressions to be found in his humor and have neglected the evidence to be found in the autobiographical writings, the letters, and the notebooks. If we are to encompass anything like the whole truth about Clemens's comedy, we must take into account a bitter, destructive, sadistic side of the man that makes itself obvious in his barbed aphorisms, his diatribes, and his virulently dehumanizing social satires. I find in many of his writings little or nothing of what Mikhail M. Bakhtin describes as the revivifying carnivalesque spirit.

The jokes that Clemens set down in his notebooks (which he started at the age of nineteen while on the Mississippi River as an apprentice pilot) are richly symptomatic of this darker side of his nature: they tell us something of his attitudes toward society and morality, drop clues to his sexuality, and are fertile in suggestions concerning his underlying feelings about race and gender.

Clemens's practice of jotting down reminders for jokes and anecdotes began early, increased during the years that were most important to his literary career, and became obsessive toward the end of his life.[1] That most of the jokes are unoriginal is not of great importance; that he selected them, recorded and rerecorded them, and sometimes created original settings for them makes them revealing.

Distribution of the jokes in the notebooks is very uneven. Clemens sometimes gathered a number of jokes at the end of an opuscule: they tend to disappear when he has a secretary keeping records for him or when he is making specialized notes for topographical descriptions. They may come thick and fast when he has been in the company of raconteurs (the officers of a steamboat, for example), expects to be called on to amuse a male audience, or hopes to use cleaned-up anecdotes to enliven a sketch or a travel book. Those notebooks are unfortunately missing that might have told us whether he continued to enter dirty jokes while paying court to Olivia Langdon and portraying himself as what she and her mother wanted him to be: a high priest of purity. In his letters of the period to the Langdons and to Mary Fairbanks, he endorsed purity and social order in all their aspects. Letters to his old friend Frank Fuller make him seem less regenerate. Would the notebooks have revealed a dissociation in his intellectual and emotional nature? Conflicts came, we know, soon enough.

Psychiatrists perceive discords such as those which beset Clemens as evidence of unconscious fears, defense mechanisms, and hostilities. We have noted his obsession with purity, and I now exhibit his simultaneous delight in the scatological and the erotic; contrarieties possessed him. The case resembles that of the man who loves filth but washes his hands a hundred times a day. My discussion here focuses on a few jokes and anecdotes that dwell on odors, corpses, feces, and defecation; aggress against blacks; or aggress against women. No attempt is made to distinguish jests from jokes or jokes from anecdotes; the terms are used pretty much interchangeably.

Taboo language runs like a warp through the fabric of these jokes. Against the grain of polite expectations, Clemens regularly introduced the aggressive, polluting words *fart, piss, cunt, ass, ass-hole,* and *shit*—usually blanked out or represented by dashes. *Fuck* is, I think, never spelled out and appears rarely, perhaps only during 1867.[2] Taboo words become formulaic, are comic automatisms: when we reach one of them we have arrived at some kind of climax; it is time to laugh. There is no amiability about the words; yet, under certain circumstances, they may relieve tension.

A number of the jokes and anecdotes in the notebooks appear only as jottings that are too curtailed to be meaningful, but some of the fragmentary items are recorded two or more times in such varying ways that we may reconstruct the basic jokes. Of special help in examining compositional technique are those items in which Clemens registered an allusion and later constructed a dramatized anecdote. Representative instances show a movement from simple, raw obscenities toward that distancing and enhancement by means of form which, in polite society, is constitutive of comedy, ensuring conservation of psychical expenditure and derivation of pleasure from sources that have undergone repression.

Although the jokes discussed here are, in Freud's terminology, tendentious, having objects, some of those on which Clemens made notes might be classified as innocent—if any jokes are truly innocent. The telling of these innocent jokes may be equated, at least in Freud's eyes, with exhibitionism in the field of sex. Aggressive tendentious jokes (if we may forgive any implied tautology), which Clemens's generally were, succeed best, Freud thought, with tellers or auditors in whose sexuality a potent sadistic component, more or less inhibited in real life, is demonstrable.[3]

Like the southwestern writers of sketches and tall tales, Clemens indulged himself in manic fantasies—resembling capriciously sadistic versions of paintings by Chagall—wherein small, airborne, stylized figures are blown to bits or otherwise made to suffer pain and injury. The ferocity inherent in such frontier tales may be palliated by its very excess and by our recognition that these stories, like folktales, belong to a mode—we know that we are in a realm characterized by frenetic invention. Edmund Wilson is too harsh in his animadversions on the sadistic nature of George W. Harris's Sut Lovingood stories, and, although jokes can be therapeutic, too kind in discovering in Mark Twain's early sketches "a kind of purgative function in rendering simply comic stark hardships and disastrous adventures."[4] Clemens's predilection for the grossly physical and the malicious did not end with the close of his western experiences. He sought to disguise the savagery and reduce the malice of the stories, especially when he adapted them for publication, but they retained a substantial fraction of the qualities that made similar jokes and anecdotes risible to the storytellers of the West and Southwest and to the readers of newspapers like the Virginia City, Nevada, *Enterprise* and the New York *Spirit of the Times*.

By current standards, comedy of this kind that appears unmodified in the notebooks is either primitive or childish. We tend not to be amused by adolescent bathroom humor or by the humor of schadenfreude. (Ancient Greek auditors, however, are supposed to have found that famous instance of schadenfreude, Homer's account of the beating of Thersites by Odysseus, to be laughable.)[5] Schadenfreude feeds on the misfortunes of others; and it may involve hatred, envy, scorn, or sadistic eroticism.

Devoted as Clemens was to the bathroom mode (with its accompanying taboo words) and to schadenfreude, when he elaborated these jokes he usually found some masking of the filth or of the pain and malignity to be necessary. Because he was in his maturity the product of and mainly the exponent of genteel nineteenth-century society, it could hardly have been otherwise. A favored device for masking involved the appropriate inclusion among the dramatis personae of blacks, lower-class women, children, and foreigners: they are set apart by being unlike us. By the conventions of the comedic tradition (and to a degree by the conventions of ordinary life) these characters belonged to a world of feeling not quite like that of normal human beings. No matter what Clemens taught us to understand about Jim's emotions in *Huckleberry Finn,* in the jokes that Clemens cherished, blacks bleed very little.

Although nothing indicates that Clemens was afflicted with parosmia, psychiatrists would probably consider as evidence of coprophilia his strong interest in flatulence, defecation, feces, and fecallike odors. The more macabre, apparently, the better: he was captivated by anecdotes that involved both corpses and odors. Readers of *Innocents Abroad* are familiar with the attraction that everything surrounding death had for Clemens. He was, of

TENDENTIOUS JOKES ▲ 165

course, not alone in being fascinated by graves, cemeteries, and morgues: this was a nineteenth-century preoccupation. Nor was he alone, especially among western humorists, in conceiving of corpses as dehumanized, an appropriate focus of charnel house comedy.

The charm of engaging in forbidden aggressions was, for Clemens, heightened by a special sensitivity to taboo words, to their hard, nominalistic particularity. Western influences, the practice of his trade as a writer, and the pressures of eastern gentility could be partly explanatory. The taboo word was less a signifier relating to a signified than a symbol homogeneous with that which was symbolized. That is to say, the symbolized was immanent in the symbolizer. This partakes of what is said at one point in Plato's *Cratylus*: an exact name would be, though impossibly, a copy of the thing or action imitated. John Locke pointed out that men often mistakenly suppose their words to stand for the reality of things. In Peircean terms, the supposed relationship could be called iconic.

According to the findings of psychiatrists, the taboo words that Clemens delighted in may well be associated with constraints imposed on him during toilet training (as also may be his obsession with purity). To the infant defecation is gratifying, and the feces are captivating. The child, it is said, may wish to hold on to these pleasures beyond toilet training or, conversely, may react against them, or the two responses may appear in combination. Rejection of the function may contribute to an inclination toward excessive cleanliness.[6]

Because many of Clemens's entries in the notebooks do not spell out a joke or anecdote in complete form but set down instead a "nub" as reminder, the unusual power that taboo words had over Clemens's puritanical affective life may be exposed by the frequency with which the nub is little more than one or two vulgar words: the heart of these precious verbal constructions consists in the unspeakable terms that are, nonetheless, spoken. In these barren, flavorless nubs, the aggressions remain, comedy is yet to be supplied or has been drained out.

Within a few lines of the beginning of his second opuscule (1860), Clemens entered a short series of jokes. One ran:

"What you done—Murder—rape—Theft—worse'n that.
"Hold my coat Bro—I've found th man sht in" [1:50].

Another entry, this one in 1865: "Scene—In a country cabin in Mo.— Traveler asks 3 boys what they do—last & smallest says 'I nusses Johnny, eats apples & totes out merde'" (1:83). As late as 1888 Clemens considered

the following amusing enough to record: "Miss, would you be so kind as to
ft here & go outside & shit" (3:370).

One of the few carefully worked up early burlesques (January 1865),
although presumably prepared with publication in mind, is marked by the
juvenility of its humor. In this long comment on a report supposed to have
been prepared for a mining company by a Professor W. Bilgewater,
Clemens writes,

> The Prof feels satisfied that the Company have got the world by the
> ass, since it is manifest that no other organ of the earth's frame could
> possibly have produced such a dysentery of disorganized & half-
> digested slumgullion as is here presented.
>
> Upon one pile of these croppings the prof found a most interesting
> formation—one which, from its unusual conformation & composi-
> tion at first excited in his breast a frenzy of professional enthusiasm.
> The deposit was cylindrical in form, & 3 inches long by 3/4 of an inch
> in diameter, tapering to a point like the end of a cigar at one end &
> broken off square at the other, exposing several projecting fibres re-
> sembling hairs. The object was of a dull light gray color, dry & capable
> of disintegration by moderate pressure between the fingers. The pro-
> fessor at once applied the tests of handling, smelling, & tasting, & was
> forced to the conclusion that there was nothing extraordinary about
> the seeming phenomenon, & that it had doubtless been deposited on
> the croppings by some animal—a dog, in all probability [1:88–89].

The comment on a presumably scientific report turns out to be characteristically western comedy: a burlesque; a scatological hoax.

Taboo words and their implication of rebelliousness are all that can
conceivably give spice to some otherwise banal entries, as in the two
following examples: "In the revised edition of the Koran it is asserted that
no man can —— literature; but this is disproven by David Ker's travel-
papers in the Cosmopolitan. Pity to put that flatulence between the same
leaves with that charming Chinese story" (3:457). And "*Diffusion.* 'That
man (a writer) would be competent to inflate a balloon with a single ——'"
(3:519).

One of Clemens's more elaborated anecdotes, set down in the summer of
1887, combines corpses and odors: "Fireman wants the widow to put off
her son's funeral a day because the boys want to turn out on that day, &
must lose the chance to turn out for *him* (a member) otherwise. The widow

explains that the weather being warm, is afraid Jimmy won't keep. The fire laddie asks to examine the body—the weeping widow stands by:

"(Bends over body & snuffs.) Smf! smf! Hell! Sweet as a nut!—keep a week!"[7]

Another anecdote exploits three favored topics: corpses, odors, and feces: "Procession of men hired to follow the corpse of an unpopular man at $2 apiece, & look down sorrowing; if they looked up, to be docked half. There was an evil smell. Finally, they agreed that one should look & they would stand the loss between them. They found they had switched off & were following a night cart" (3:233).

In late March (?) of 1878, Clemens reminded himself of a series of "undertaker stories" that he intended for *A Tramp Abroad* (1880). (An undertaker does appear prominently in chapter 43 of *Life on the Mississippi*, 1883.) The proposed sketches have to do with corpses on ice, corpses shipped as turnips to profit by the advantageous freight rate, the undertaker who crossed the hands of a dying man and requested that he keep them so, and the man who dropped a nickel into a child's coffin on the absentminded assumption that it was a collection box. One of the stories on the list (about Limburger cheese and a coffin box) had a long prepublication history. On Howells's advice, Clemens omitted it from the version of "Some Rambling Notes of an Idle Excursion" that appeared in the *Atlantic* in 1877–78. Later he consulted Howells again and omitted the tale once more, this time from *A Tramp Abroad*. At last, he mutinously published it in "Some Rambling Notes" in *The Stolen White Elephant* (1882).[8]

On August 23 (?), 1883, Clemens entered, with revisions and expurgations, a brief, unusually provocative note portraying, as I interpret it, the act of defecating as habitually performed by some unnamed but supernally magnificent personage whose surroundings and entourage, even for this duty, are of a splendor that occurs only in a dreamer's most florid imaginings. The meaning is obscure. No clues tell us whether Clemens is fantasizing about a hated God; a megalomaniacal acquaintance; or, for that matter, his imagined, lordly self. All that seems clear is that the dignitary concerned goes to defecate in a house or room made of precious jewels (the floor is a polished ruby—compare Fitzgerald's "The Diamond as Big as the Ritz") accompanied by exalted servitors (a Roman emperor, a pope) and, for the humblest service of all, not a goose but an Irishman.[9]

In the tall tales and anecdotes of southwestern comedy blacks occupy a position inferior even to that of members of the poor-white class. Their injuries were laughable, not painful; their ignorance and simplicity were proper subjects for derision: when they were objects of ridicule, schadenfreude carried no after-burden of remorse or guilt. This southwestern humor was the kind that Clemens knew best from his earliest years, and its openly racist bent clearly did not distress him after he had made himself a member of the eastern establishment.

In April-May of 1882, while on his Mississippi trip to gather facts and impressions that were to go into *Life on the Mississippi* and, as it happened, into *Adventures of Huckleberry Finn,* Clemens indicated his fondness for using Negroes (generally assumed to be oversexed and morally lax) for sexual comedy by reporting a supposedly overheard conversation on board ship between two black laundresses. One says that if she were a girl, she "wouldn't sleep with no stranger, don't care what he'd pay" and remarks of "a young colored chap" who apparently had been caressing her, "That's just as close as I allows one of them young fellows to go. I don't want anything to do with boys. If I want anybody, I want a *man*" (2:501).

Equally stereotyped (reminding one of the widely told anecdote about Negroes and alligators that ends, "I *thought* somethin' was gettin' them chillun") is a seriocomic note on parental unconcern on the part of Negroes: "When the niggers move from one plantation to another by these boats they carefully get all their dogs aboard—mangy, yellow dogs—and are so interested in the dogs that they sometimes forget their children. In one instance they brought six miserable dogs and left a child on the landing. The people had to take care of that child."[10]

Over and over the notebooks show Negroes as supplying comedy. These jests, jokes, and anecdotes tell us what Clemens thought might be valuable, when developed, as material for sketches, letters to newspapers, or books. They reflect his opinion of the taste of his readers, and they add to our understanding of his racial attitudes and his sense of comedy.

In 1866 Clemens entered an exceptionally brutal joke for which his editors seek to find an extenuating explanation:

"Where did you get that excellent venison at this time of the year?"
"It isn't venison—it is a steak off that dead nigger" [1:136].

The editors believe that Twain's "grotesque levity may be a reaction to the methodical butchery" performed by famished sailors as described in a book that Clemens was reading. But that Clemens was expressing humane indignation is by no means certain or even probable; during this period the tone of much of his comedy intended for western readers would suggest otherwise. Consider a jest he set down while on his *Quaker City* voyage, apparently on June 23, 1867: "Extract from a Sandwich Islander's Journal: 'Had a Christian for Breakfast this morning'" (1:348).

More typically, Clemens's notebooks following his removal from the West to the East contain entries in which blacks are objects of less grisly fun. Ordinarily the words *colored* and *darkey* supersede the term *nigger*, but the Negro continues to be fully acceptable as laughingstock. Clemens made the following entry in 1878 while on shipboard en route to Europe: "3rd day out, Bayard Taylor's colored man, being constipated, applied to the ship's doctor for relief, who sent him 6 large rhubarb pills, to be taken every 4 hours; the pills came by a German steward, who delivered the directions in German, the darkey not understanding a word of it. Result: the darkey took all the pills at once & appeared no more on deck for 6 days."[11]

In August 1880, he tried his hand at a sketch (particularly venomous with respect to the French) which he intended to work into "Captain Stormfield's Visit to Heaven": "Early, in heaven Stormfield is delighted with the social equalities—a nigger, a Digger, an Esquimaux, & a Fejeean invite themselves to dinner with him—'if we had another animal or two, we could start a menagerie.'" Finally Stormfield concludes, "'Heaven is a most unpleasant place; there is no privacy in it. I must move'" (2:368–69).

While preparing for his return to the Mississippi in 1882, Clemens made notes on things he should do or should write about. In one note he reminded himself to write a comic sketch of a fat, black chambermaid (placing her in Arkansas) whom Clara Spaulding, Livy's longtime friend, had told him about: "Make her good natured & perfectly overflowing with variegated profanity." The chambermaid is to protest that she has been converted and "doan use dem kine o' words no mo', now." After that, Clemens concludes, "let her heave in Scripture & piety honestly, & occasionally forget & hurl in a sounding oath" (2:458).

During April, while on the river, Clemens recorded in detail what he called "The Handcar Episode" as told him by a second mate who went with two rich men—Elevator Dodge and Joe Smith—to look at some property that they wanted to buy. The men took a "God-damned" handcar propelled by a couple of "damned niggers" and coming to a downgrade encountered "a lot of shanties occupied by a lot of damned niggers." Out came an old sow that the handcar chopped into two pieces. The men fell down the bank but scrambled up unhurt. "Wasn't nobody hurt but that hog, and by God they taxed us $16. for that hog. If it was to do over again I would come on those niggers for damages to myself" (2:531–32).

A handful of the jokes and anecdotes that may be found in the Mississippi River notebooks (as now printed numbered 21 and 22) get into *Life on the Mississippi*. There (chapter 14) Clemens portrays the childish pride that Negroes take in status-by-association, telling stories about the fireman on the *Aleck Scott* and the barber on the *Grand Turk*. He also tells two comic tales about steamboats that stress Negro simplicity (chapter 30), and puts into black face (chapter 45) an anecdote illustrating southern exaggerations of the charms of antebellum days: "Ah, bless yo' heart, honey, you ought to seen dat moon befo' de waw!" He includes, too, a story of the difference between country time and town time that was expounded to him by a coachman in Hannibal (chapter 56).

During this period, critical as it is to his reputation as social moralist, his jokes and anecdotes that contain black characters are no more sympathetic than would be expected of an only partly reconstructed southerner with a quick eye, a practiced ear, and the professional habit of assembling materials for comedy. The Negro remains what he had been for Clemens for some years: a separate case—good-humored, childlike, superstitious, coarsely salacious, at many points laughable, and to be pitied for past offences committed against him—separate because he is not quite a man.

Like the jokes about Negroes, Clemens's jokes at the expense of women must be of great interest to biographers and critics. They occupy an important place in the notebooks and have their parallels and counterparts elsewhere. In Clemens's "1601," his best-known piece of bawdry, written in 1876 and first printed in 1880, the self-induced shock of having vulgar language used in the presence of noble ladies or placed in their mouths excited him to almost uncontrollable merriment, and he joyously circulated copies among male friends and acquaintances.[12]

Joseph Twichell and Howells—both timid about coarse language— would not have been amused if "1601" had been printed in the *Atlantic*; but they could accept it as intended for private circulation among men. Even so, masking must have been important for securing acceptance: the imagined scene was distant in time and culture, the language as spelled had a pleasing, softening tinge of the obsolete about it,[13] and the whole was framed as literature. For Clemens and his friends, "1601" humorously lowered the dignity of highborn ladies, but it could be enjoyed as not really having anything to do with Harmony Twichell or Elinor Howells or Olivia

Clemens (whom Clemens called during courtship "a visiting *Spirit* from the upper air"), all creatures of a better and purer age. The sketch may be read, however, as a timorous, exhibitionistic substitute for overt sexual aggressiveness, furnishing a kind of paradigm for the jokes and anecdotes in the notebooks whose effect is to render women comic and, very often, to sully them.

If one may judge from entries in the three volumes of the notebooks that are now in print, the character of Clemens's jokes relating to women underwent no notable change with the passage of time, but they are recorded in increasing numbers. From the beginning the range was wide, extending from an apparently mild reference to the "old sow" and a man's assertion that his wife is perfect "but blamed if she suits me" to thoroughly noisome anecdotes (1:83, 110).

One finds, for example, a story of a husband who mistook the druggist's meaning and applied the halves of a plaster to the outlets of his wife's body with explosive results; and there is the more repellent story of a girl who "used" a sausage and then threw it out of the window to the street, where it was picked up by a beggar who decided that there "must be rich folks here" who buttered their sausages (1:164). Later notebooks contain stories of much the same order of jarring vulgarity: "Old maid newly wedded—I never *could* worth a dam on a steamboat"; and "Our John just slaps it in dry. Well have *you* noticed that wart?—you're the millionth man" (2:347). In April 1886 he entered an especially unpleasant jest—one that circulates in many cognate forms—based on the odor of unwashed female genitals: "Texas girls [*sic*] lassos wild horse & rides home; Boston girl captures codfish & rides him home astride. Burdette—'This accounts for the peculiar smell of the codfish.'"[14] Immediately following is a punning jest (which may have serious psychological implications) translated into German:

Wie fühle ich? Ich fühle unbeschreiblich wohl.
Weisst du warum du die —— eine Frau Gleichest?
Weil du so viel besser fühlst als du aussiehst.

Taboo language and erotic references in these jests which range from the mildly improper to the unrelievedly obscene classify them as aggressive; but many of them obscure their aggressions (particularly against gentlewomen) by some kind of distancing or occultation. One characteristic distancing— difficult to reconcile with Clemens's reputation as a partisan of the folk—is accomplished by placing vulgarities in the mouths of lower-class characters, male or female: either their ignorance protects them or they possess so little essential dignity that it is safe to disesteem and deride them. Some of Clemens's anecdotes with poor whites as characters are so rudimentary as to lack all of the elements of successful comedy, unless vulgar language in itself is taken to be such an element. I have cited above one entry, altogether primitive as it stands, which reads, "Miss, would you be so kind as to ft here & go outside & shit."[15] Another, hinting at a narrative framework and therefore slightly more comedic, says, "Sis, don't you drink a drop of water in this tavern—I've ——'d in the spring!" (3:465).

A child as purveyor of taboo words or pornography may serve the same veiling purpose as a lower-class person as speaker or as a character in an obscene playlet. Clemens was impressed by an incident involving the small son of Charles Hopkins Clark, the assistant editor of the Hartford *Courant*: "Company at Charley Clark's—his little boy of 7 runs out to a fire alarm: 'Well, where was the fire, Johnny?'—'Nothing but a whore house in Front street,' Tableau. He had heard the firemen say it."[16]

In this last story, as in many that Freud observed as circulating in polite society, the child, in his innocence, has no inhibitions about what he says before company and may not be severely blamed. Perhaps the first audience was free to titter unrestrainedly; the auditors for whom Clemens intended the anecdote would certainly laugh—their normal habit of suppression would be circumvented because they are removed from the actual situation, are set free by the innocence of the child, and are able to enjoy the discomfort of the original audience. The anecdote counteracts the repression of sexual topics in the presence of ladies and exposes the ladies to a mentioning of forbidden sexuality under such circumstances that they find it difficult to object. The inferential exposure of the ladies in the story (and of any ladies who may hear the story) to sexual aggression intensifies the pleasure derived by erotically or sadistically inclined male or female auditors and, through them in part, by the teller of the tale. Perhaps we may conclude that an act of symbolic seduction or ravishment has been performed by Clemens, the teller.

Certain dirty jokes stuck so like burrs in Clemens's mind that he could not let them go: he refreshed his memory of them repeatedly with nubs or catch-lines. A few he purified and worked up into publishable form; and he probably used them uncleansed to regale such heartily convivial male companions as James R. Osgood, the publisher, Thomas B. Reed, the political figure, and Henry R. Rogers. In the southwestern tales that were Clemens's

early models, backwoods characters—yeomen and poor whites—are ordinarily figures of comedy, like Shakespeare's rustics and bumpkins. For
Clemens and his companions, otherwise socially forbidden matter was
made palatable by using poor or socially inferior persons as speakers or
butts: their sensibilities are not our sensibilities.

The tale of Mother Utterback occurs twice in the notebooks (through volume 3), entered in almost unintelligible abridgments. The second, of July
27, 1886, suggests identity only by the words "Fly around gals," but the
first, in October (?), 1878, is assured: "Sitting on that cold rock just married!"[17] This jotting is a reminder of a vignette which Clemens published in
the San Francisco *Golden Era* in 1866 about Mother Utterback and her six
gawky gals who lived in the bend, over on the Arkansas side, below Grand
Gulf, Mississippi. Captain Ed Montgomery, out of the goodness of his
heart, always bought wood—though it "wouldn't burn any more than so
many icicles"—from Mother Utterback simply because she was poor and
because the other captains would not trade with her. In Clemens's vignette
Montgomery "brought some fine ladies with him to enjoy the old woman's
talk." With many a flirt and flutter, like Poe's raven, Mother Utterback
welcomed them to "her shabby little floorless log cabin":

> "Good morning, Captain Montgomery!" said she with many a bus-
> tling bow and flourish; "Good morning, Captain Montgomery; good
> morning, ladies all; how de do, Captain Montgomery—how de do—
> how de do? Sakes alive, it 'pears to me it's ben years sense I seed you.
> Fly around, gals, fly around! You Bets, you slut, highst yoself off'n that
> candle-box and give it to the lady. How *have* you ben, Captain Mont-
> gomery?—make yoself at home, ladies all—you 'Liza Jane, stan' out of
> the way—move yoself! Thar's the jug, help yoself, Captain Montgom-
> ery; take that cob out and make yoself free, Captain Montgomery—
> and ladies all. You Sal, you hussy, git up f'm thar this minit, and take
> some exercise! for the land's sake, ain't you got no sense at all?—settin'
> thar on that cold rock and you jes' ben married last night, and your
> pores all open!" [18]

As published, the vignette of Mother Utterback fitted precisely into the
mold of southwestern and western newspaper humor and is one of the
most successful of Clemens's early squibs. The devices of some of his most
admired sketches are already solidly in place, borrowed as they were from
his comic predecessors in the genre. Although as in his notebook stories he

was not particularly careful about consistency in misspellings and abbreviations intended to represent folk speech, Mother Utterback's vernacular diction and speech rhythms capture the sophisticated, condescending reader; by their amusing novelty they contribute as much to the story as does the indecorous nub. The narrator clearly expects us to join Captain Montgomery in smiling at voluble Mother Utterback; but we also find as productive of possible delight a latent aggression, which we may or may not willingly enjoy, against the "fine ladies" and against ladylike readers. Mother Utterback's grossness is privileged, protected by her backwoods ignorance. Because what would be indecent in another context is simply natural to her, neither the fine ladies of the sketch nor women readers of the *Golden Era* were free to take great offense. In the simple, uninhibited boondocks a Mother Utterback may invite ladies to drink whiskey from the jug and expect them to appreciate the danger to Sal's health of not cooling down gradually; but in the world of the readers, the tale partly draws aside polite concealments. The pleasure of gentlemen and of less-repressed ladies is heightened because of the distanced yet naughty sexual reference.

There are Chinese boxes here: meanings manifest and latent. Complex psychological vibrations may be overheard. In another context, Leslie Fiedler offers the general theory—which may hardly be taken seriously— that because the nineteenth-century myth of the Immaculate Young Girl has failed to survive in any felt way into our time, male revenge is taken in dirty jokes directed against women for having "flagrantly betrayed that myth."[19] Women were the objects of dirty jokes, however, before the nineteenth century and during it. A more likely supposition is that women—especially gentlewomen—are aggressed against for being at once desirable and relatively untouchable, not for having destroyed the myth.

With Clemens the eroticism is presumably a reverse accompaniment of his neurotic dread of pollution and of his attachment to the idea of innocence. On the part of the listener, his deeper, subversive laughter arises— according to the psychoanalytic doctrine—from a momentary relaxation of conventions that bind polite society; the unconscious has its small triumph.

The French language was amusing to Clemens, but German had for him an inexhaustible comic appeal, so much so that I question whether for all his years abroad and for all the intermittent attention he gave to French and German he had any sensitivity for languages other than his own. He seems to have been in actuality—not just through the personae he chose for writing—insulated from the nuances of European languages and cultures.

In shielding his introduction of words that are, or were, taboo in English by using phonetic equivalences in German, he exploited German in such a way as to mask an aggression. Several of the components that he often worked into anecdotes appear in a story about Germans and profanity for which he first entered a note in 1879: "Baroness—God-dam is swearing in English—Baron—Yes, God dam, god-dam. (Baron prides himself on knowing this one English word")" (2:273).

Here we see only the irreducible rudiments of the appealing components: the oddity of foreigners; the delight in hearing an impious oath, particularly if it issues from aristocratic female lips; and the titillation attendant upon despoiling a lady of her customary dignity, a diminution which is the more permissible because the baroness is German, not American. Because she is German, she doesn't know any better; like Mother Utterback, she is privileged by virtue of ignorance.

The supernumerary baron is whisked offstage, the German language is brought on, and the operative comic elements of the story are established a little more securely in an entry made late in May: "That dear sweet old German baroness who loved to find similarities between G & E—'Ah the 2 languages are so alike—we say Ach Gott, you say Goddam.' To laugh when people are serious is not a fault of mine, but this 'fetched' me" (2:310). Clemens wrote down the key words—"Ach Gott—God-dam"—among a great many other reminders for jokes in June 1891 while en route from New York to Le Havre (3:644), and he finally made the tale as publishable as many that he entered in his autobiographical writings but not, it seems, until 1906. He then returned to the incident in "A Family Sketch" to give it a fully fleshed-out anecdotal setting, explaining that one has to like German profanity because it is so guileless, picturesque, and alluring. A baroness in Munich "of blameless life, sweet & lovely in her nature, and deeply religious" was a winning swearer as reported by the Clemens's traveling comrade, Clara Spaulding: "The Baroness was fond of believing that in many pleasant ways the Germans & the Americans were alike, & once she hit upon this happy resemblance: 'Why, if you notice, we even talk alike. We say Ach Gott, & you say goddam!'"[20]

In this development the baroness becomes deeply religious and Clara Spaulding appears on the scene. Now Clemens has brought together, most happily for himself, several kinds of authority; and he exposes each in turn: aristocracy, which as an institution he attacked openly and often; piety, which he attacked frequently but less openly; and the moral and cultural preeminence of gentlewomen, which he publicly subscribed to and assailed rarely and generally covertly. Here he implicitly shadows the virginal gentility of Clara Spaulding (and domesticates the aggressions?) by making her an auditor.

Clemens's interest in languages, reinforced by long stays in Europe, began very early. His first notebook, started in 1855, was intended as a "French lesson copybook." When in 1857 he entered upon his brief career as a pilot, he encountered the French-speaking residents of Louisiana and became even more ambitious to learn French. He seems not to have worked on German, however, until he planned to go abroad in 1878; and he seems never to have learned either French or German at all well. (His written German is often wretched.)[21] His knowledge of Italian seems to have been very superficial. He persisted, moreover, in the faith (useful to a writer of comedy) that semantic and idiomatic differences between English (the norm) and French or German (the aberrations) are essentially farcical. The use of a foreign language permitted the affective shock of a vulgar word to be delayed, heightened, and distanced when it could be introduced by way of homophony, establishing a kind of bilingual equivoque. Thus covert rebelliousness or aggression could be substituted for open; immanental language, for action.

Immediately after Clemens began the study of German, he discovered the possibilities for comedy in falsely analogous English-German homophones. He entered the nub of an anecdote in a notebook: "Pupil Könnt—Fahrt—draw the line at ⟨a-hole⟩."[22] This naive vulgarity—set down toward the end of March (?), 1878—alludes only in the word *Pupil* to a possible dramatic setting, a development that clearly would be necessary if simple vulgarity were to be converted into comedy for any audience. Approximately a month later Clemens attempted a slightly more detailed version:

> Hamburg-Amerikanische Packet*fahrt* Actien Gesellschaft.
> Lady teaches gentleman how to pronounce the words, one after the other.
> Draw the line at ——.[23]

The adumbrated setting seems not to have been completely satisfactory, perhaps because Clemens consciously accepted the privileged position of gentlewomen unless they had somehow offended him or otherwise degraded themselves, perhaps because he believed that any audience would find shocking his use of a gentlewoman to mouth vulgarities. Although he used European ladies as buffers to protect Americans, he seems to have found their use of profanity to be shocking as well as amusing. He was careful to note, citing examples, that profane language was freely used by both sexes in "German good-society conversation" (2:68). At any rate, it was nearly a decade after Clemens first mentioned the intriguing German-English homophones that (at the end of August 1887) he effected a strategic transformation of his materials. By drawing upon the devices of southwestern humor, he constructed a vernacular sketch that would, for his purpose, pass muster. He places an "Arkansas girl" in the foreground, thus obscuring the reduction of gentlewomen and emphasizing the comedy that the sophisticated may discover in the blunders of the ignorant.

The Arkansas girl remarks, "I ain't no more particular'n most folks, but all the same I can't stand only jist *so much*, & I got to have a *limit* set up. Now, all in jist this fust week we've had ⟨Schütz⟩, & ⟨Fahrt⟩ & ⟨Konnt.⟩ I don't wish to crowd marters & 'pear to be *over*-finicky, but I want to give you notice here & *now*, that I'm goin' to draw the *line* at a-h" (3:310).

This satisfaction in the scatological and the vulgar which derives from subverting bourgeois sanctities suggests that these same sanctities had their place in Clemens's own system of verbal and social taboos. By temperament and as a jokester (perhaps we may assume that initially causation flows from the first toward the second) he had strongly ego-syntonic as well as syntonic tendencies. Jokes are among the devices which make the resulting stresses bearable. An individual who is both severely inhibited and unusually rebellious finds the relaxation of psychic controls exceptionally satisfying. When we consider Clemens's horror at the idea of seduction or adultery, something of this pleasure in subversion is conveyed in a jest that he set down in December 1889: "He said he would rather sleep with ⟨Adelini⟩ Adelina Patti without a stitch of clothes on than with General Grant in full uniform" (3:537).

Key elements in the repressions and aggressions which the jokes both reveal and serve to relax were, as I have intimated earlier, conflicting twin devotions: to a probably extreme eroticism, and to the ideal of sexual purity in women. Even when taken alone—read in a vacuum, as it were—the notebooks speak convincingly of the intensity of Clemens's opposed positions: prudery matches scopophilia; purity is paired with pollution. Jokes and other notebook entries indicate an endless prurience.

Clemens was fascinated by the sight of nude women in the Sandwich

Islands and in Egypt (1:208, 219, 221, 444). In May 1885 he made a note reminding himself of a merely typical Slavic event, a pictorial souvenir of nudes seen eighteen long, busy years earlier: "At that port near Sebastopol we saw Russian ladies strip themselves stark naked for a sea bath & walk down into the water so."[24] In 1878 he was scandalized by the erotic nature of a painting in the Cathedral of St. Mark and wondered, also, if women did the handling that made the private members of statues black and polished. A little later, in 1879, he considered Titian's *Venus of Urbino* to be grossly obscene; mulled over the appearance of a nude model he had seen in Rome; deplored the immodest pictures on French matchboxes; and tried his hand at a passage of (French-style?) pornography: "He put me on the sofa, & put his hand on my ancle & pushed it up above my stocking & then up between my naked thighs & then . . ."[25] Was he translating the inscription on a matchbox or had he been sampling *le roman noir*?[26]

During this same period he railed, horrified, against the practice in early France of le droit du seigneur (2:321). The modern French also rendered Clemens semihysterical with, as he saw it, their omnipresent adulteries and wholesale indecencies. Statements made in 1879 in a set of censorious notes directed against the French give some idea of his fear of sexuality, the high value he gave to chastity, and, in all probability, his covert longing for uninhibited sex relations.[27] Every man in France over 16 and under 116 has, Clemens asserted, at least one wife to whom he has never been married; and most married ladies have paramours. The country has neither winter nor summer nor morals. The French language, a "mess of trivial sounds," is right for illicit love and the conveying of pornographic double meanings. For a thousand years France has been governed by concubines, because every man from king to rat catcher has a foul, selfish, trivial-minded concubine who governs him. A Frenchman's home is where another man's wife is. The French practice bestialities which are unknown in civilized lands. America is, by contrast, the most civilized of nations, where pure-minded women are the rule among "the native-born" in every rank of life. American men are "clean-minded, too, beyond the world's average."

As Clemens worked on *A Connecticut Yankee,* his adverse attention fell upon the English nobility, though his censures were not as extravagant as those which he directed against the French. To his customary horror at the libertarian sexual proclivities of the nobility was added his fury at privilege and undemocratically imposed authority.[28] Again the idea that the *jus primae noctis* was once exercised excited his indignation. That kings had mistresses and that nobles engaged in casual amours angered him, but he may have been more outraged that presumably chaste American heiresses (and their wealth) should be given to presumably profligate and probably diseased English or European noblemen.[29] His emotions were vehement when he read in 1889 that Alan Plantagenet Stewart, earl of Galloway, had been acquitted of "using lewd, indecent and libidinous behavior" toward a ten-year-old girl; he wanted to put an account of the case into a footnote or appendix of *A Connecticut Yankee* (3:523). Like the New York *World,* he assumed that the earl secured his acquittal by means of power and wealth. In view of Clemens's tendency toward pedophilia during his later years, this case involving the earl may have been to him particularly titillating, particularly deserving of punishment.

Offences against chastity charged to Americans could be as lacerating to Clemens as those charged to Europeans. In August 1881 the body of a twenty-year-old woman was found on the New Haven shore; an autopsy disclosed the presence of arsenic. Two young men—cousins, each of a well-to-do family—and a woman were brought to trial. One of the young men was charged with seducing the murdered woman, refusing to marry her, and engaging the other defendants in a conspiracy to kill her. Clemens, writing while in New Orleans, feared, rightly, that those charged would be acquitted. His emotional involvement suggests that the assumed prefatory seduction was to him more heinous than the alleged murder: "Give the Malley boys a shot, & a good strong one—for they are guilty, no matter what the evidence may fail to prove. They ought to be taken from Court & lynched—if I were kin to the girl I would kill them on the threshold of the court."[30]

A few of Clemens's indecent jokes and anecdotes were useful or possibly useful as literary provender; they were or could have been stuffed into letters to the *Alta* or sprinkled into sketches and travel narratives. Most were, however, literarily useless: they were set down for his private benefit or for that of friends. This iterative recording of dull jokes speaks unflatteringly of an aspect of Clemens's sense of comedy and hints of serious personality disorders. They may not be passed off as demonstrative of simple high spirits, affectionate good humor, or a healthy interest in sex. Nor are they mere unindicative ribaldries of which he, a professional jester, availed himself in order to court cultural mediocrities. His comedy is not to be compared to that of Hogarth or, as it often has been, to that of Rabelais; it is certainly not like that of Goldsmith. It is southwestern, anarchistic, and deeply personal; and it runs counter to his generally commonplace, socially normative notes made for business and journalistic purposes.

There is nothing spontaneous about these jokes: they were calculated, mulled over. Some could have been used for ritual joking as appropriate to a male, smoking-compartment camaraderie. They testify to a conflict of values in Clemens and, if they found an appreciative audience, to a comparable conflict in the society.

Without a conflict joking cannot occur. A joke attacks repressive control, intimates the possibility of alternative patterns, values, or ideas, and effects the pleasurable conservation of psychic energy. Although Clemens's conflicts were at times noticeably neurotic, his society, too, recognized similar dominant and subdominant values: Clemens made himself into a genteel easterner but retained western biases; eastern society had its moments of revulsion against gentility and thus could profit from subversive joking. If there had not been congruence of the joke structure with the social structure, Clemens would have had no audience for even his milder anecdotes. The jokes, perhaps fundamentally antiparental, express an exceptional rebelliousness against persons and institutions, against social taboos and lexical taboos; and if the vulgarities of the jokes had not introduced an alleviatingly novel suborder to the burden of the superordinate in Clemens, he would not have been their devotee.

Much of the comedy that Clemens enjoyed, like much that he wrote for publication, depended on sharp contrasts, exaggeration, or the shock of the unexpected; his jokes tend to rely on favorite topoi with thematic affiliations. As we have seen, distancing, both formal and social, is necessary to obscure (even from Clemens himself) the fears, animosities, stresses, and, in addition, the subversions of an accustomed order that the jokes make dimly visible. To achieve distance Clemens utilizes transferences and displacements. Blacks, foreigners, and lower-class Americans become devices for securing this necessary distancing, for muffling deep subversions. No veiling or transformation serves, however, fully to eclipse the revelation of Clemens as a man partly at odds with society and with his conventional self—a man under stress, in a state of psychic imbalance.

As a person and as a writer Clemens was quite capable of changing roles. He could set aside his gentility; or, he could set aside the jokester and become the ritualist defending established values, as in "A True Story," *Joan of Arc,* and his many statements on purity. The jokes reverse the standard. They show him, for example, as not especially compassionate, at bottom, toward the blacks and poor whites who populate his anecdotes. He sees these people from above. Their culture is inferior, at times scarcely removed from animality. Although such persons were the accepted butt of crude humor in all but the choicest society, for Clemens to take pleasure in framing vulgar jokes about them is, nonetheless, revealing of racist and elitist sentiments. He exhibits no inclination to find among them a liberating ethos with which to revivify a nerveless, genteel America.

Clemens's jokes which manifest a fear of, a loathing for, and a longing for the sexuality of women support what we know from other sources: in psychoanalytic terms, they are indicative of sexual arrestment before arrival at the genital stage and are congruent with Clemens's sadomasochistic tendencies. They are, furthermore, polar accompaniments of hypertrophied solicitude for cleanliness. They often reveal the other face of his obsession with chastity in women, caught as he was between the appeals of purity and impurity. His anecdotes expose, excite, or seduce: they tumble women from those pedestals on which he ostensibly wished to see them safely fixed forever. The actuality of women's bodies is more to be verbally abused than physically enjoyed: women are to be punished in vulgar jokes for their dangerous fleshly powers. It was his pleasure to avenge himself on them by diminishing their dignity or insulting their sexuality; he is jealous of them and of the Oedipal father.

The jokes that degrade women obviously contradict the usual posed portraits of Clemens as the worshipful husband who naturally extended his chivalrous idealizations to cover all women. They must be read in the light of his urgent demand during courtship that Livy be pure, his later insistence that his daughters keep themselves above suspicion of unchastity. They shed light on his horror at the alleged immorality of the French and the sexual diversions of members of the British aristocracy. They have bearing, too, on his infatuation with the image of a sexless Joan of Arc. Safe sex is romantically distant and disembodied.

When the dirty jokes that pepper the notebooks are bare of dramatic settings, as are dozens of those recorded, they must seem to the most receptive of readers as less *lebhaft* and ludic, warm and spontaneous, than labored, banal, and brutal. Even when carefully dramatized, most of the anecdotes lack wit or grace. One may make allowances for the conventions of the southwestern subgenres and yet find the general effect to be less a democratizing than a sansculottish pulling down, less a correction of social absurdities than the revelation of a drive toward symbolic vandalism and hierarchical, racist, or sexist soiling. Jokes and anecdotes yield evidence that tends to upset the conception of Mark Twain as a hero of American democracy: they contradict the almost universal assumption that he was a kind of secular Buddha, brooding quizzically and wisely, if not always serenely, over the American nation.

RACISM

AND

HUCKLEBERRY

FINN

9

▲ ▲ ▲ ▲ ▲ ▲ ▲ ▲ ▲

A number of attempts, usually superficial, have been made not only to demonstrate that Mark Twain was a racist, especially with respect to blacks, but that because of its racist contents *Adventures of Huckleberry Finn* should be withdrawn from schools. A conventional recent complaint is that reading the novel inflicts psychological damage on young blacks. Denials, often vehement, that Clemens was a racist or that his masterpiece displays racist sentiments have been entered by both scholars and journalists. Journalists are likely to bring into play arguments against book-banning and book-burning. Controversies over Clemens's racism extend to his attitudes toward Indians and Jews. Defenses against these additional charges of racism have been somewhat more successful with respect to Jews than with Indians.

Clemens's attitudes toward Indians and Jews may be illustrated only briefly here. He was generally in tune with that harsh strain of thought that took the red man to be ignoble, not noble, suitable for subjection. He was contemptuous of the idealizing engaged in by writers like Cooper and Longfellow and considered the actual Indians that he saw in the West to be of their own natures utterly degraded. Over the years, of course, as we shall see with respect to the black, his attitudes were not entirely constant.

For exploitative Europeans the theoretical justification for harassing and killing Indians was given classic expression by Vattel a century before Clemens joined the westward movement.[1] According to this theory, by the will of God, for the sake of progress, and for the greater good of the greater number, land everywhere belongs to civilized occupiers who know how to populate it better than do savages, who, by reason of their natural inferiority, can populate it only thinly. Thus, to achieve the greater good, any claims in favor of savages could be ignored: their land was free land. Thus the subjugation or elimination of Indians was made palatable by an insistence on their subordinacy.[2]

In his more extreme denunciations of the filth and cruelty of Indians Clemens was voicing the dominant American position as expressed by the Topeka *Western Leader* in 1867, during a period of "unrest." The newspaper characterized the aborigines as a set of as "miserable, dirty, lousy, blanketed, thieving, lying, sneaking, murdering, graceless, faithless, gut-eating skunks as the Lord ever permitted to infect the earth, and whose immediate and final extermination all men, except Indian agents and traders, should pray for."[3] Clemens complained in a letter of June 5, 1867, addressed from New York to the San Francisco *Alta California* that although the "Indian Row" is a topic of conversation, easterners know nothing of the West and of where the Indians could be dangerous. He, himself, is waiting, not altogether patiently, to hear that "they have ordered General Connor out to polish off those Indians." Connor, Clemens added, knows how to fight the Indians that God made, "but I suppose the humanitarians want somebody to fight the Indians that J. Fenimore Cooper made." Cooper's Indians are dead, and "the kind that are left cannot be successfully fought with poetry, and sentiment, and soft soap, and magnanimity."[4]

Although Clemens was of two minds about Jews, he was more often than not depreciatory in common ways. The Jew is ugly, aggressive, and a fit subject for tendentious humor, much as is the Negro. Opinions of this kind may be drawn from Clemens's letters of December 20 and December 28, 1867, written for the *Alta California*. On board ship, headed for Panama, Isaac is his natural self: "His vanity, impudence, obsequience and utter imperviousness to insult trench upon the wonderful." Isaac raffles off the jewelry of his dead wife; the passengers feel ashamed and unmercifully snub him. A passenger puts something in Isaac's tea that came near "making him throw up his boots. But some people will never learn anything. He went into the Captain's room to-day, uninvited, and fell into another trap provided for him by a passenger. He found a bottle—he always drinks from bottles wherever he finds them, whether asked to do it or not. He drank from that bottle, and then retired to his stateroom and has been patiently disgorging ever since."[5]

Only a handful of statements by white scholars and critics suggest that Clemens was a racist with respect to blacks. Louis Budd has observed that "a number of anecdotes in *Life on the Mississippi* carelessly pandered to the sense of innate white superiority still felt in almost every quarter" and that because Twain's sympathy for the freedman had a condescending base, *Huckleberry Finn* could mistreat Jim so crudely at the end that its total effect is seriously weakened.[6] Ellen Moers (not a Twainian) sees Clemens as lacking in social conscience and adds that "stupidity, shiftlessness, superstition, helpless immaturity, and ineradicable ignorance are the qualities we find in Twain's Negroes, relieved only, in *Puddn'head Wilson,* by depravity, viciousness and cruelty." Henry Nash Smith says very moderately that Roxy, in *Puddn'head Wilson,* takes over the role of Hank Morgan, in *A Connecticut Yankee,* "as adversary of the dominant class" but that Clemens could not identify with her as he could with Hank because she is a Negro and a woman. Wayne Booth rather reluctantly concludes that, although *Huckleberry Finn* is a wonderful book, its racist attitudes make him question its morality.

Uneasiness about Clemens's possible racism began early. A. B. Paine was careful to write that Clemens, of slaveholding stock (which is to say, an aristocrat), was, nevertheless, desouthernized, a rampant abolitionist, and a champion of justice and liberty (which is to say, a progressive, modern man, fit subject for an adulatory three-volume official biography).[7]

Some defenses are exclamatory. A recent scholar writes, "The evidence for Clemens's deep love for the Negro people and their music is well known; it is no exaggeration to say that at times it went almost as far as complete psychological identification."[8] Even more fanciful is the opinion that the coldness of Clemens's father helped to create in young Sam a sense of inadequacy and that he identified his helplessness with that of the slave: his real self was a black child disguised as a white man.[9]

Standard opinion is less extreme but almost uniformly protective. Biographers think him tenderly humane and stanchly nonracist. DeLancey Ferguson holds that during Sam's early childhood he learned superstitions and folklore from family slaves and developed "a lifelong fondness for the simplicity and kindliness of the Negro race."[10] Ingenuous formulae of this kind run throughout the scholarship. When Ferguson quotes from a letter that Clemens wrote home in 1853, saying, "I reckon I had better black my face, for in these Eastern States niggers are considerably better than white people," he notes no contradiction between Clemens's "lifelong fondness" and his frank assumption of black inferiority except by remarking that young Clemens "was still thoroughly Southern in feeling." Nor does he comment when Clemens wrote to his brother Orion apropos of the Free Soil movement, "I would like amazingly to see a good old-fashioned negro." ("Old-fashioned" meaning one who knows his place.) Ferguson found ample material in *Huckleberry Finn* and in *Pudd'nhead Wilson* to lead him to commend Clemens's "fearless and dispassionate" treatment of blacks.

Edward Wagenknecht, whose biography was long popular, calls the commonplace rhetoric of Clemens's rather saccharine praise of Negro spirituals "perhaps the loveliest passage in all Mark Twain's criticism" and thinks the influence of the spirituals shows "in Mark Twain's never failing love and sympathy for the Negro race."[11] He explains away Clemens's decision to employ a Negro butler because he did not feel comfortable giving orders to a white man and thinks that in his youth Clemens "shared mildly" in the Know-Nothing suspicion of "foreigners." Wagenknecht acknowledges, however, that not much may be claimed for Clemens's sensitiveness to abuses of Indians and that although Clemens was considered a friend and admirer of the Jews he perpetuated—through ignorance, not malice—some stereotypes in his "Concerning the Jews." Wagenknecht sees no "sense of racial superiority" in *Pudd'nhead Wilson* and observes, "When Negroes object to Jim in *Huckleberry Finn,* one can only regret that they are behaving as stupidly as white folks often do, for surely Jim is one of the noblest characters in American literature."

Dixon Wecter joined the chorus of biographers who have claimed that Clemens was thoroughly southern but loved blacks. Wecter tells, incidentally, the story of how John Marshall Clemens, Sam's father, sat on a circuit court jury at Palmyra, Missouri, in 1841 and assisted in sending three abolitionists to prison for twelve years for trying to help five young Negroes escape.[12] Young Sam, Wecter says, "was prone at first to take for granted the South's 'peculiar institution'"; yet during summers spent on the farm belonging to his uncle by marriage, John Quarles, at Florida, Missouri, he came "to know and love" the slaves. Clemens, himself, made much of his memories of those slaves. In an unpublished story ("Adam Monument," 1879?) he says of one of the black slave women who had the grit and warlike bearing of a grenadier that, nevertheless, "being black, she is good-natured, to the bone. It is the born privilege and prerogative of her adorable race. She is cheerful, indestructibly cheerful and lively." In his Autobiography, speaking of the slave Uncle Dan'l, he remarks, "It was on the farm that I got my strong liking for his race and my appreciation of certain of its fine qualities."

As is frequently remarked by biographers, in Clemens's later years he often expressed a liking for and sympathy with Negroes; and he made gifts to Negro students and to Negro colleges. It is not necessary to consider the gifts to be evidences of bad conscience; they do not go beyond what could be expected during the last quarter of the nineteenth century of an affluent white who enjoyed thinking of himself as "reconstructed." And there are, to be sure, different ways of liking Negroes. In "Benito Cereno" Melville reminds us that Johnson and Byron "took to their hearts, almost to the exclusion of the entire white race, their serving men, the negroes, Barber and Fletcher." Melville also assures us, not, one supposes, without irony, that in "Benito Cereno" Captain Delano, a man of good, blithe heart, "took to negroes, not philanthropically, but genially, just as other men to Newfoundland dogs."

Some slaveholders together with members of their families were, after their fashions, unquestionably fond of certain slaves; and Clemens may well have felt affection for slaves on the Quarles farm. His roseate recollections of his relations with blacks may be no more intentional falsifications than are his memories of Hannibal in "Villagers of 1840–3" as a community which took little interest in money, paid no undue attention to wealth, and bred only virtuous young women.[13] In each instance he was, nevertheless, offering an interpretation of the past as seen through a momentary golden haze. Early letters and early entries in his notebooks are particularly useful in revealing the extent to which these late recollections idealize and sentimentalize his youthful views of Negroes.

Until he was thirty-two years old, Clemens was by almost any standards blatantly racist. A dramatic change in his written references to blacks began after he sailed from San Francisco for New York in 1867. Within a year, by the standards of his own time his published writings were free of anything like frank racism. By our current standards, however, evidence that he retained racist sentiments is overwhelming. His later racist attitudes may be seen in part as the residue of boyhood biases; but in part they belonged to his time. They were very much those of his genteel friends and of his rich relatives by marriage.

Overt expressions of contempt and distaste for Negroes began to disappear from Clemens's writings, then, in 1867 and, more noticeably, in the summer of 1868, during his courtship of Olivia Langdon. With Livy's regulatory assistance, Clemens made himself fit to be a valued contributor to William Dean Howells's *Atlantic Monthly* (his first contribution was "A True Story," in November 1879, a sentimental tale of a black woman) and to be the platform companion of George W. Cable, a prolific essayist in defense of civil rights for the Negro. At his most eastern and bourgeois his beliefs about blacks could even be thought of as scientifically sound: they came to resemble less analytical versions of beliefs held by a great many prominent American and British practitioners of the new "science" of eugenics.

Passages illuminating aspects of the temper of the nineteenth century may be cited from Hawthorne, Emerson, and Carlyle. Matters had not changed greatly since David Hume declared, "I am inclined to believe that Negroes are naturally inferior to whites."[14] Approximately a decade before the period in which Clemens sets *Huckleberry Finn*, Hawthorne, while traveling, noted a small irony: "A young man from Ouisconsin said, 'I wish I had a thousand such fellows in Alabama.' It made a queer impression on me—the negro was really so human—and to talk of owning a thousand like him." This notebook entry of 1838 portrays a "negro respectably dressed, and well-mounted on horseback, . . . calling for oats and drinking a glass of brandy and water at the bar—like any other Christian."[15] Emerson, the "transparent eyeball" of American Transcendentalism, in his essay "Fate" (finished in 1852?), quotes approvingly "pungent and unforgettable truths" from Robert Knox, *The Races of Man* (1850): "Nature respects race and not hybrids." "Every race has its own *habitat*." Emerson adds with appropriate resignation to the iron necessity that governs mankind, "The German and Irish millions, like the Negro, have a great deal of guano in their destiny."

Although Clemens attacked Carlyle in a column in the Buffalo *Express,* August 27, 1869, for his supposedly antidemocratic tendencies, he almost surely would have sympathized with the substance of "The Nigger Question" (1849), where Carlyle, without defending slavery, argues that "masters" and "servants" there must be: we must not treat the black man unfairly; but he must serve the state, the power of which (Carlyle regularly held) must be maintained. Clemens, too, could have written that no one "who will not work according to what ability the gods have given him for working, has the smallest right to eat pumpkin," that he did not hate but decidedly liked "poor Quashee. . . . A swift, supple fellow; a merry-hearted, grinning, dancing, singing, affectionate kind of creature, with a great deal of melody and amenability in his composition." The work for which poor Quashee was fitted was obviously menial.

Purity of race was a matter of deep general concern. A depreciatory conception of hybrids appears in Gobineau's influential *Essai sur l'inégalité des races humaines* (1853–55). In William Gilmore Simms and in a hundred other southern writers, in Melville's *Omoo* and *Typee,* and in Cooper a mingling of races or of cultures is censured. Melville held that a Polynesian should remain a Polynesian; the people of Oahu are not as good as the savages of islands less visited by the Europeans. In many American writings about the West, a half-breed is represented as being by nature a villain. The expository and argumentative literature of the Old South frequently made Negro-white hybrids out to be physically and morally weak, though possibly quicker and more intelligent than the pure Negro. An exception might be made for females: the part-Negro could be represented as gaining in culture and in sexual attractiveness; but in general blacks were represented as inferior, and hybridization was to be deplored. A small emotional countercurrent to the customary may be seen in fiction about "the Tragic Mulatto." Clemens's complex, sometimes confused treatment of hybrids constitutes a subject in itself.

Even before Clemens left the West for New York, he was generally opposed to cruelty directed toward individuals of any race. He was, nevertheless, unquestionably a racist.[16] Like his mother, Jane Clemens, he used the word *nigger* freely, obnoxious though it was in polite circles. Negroes are, he frequently complained, malodorous. In 1853 the seventeen-year-old Clemens noted that "niggers" in Hannibal sweat more and look more greasy than do whites. Later, in San Francisco, he compared the stench of a police courtroom with that of a black man and a polecat. In 1866 he jotted down a little ditty about white men who "smell berry strong but black man stronger"; to stand to leeward of a sweltering Negro was a "rough" experience. In 1867 he wrote that in Key West's "nigger quarter" "black & jolly rascals" were valuable to the maritime industry because storm-tossed sailors with a delicate sense of smell could follow their fragrance into port; and he complained that when he went to church he was placed in the aftermost seat "with the niggers."

He regularly found Negroes to be a fit subject for slurs and comedy. One of his companions on his Holy Land excursion was "a splendid fellow" because he never became angry though Clemens "always called him a nigger & told him niggers were not allowed in the after cabin after eight bells." A notebook entry of the time remarked on the "inhuman d—d ugliness" of Moorish women and mentioned blacks who resembled the "original nigger," a phrase that was modified when put into a letter to the San Francisco *Alta* to "original, genuine negroes, as black as Moses." Learning that in Tangier blacks able to read the first chapter of the Koran could no longer be slaves, he added that it would have been well to adopt the educational test for the "nigger vote" in America.[17] In one of Clemens's newspaper letters written in 1867 opposing and satirizing the movement favoring suffrage for women, he thought it would be best to leave American society divided permanently into its three logical classes: men, women, and niggers, in that order.

One stereotyped comic resource was to pretend to be strongly attracted to blackness; thus, in after-dinner remarks delivered in 1867 Clemens asserted that he loved all women, "irrespective of age or color." A letter of 1869 to Elisha Bliss, the publisher of *Innocents Abroad,* declared that an illustration reminded him of "a lot of niggers & horses adrift in a freshet."

During the watershed period 1867–68, Clemens, eagerly seeking a place in the eastern establishment, submitted gladly to having his manners corrected and his written vulgarities excised. He praised Mother Fairbanks in letters to relatives and editors for the help she gave him. Perhaps because of the influence of Livy—whom he was soon to marry—when he read final proofs for *Innocents Abroad,* he revised *nigger* to *negro* and removed many of the derogatory comments he had made about Jews and Arabs as well as about blacks. In editorials for the Buffalo *Express* in 1869 and 1870 he sometimes went so far as to capitalize *Negro*, a nicety that was not observed by many American newspapers for another half-century or longer. During this same period he gave increasing awareness of infringements against the rights of Negroes and an increasing hatred of the brutalizing of persons of any race. In 1869 in an editorial in the *Express* he printed his first public indictment of violence against Negroes in the South. At the same time he began to concede the possible virtue of the enfranchisement of blacks and to express the belief that some blacks might benefit from education.

His own redemption, however, was not complete. Clemens printed in the *Express* some crude sketches that concentrated on dialect and humor as being what he called (omitting for the moment the ingredient of pathos) "the two indispensable—if not sole—ingredients of Black character." In these sketches Negroes take the Bible as literal fact, are ignorant, gullible, superstitious, and use a variant on the vernacular. Black English is of interest, it appears, because it is humorously picturesque.

In the notebooks kept during Clemens's Mississippi River trip preparatory to completing *Life on the Mississippi* and *Huckleberry Finn*, Clemens's interest in Negroes was almost solely for coloristic and comic purposes. He notes that white men are said not to keep Negro mistresses "as much as befo' the waw," mentions "Boodoo" superstitions, describes a cockfight in which a Negro handles one of the birds, and records the conversation of black washerwomen as they comment unfavorably on the hazards of slavery times.[18]

If Negroes did not supply color or comedy, they were of no particular benefit to him, as is indicated in his notes on a visit while in New Orleans to Winans Chapel (the First Street Methodist Church): "Opened with singing of a choir, 12th Chap. Daniel read by a black clergyman, during which an aged deacon back by the door chided some young, dusky damsels saying 'Takes yo' long time get seated. Settle yo' d'rectly ef you do' get seated." The clergyman lined out a hymn and offered a prayer, which was better than those of some white ministers, because it was short. "The thing a failure because too good for literature."[19]

Even during Clemens's later years, when the circumstances were propitious he felt free to use the word *nigger*. He used it in speeches made in 1886 and in 1892 in contexts intended to be comic.[20] Writing from South Africa on June 18, 1896, to Henry Rogers to congratulate him on his second marriage, Clemens drew up a facetious list of presents that he is sending by the first vessel. The list ends with the comically climactic, "Herd of niggers."[21] Rogers, a self-made man, yacht and all, liked Twain's vulgarities; and *nigger* was a word suitable for the jesting tone that marked their exchanges.

For an overview of Clemens's late, consciously expressed public attitudes toward nonwhites, *Following the Equator* (1897) offers excellent resources. There Clemens frequently satirizes the white man's treatment of aborigines in Australia and of blacks in Africa. In Ceylon he praises the forms and faces of the people, contrasting their natural free movements with the stiffness of a group of girls from a missionary school. Similarly, the nudity of a little boy is contrasted with "the odious flummery in which the little Sunday-school dowdies were masquerading."

The weight to be given these favorable views of "natives" and their traditional ways depends to a degree on how much one judges them to have been influenced by Clemens's long-standing distaste for missionaries and all their works and by his more recent hatred of empire-building. Demonstrations of respect for dark peoples are to be balanced, moreover, against the generally condescending tenor of Clemens's remarks on natives. What was right for young natives was right because they were natives. Their norms are not our Western norms; what was right for young natives would have been a failure in decorum for the Clemens girls when they were small. In Australia, India, and Africa, the aborigines are all "natives" and may be considered "picturesque." Indian architecture is "quaint and showy." Indian servants are described for comic effect, and along the road at Jeypore Clemens seems as distant from the "tossing and moiling" flood of people as he is from their "strange and outlandish" vehicles.

As Arthur G. Pettit points out, live Africans did not appear to Clemens to be worth much. He started to write in his African notebook that the mass slaughter of blacks in South Africa had been a great loss to the country but scratched this opinion out and scribbled, "No, not that."[22] At Delagoa Bay (chapter 64) most of the blacks "are exactly like the negroes of our Southern States—round faces, flat noses, good-natured, and easy laughers." The splendidly built Zulus are so overflowing with strength that "it is a pleasure, not a pain, to see them snatch a rickshaw along." He wonders (chapter 69) that the diamond mines were not discovered five thousand years ago instead of about 1869, for the first diamonds were found on the surface of the ground "and in the sunlight they vomited fire. They were the very things which an African savage of any era would value above every other thing in the world excepting a glass bead."

This comment on the Negro's love of glitter, made *de haut en bas,* may be compared with Clemens's opinion of the best gift for John T. Lewis, the black farmhand who, in August 1877, by stopping a runaway horse was thought to have saved the lives of Charles Langdon's wife and daughter. Lewis received other gifts, but Charles Langdon's wife presented him with a "sumptuous gold Swiss stem-winding stop-watch." Clemens considered Lewis to be both modest and heroic; nevertheless, he explains: "I was asked, beforehand, if this would be a wise gift, & I said, 'Yes, the very wisest of all; I know the colored race, & I know that in Lewis's eyes this fine toy will throw the other more valuable testimonials far away into the shade.'"23

Clemens's habit of condescension is also illustrated by the implications of a remark by Livy which he liked well enough to quote in a notebook (August 1884) and to repeat in a letter of September 17, 1884, to Howells. Livy observed that Clemens tended to lose his temper over begging letters, except when they came, as Clemens put it, "from colored (& therefore ignorant) people." With this in mind, she urged him to adopt as a motto, "Consider everybody colored till he is proved white."24 The opening pages of "In Defence of Harriet Shelley" (written in 1893; published in July 1894), in which Clemens defines a cakewalk, present a later example of Clemens's condescending attitude toward Negroes.

Whatever Clemens knew of eugenics would almost certainly have pressed him toward racism. He obtained and read the treatise of Francis Galton on fingerprints while composing *Pudd'nhead Wilson* during 1892–94 and may have read some of Galton's early writings on eugenics. He could hardly have avoided knowing what Galton and other eugenicists had to say about race and evolution; and he must have read articles on the avoidance or containment of bad traits. The periodical literature on inherited capacities usually reinforced conservative notions concerning the inferiority of blacks, Indians, Jews, and South Europeans.

Galton, who coined the word *eugenics* in 1883, helped to popularize an interest in "natural ability."25 He confidently equated science with progress and pondered what might now be called a kind of genetic engineering, for it seemed to him that heredity determined both talent and character. His early, extended travels in Africa confirmed him in holding depreciatory views on "inferior races." Moved by Darwin, he dismissed the superstitions of religionists (as Clemens did) and thought hereditary aristocracy a "disastrous institution." He propounded instead a biological program that would lead to a conservative meritocracy. Again like Clemens, he did not believe in natural equality or that the political rights of all should be equal. Clemens, of course, equivocates about determinism. He tells us plainly that biology is destiny, but he also tells us plainly that training (environment) is destiny.

The aberrations of Galton did not die with the nineteenth century. Early in the twentieth century, Charles Davenport, a well-known American Mendelian, argued for the heritability of, among other things, "feeble-mindedness," a term that included a range of mental deficiencies. In conformity to the ordinary racism of his day, Davenport thought that heredity determined the inferior characteristics of Negroes and of the immigrants that were flooding into the United States. Like Galton and Arthur Pearson (the English biometrician) before him, Davenport identified good human stock with the middle class, "especially 'intellectuals,' artists and musicians, and scientists." He esteemed in America "the native white Protestant majority."

It becomes obvious that the attitudes toward race that Clemens held during his maturity were unremarkable and essentially unambiguous. He had moved from being blatantly racist to being paternalistically racist— though, as we have seen and shall see again, with curious lapses. On December 24, 1885—*Huckleberry Finn* had appeared in the United States on February 18—he wrote to Francis Wayland, dean of the Yale Law School, explaining his interest in helping blacks rather than whites: "We have ground the manhood out of them, & we should pay for it."[26] His attitude of kindly superiority was dependent on many factors: family stories of aristocratic slaveholding antecedents; eastern associations; marriage into a rich, antislavery New York state family; his reading; and the pride he took in thinking that his Missouri, slaveholding origins made him unquestionably privy to the minds and hearts of all Negroes.

The notebooks and *Life on the Mississippi* intimate that even during the period that gave final shape to *Huckleberry Finn,* Clemens took only a minimal interest in the sociological, political, and economic conditions of Negroes. He seems to have learned little or nothing of the problems of class and caste in the postwar South from his return to the Mississippi, from Cable, from Edward King's "The Great South" series in *Scribner's Monthly Magazine,* or from the numerous sociologically oriented articles on the New South and "the Negro Question" that appeared in northern periodicals in the late 1870s and the early 1880s. His emphasis falls on the immorality of slavery, southern barbarism, the aesthetic pretenses of rural aristocracy and the middle class, Walter Scottism, and the commercial and industrial progress of the upper Mississippi Valley.

Throughout Clemens's career as a writer, Negroes interested him primarily because they were useful to him for local color, pathos, and comedy. It is, indeed, untenably sanguine to hold that *Adventures of Huckleberry Finn,* the favorite ground for debate on the subject of Clemens's racism, exemplifies unequivocally nonracist attitudes. Most readers now agree that Jim serves as a moral stimulus to Huck and as a moral center for the book; but we may not therefore assume that either Clemens or the novel was without racial biases. The book itself tells us in many ways that it is in fact prejudiced.

Huckleberry Finn is fully peopled, but not with "round" characters. Clemens offers a sheaf of quick sketches, though some are as knowingly drawn as an engraving by Hogarth or a lithograph by Daumier. To supplement the caricatures and stock figures, the novel—by most criteria for nineteenth-century literary realism—requires one or two developed, centralizing individuals. Only at times do Huck and Jim fill this need. Huck's sense of his own identity and Clemens's sense of Huck's identity were equally unsubstantial.

Unless we give a very positive reading to a few enigmatic words in the novel's last paragraph ("I reckon I got to light out for the Territory . . ."), the moral choices that Huck makes during the course of the action do not lead him, even if they do lead the reader, to a climactic, permanent renunciation of at least some of the false values of a slaveholding society. At the end of the novel his positions vis-à-vis Jim and Tom are very much what they were in the beginning: the story in the end is not a fulfilled bildungsroman, and the fact that Huck's posture is debatable does not help in fixing the character and function of Jim.

Contrary to textual evidence and central though Jim is to any interpretation of *Huckleberry Finn,* his character is almost habitually misconceived as being unitary, a model of all the virtues. If we consider only the Jim of the central portion of the book, he may, with much justice, be held to be an archetypal figure, enormous on the American moral landscape; but to think of him as a revered hierarch—uniformly priestly, able, and benevolent—is to deny the rest of the story. Walter Blair in his genetic study of *Huckleberry Finn* points out that in Clemens's preliminary thinking about the book, in his notes, and in his early chapters "Jim is little more than a type—the ignorant, superstitious Negro of ante-bellum humorists—though with affection for Huck and dependent on him like the faithful servitors emphasized by writers in the plantation tradition."[27] This description fits Jim for the first fourteen chapters of *Huckleberry Finn,* and it is apposite again in the later chapters, beginning when he reenters the story in chapter 34. Additional, though less obvious, evidences of racism may be noted even in the central portions of the novel.

A minstrel show darkey is very decidedly the Jim that Edward W. Kemble drew in illustrating the novel. As Kemble submitted drawings, Clemens scrutinized them with what was for him unusual care. He didn't like the first pictures of Huck, complaining that the mouth was "a trifle more Irishy than necessary" and that Huck should have a "good-looking face."[28] The request to Kemble for changes in drawings of Huck lends added significance to the fact that Clemens did not call for revisions in drawings of Jim, who appears—especially in the early illustrations—as awkward, one-gallused, ragged, big-footed, scraggly bearded, often with large, frightened eyes and a foolishly gaping, thick-lipped mouth. A comparison suggests that Kemble in no way distinguished Jim from the other comically represented Negroes.

Clemens's own statement on Jim's origins asserts, as he commonly did, that he was following life. His model (as for several other blacks given genially patronizing portrayals) was Uncle Dan'l, a middle-aged slave owned by John Quarles. The man's "sympathies were wide and warm"; his heart "was honest and simple and knew no guile"; "patience and friendliness and loyalty were his birthright." In short, he was recognizably a type, a stock figure in white southern fiction and in the white southern mind, not a real person.[29]

In the unhappy sequels, both complete and incomplete, that Clemens attempted, Huck reverts to being Tom's pawn; and Tom is a boy who—whether seen as converting the world into a fiction through the power of a literary imagination informed by faulty models or as representing the real world in all of its hypocritical horror—cannot possibly help Huck to sustain a fully enlightened moral vision. As for Jim, he dwindles at once into being, in a phrase used by Huck in *Tom Sawyer Abroad* (1892) and in *Tom Sawyer Detective* (1896), "our old nigger." The Jim of the sequels is even more a butt for humor than is the Jim of the opening and closing chapters of *Huckleberry Finn*. He is an eye-rolling figure of fun: gladly subservient, foolish, easily frightened, mindless in crisis. Nothing remains of that Jim who has been considered iconic; one is compelled to wonder whether Clemens had any understanding of what he had created.

Nothing suggests, in fact, that Clemens ever viewed Jim as a monumental figure. Nor did early critics see Jim as heroic. *Huckleberry Finn* sold well, but it was not perceived as a classic overnight. Becoming an American masterpiece was a slow process; entering the canon of world novels, a slower one. Indeed, its achieved status continues to remain in doubt; and any reservations concerning the novel apply with added force to our conception of the undiminishable nobility of Jim. It may be argued that even in the central portions of the novel, important though Jim may be both thematically and to Huck's putative moral development, he is never more than a remarkable stage device, or, in Henry James's phrase for Maria Gostrey, "the most unmitigated and abandoned of *ficelles*."

Incidental light thrown on a passage important to Clemens's characterizing of Jim may tell us something of the method of composition and of the serendipitous whimsicality of authorial processes. The modern conception of Jim as the moral center of the book depends in considerable part on a few small, sometimes almost incidental components. A particularly telling, humanizing passage occurs in chapter 23 when Jim speaks in moving detail of discovering, after he had given his little daughter "a slap side de head" for supposed failure to obey, that she was "plumb deef en dumb," made so by "sk'yarlet-fever." Clemens prepares for the story with an ironic reassurance that blacks are human. Huck contradicts the ethos of the slaveholder and the jokester: "I do believe he cared just as much for his people as white folks does for their'n. It don't seem natural, but I reckon it's so."

As it happens, written sources for this episode are known. Chance and Clemens's skill as mosaicist combined here to transform what might have been waste material, like so much in the notebooks, into what is usually taken to be an operative jewel.[30] In late September 1872 Clemens made a brief entry in a notebook: "Some rhymes about the little child whose mother boxed its ears for inattention & presently when it did not notice the heavy slamming of a door, perceived that it was deaf." In 1882, shortly after returning from his Mississippi River trip (April 18-May 24), Clemens made a longer entry among notes intended for use in composing *Huckleberry Finn*. In this entry "L. A." punished her child only to discover that it was deaf and dumb. The pathos of the situation is now emphasized: the child "showed no reproachfulness for the whippings—kissed the punisher."

Scarlet fever was prominently in Clemens's mind during that summer of 1882, for his daughter Jean had it. In January 1884 the disease was on his mind again. Howells's son, John, was ill of it; and Clemens wrote to

Howells warning that John should not be let out of bed too soon. Presumably Clemens believed that because of inadvisable activity following a case of the fever, one of the children of his coachman, a Negro named Patrick McAleer, became deaf. As the editors of the Twain-Howells letters suggest, this odd combination of aides-mémoire and events from life lies behind Jim's "Oh, de po' little thing! De Lord God Almighty fogive po ole Jim, kaze he never gwyne to fogive hisseff as long's he live!"

A second passage, only wryly pathetic, smacking indeed of a stock jest, has close affinities with the scarlet fever episode. Huck explains (chapter 32) that his arrival at the Phelps farm was delayed by a "blowed out cylinder-head." Aunt Sally asks, "Anybody hurt?," and Huck replies, "No'm. Killed a nigger." Relieved, Aunt Sally adds, "Well, it's lucky; because sometimes people do get hurt." Taken together—especially if one has in mind the contrast between Pap Finn as father and Jim as father and surrogate father—these two segments comprise a bitingly ironic commentary on the mentality that devised and institutionalized a racist ethos, that conceived of blacks as less than human and in consequence incapable of emotions like those felt by whites.

Apt though the scarlet fever passage is, however, for heightening the reader's appreciation of Jim, it would seem to be more strikingly fortuitous than a natural outgrowth of Clemens's conception of Jim's character. Neither it nor the book as a whole nor the relevant letters and notebooks support the portrayal of the Clemens of *Huckleberry Finn* as a social idealist who for the moment worked out principles that almost completely satisfy the demands of a new, superior, vernacular ethos. Clemens neither experienced nor portrayed a social epiphany or a moral rebirth.[31] His social morality in *Huckleberry Finn* is more standard-genteel and more a function of technique, in a broad sense, than has been supposed; and after *Huckleberry Finn* one finds no residual evidence of a hypothecated vernacular newness in his treatment of blacks. He accepted the exigencies of character, plot, tone, and intent—of everything novelistic, much as he accepted the role of pragmatic showman in planning platform readings.[32]

By themselves, Huck and Jim are not sufficiently developed or sufficiently coherent to unite the disparate parts of *Huckleberry Finn,* turning it into a well-made novel. They are, nevertheless, quite enough to serve a picaresque novel when taken together with other strong binding sinews: the vernacular voice, the wonderful gallery of village eccentrics and frontier types, the mythic River and a dream of nature, the terrors, and the comedy. The book is a compendium of the shared beliefs, hopes, and fears of Mark

Twain's America, of everything that made up the *mentalité* and ideology of that epoch and to an extent of ours. It contains reverberant, literarily just anecdotes that tend to overpersuade us of the writer's social and moral percipience; it is suffused with emotions in which we wish to share, and we incline to the belief that we are absorbing great human truths. But not all of these truths withstand inspection; they are not at all points poetically, ideally sound, nor is the text a reliable document from which to learn history.

Radical changes took place, as we have seen, in Clemens's public attitudes toward blacks, and we may safely hold that substantial changes took place in his private attitudes as well. From 1868 or 1869 until quite recent decades, most enlightened Americans have not thought of him or of his books as being racist. The evidence makes clear, however, that Clemens never became thoroughly informed, positively *engagé,* or free of racial bias. His conception of the Negro was clouded over by his past, by his southwestern literary models, and by his culture-bound deficiency in social and political comprehension. A few plainly derogatory references to blacks continued to appear in his letters and notebooks; and late, unfinished writings suggest that he was affected by the anti-Negro hysteria of 1889–1915. To our current sensibility, a particularly objectionable form of insensitivity is registered in his persistent recording of jokes that aggress in the old, openly bigoted way against blacks.

During his return to the Mississippi in 1882, Clemens thought he saw a South in which whites were tyrannized over by a one-party system but where blacks were free. The period was in fact one in which blacks remained in subjection and white yeomen were losing their economic independence to commercial interests and an emerging capitalism; but we get no understanding of this from Clemens. What he left out of his notebooks for the period is as indicative as what he put in: his eye for local detail and his ear for colloquial speech were not matched by accurate social and political insights.

Clemens is not a good informant on the sociology of the South or on the ethics of American democracy. He made no effort in his notebooks to set down a taxonomy of southern society or to develop a democratic ethos. He had almost nothing to say about poor-whites, yeomen, the urban middle class, intellectuals, or social forces. That these topics are neglected suggests that a number of recent critics tend to overread some of his major works. The upper-middle-class, progressivist spectacles through which Clemens sees the Mississippi Valley during the latter part of the nineteenth century provide us with pictures that bear little resemblance to descriptions attempted by historians and social scientists. In Clemens's case, the genteel-abolitionist-comic truths of poetry must be checked against the analytical-prosaic truths of history.

The blacks pictured in the notebooks and in *Life on the Mississippi,* except for those few who move in an atmosphere of pathos, are there to supply comedy. They are literary conveniences. They resemble blacks as Clemens interpreted them to his family, his friends, and his readers: they are at best simple, smiling, trusting, loyal, and superstitious; they are creatures of their emotions, born with music in their souls, perhaps ingenious in small ways, perhaps courageous and enduring. They are, of course, inferior in kind; even in maturity they live in a state of arrested childhood and are dependent on whites for guidance.

Although little in this view of blacks distinguishes it from that held by the more cultivated and humane among antebellum slaveholders, Clemens's attitudes seemed reasonable and just to him, not in the least ambivalent or paradoxical; he thought them the distillations of experienced judgment. Nor did his attitudes seem other than admirably understanding and sympathetic to Livy, William Dean Howells, and the cream of eastern gentility. To Howells, if Clemens's "sense of justice suffered anything of that perversion which so curiously and pitiably maimed the reason of the whole South, it does not appear in his books, where there is not an ungenerous line, but always, on the contrary, a burning resentment of all manner of cruelty and wrong."[33]

Clemens's humor at the expense of blacks aroused no objections; his compassion was highly visible, and his condescension was not. The wise and kindly image of Clemens that has been projected may not be accommodated, however, to the evidence of the writings, to his prophecies of Negro supremacy—to be considered below—and to the implications of the more brutal of the jokes about blacks that he preserved in his notebooks. Any unqualified defense of Clemens against charges of racism as racism would now be defined is impossible to maintain. He and most other humane whites of the period assumed the existence of a natural racial hierarchy, accepted as a premise the biological inferiority of Negroes. To attempt to endow him or those whom he respected with views that may now be called racially neutral or fully enlightened is, not surprisingly, optimistically anachronistic; if he, the most popular American writer of his time among those who continue to hold our respect, helped to make America's culture, he was also its prisoner.

A WORLD

TURNED

UPSIDE

DOWN

▲ ▲ ▲ ▲ ▲ ▲ ▲ ▲ ▲

Letters, notebooks, and fragmentary stories indicate that humorously in 1874, seriously in later years, Clemens was given to fantasizing precipitous declines, abrupt falls from high to low estate, and cataclysmic reversals, both individual and societal. While on tour with George W. Cable during January 1885, the month that saw the first American publication of *Huckleberry Finn,* Clemens set down in his notebook a hint for a story with reverberations very different from those of his masterpiece: "America in 1985. (Negro supremacy—the whites under foot.)"[1] This laconic note prefigures a more ominously detailed one made nearly three years later, in November or December of 1887. In this instance, in the year 1910 in the South, whites of both sexes must ride in the smoking car and pay full fare, but the "populous & dominant colored man" refuses to ride with them. "The colored brother" has had severe laws passed against miscegenation. "The whites have to vote as they are told, or be visited by masked men & shot, or whipped, & house burned & wife & d turned out in their night clothes." Before writing "turned out in their night clothes," Clemens started to write "stripped naked." Added to this same note is the line, "More religion than ever with both colors."[2]

Racist feeling may be discerned in the entry. The white man is being treated exactly as the black man has been treated, but the black man is referred to condescendingly as "the colored brother," and prejudices against him are stirred in tbe mind of the white reader by his abuse of white women. The last line would seem to spring from what were by this time Clemens's bitterly antireligious convictions; it suggests the portrayal of an America in which both whites and blacks have been corrupted by religion.

Beginning probably in the spring and running into the fall of 1899 Clemens, writing in Sanna, Sweden, and in London, composed the first third of the manuscript for a novel that he ended by calling "Which Was It?" He wrote the remainder of the manuscript in the United States between 1900 and 1902 and may then have had his notes on Negro supremacy in mind.[3]

Like many of Clemens's stories, this one, long in gestation, has proleptic origins in Clemens's life as well as in the notebooks. In a notebook entry of 1879, one surely more important to him than those on Negro supremacy, Clemens jotted down an idea for a book: "The Autobiography of a Coward. Make him hideously but unconsciously base and pitiful and contemptible." The following year he mentioned his plans for this book (and for another one) in a letter to his brother, Orion. Whether he had himself in mind at the time as the model for the coward does not appear; he could have intended that honor for Orion, but, looking back, he sometimes spoke of himself as a coward.

When Clemens actually wrote his story of a coward, joining to it the idea of black supremacy, though of supremacy only on an individual scale, he made use of elements important to form and theme that appear repeatedly in his late stories. The dream as an enveloping structure had been popular with poets and storytellers for centuries. Clemens repeatedly chose a frame-story (envelope) structure in which a happy protagonist falls into a nightmarish dream and on awakening wonders whether the dream state or the waking state is illusory. The major theme of the story proper is that of a cruel reversal in the life of the protagonist, the upset being occasioned by mysteriously ineluctable powers. Often the inversion is associated with an insistence on the insignificance of man, "microscopic trichina concealed in the blood of some vast creature's veins."

As a man of his times Clemens was affected by the sense of crisis that afflicted the still-republican mind of the Protestant middle class. What has been called a burgeoning utopian literature was structured on an image of apocalypse, with threats of fiery destruction and promise of the Kingdom of Christ. In the latter Clemens did not believe; in some form of personal or social destruction, he did.[4]

The reversals that figure in Clemens's late manuscripts had their auto-biographical origins most prominently in his bankruptcy and in the death of Susy. On August 18, 1896, alone in Guildford, near London, he received a cable saying that Susy, "his heart's pride," had died.[5] Guilt had for long been a constant in Clemens's life. He had felt guilt for the death of his brother Henry following an explosion on a river steamer, guilt for the death of his little son Langdon. Now he engaged in "daily and nightly rituals of self-accusation."[6] His and Livy's loss would, he said, with hyperbolic emphasis unusual even for him, "bankrupt the vocabulary of all the languages to put it into words"; it was, put more simply, "like a man's house burning down—it would take him years and years to discover all that he had lost in the fire."

In his own mind, Clemens linked the two most grievous reversals in his life. The death of Susy he related directly to his mania for speculating that brought about the wasting of his and his wife's fortunes: "My crimes made her a pauper and an exile," he told Livy, meaning only that Susy was not the daughter of rich parents when she died, and that Susy had preferred to remain in the United States when Clemens, Livy, and Clara departed on a world lecture tour. But as was usual with him, he also fixed on a scapegoat. In this instance, Charles Webster, whom he had installed as manager of his publishing company, was "the primal cause of Susy's death and my ruin." The result, as he repeatedly declared in one phrasing or another, was that this "is an odious world. . . . It is Hell; the true one."[7] In prose and verse, in letters and fiction, he lamented his losses, proclaimed his guilt, and sought not so much absolution as self-acquittal.

The period obviously was for Clemens one of flagging energy and diminished creative vitality; yet he continued to write voluminously, though he brought few pieces to a successful conclusion. His craving to make millions had lessened. His eminence as a public figure and his status as an established author may have been enough to satisfy his ambitions. And, as he told reporters and others, he now wished to write mainly to please himself. Thus the narcissistic, disorderly stories about his woes, guilt, and innocence; thus the literary embarrassments that tread hard on one another's heels.

His preoccupation with reversals led to Clemens's obsessively repeated "fantasy pieces or fables,"[8] generally in essence family tragedies of a fall from contentment to misery. Similar in tone, though much less important to Clemens, were his gloomy prognoses of social upheaval. As he apparently saw things, if blacks, outnumbering whites, should take over social control, that would simply be one example of his theory of power relationships; he believed that the typical correlation among individuals, classes, and nations was a "tyranny of the strong over the weak." Those in power would entrench themselves or, "with a change of circumstances the victims would become the masters." Clemens "often projected the second alternative."[9]

Clemens prophesied social reversals other than one in which Negroes would rule whites. A late marginal note in *The Memoirs of the Duke of Saint Simon* projects domination by Roman Catholics, a fear that Clemens had proposed as the basis for a play in 1883; and in chapter 7 (written in 1899) of *Christian Science,* he called it "a reasonable guess" that the Christian Scientists would in 1940 become "the governing power in the Republic— to remain that, permanently." A notebook entry of February 6, 1901, suggests that at the time of Clemens's "the Eddipus story," government may be in the hands of the Christian Scientists or of the Roman Catholics. In the story itself, the two combine to form an absolutist church-state to rule the world. The hegemony of Christian Science he adverts to again both in an article in the *North American Review* for April 1903 and in the "Later Still" section of the Eddipus story.[10]

Clemens held a consistently hostile view of Roman Catholicism. Everything that he saw as wrong with the Church when he wrote his travel letters to the *Alta* in 1868 was reinforced by his later reading in books that he admired, such as W. E. H. Lecky's *History of European Morals from Augustus to Charlemagne* (1859), and by the general darkening of his thought in the 1880s. As for the Christian Scientists, he expressed at length his contempt for Mrs. Mary Baker Eddy and all her works. For either the Roman

Catholics or the Christian Scientists to establish hegemony would have impressed him as cataclysmic. Given the universality of the reversal topos, and given the American emotional climate, it is not surprising that the idea of white-black inversion should enter his late writings. He would never have defended cruelty to blacks by whites; but despite his "reconstructed" positions and his paternalistic attitude toward Negroes, or because of it, he would have felt repugnance at the idea of a future in which Negroes would dominate.

Racial memories may or may not have bearing; in any case, a world represented as in some fashion turned upside down is a major topos rooted in antiquity. Temporary hierarchical inversions--often associated with religious institutions—have ritual functions. Early cult practices pertaining to the Mater Deum Magna could be orgiastic. Among other notably disorderly rites were the Bacchanalia; the Orphic, Phrygian, and Dionysiac mysteries; and widely scattered chthonian cults. Anthropologists have collected myths in Brazil, in the Chaco, and in Tierra del Fuego which tell how women once ruled over men by virtue of powers gained from a feast during which they impersonated spirits or demons. Men, discovering the secret of the women, killed them, letting only small girls live, then used initiation rites to maintain male dominance.

Controlled, temporally limited periods of disorder presumably dissipate potential unrest. In Rome during the Saturnalia masters sometimes served their slaves. Christian authorities, too, permitted conspicuous licentiousness during the carnival season, as in Rome and Florence. Related perhaps to the Saturnalia was the Feast of Fools, when priests dressed as clowns or as women. In England, Scotland, and France those in power accepted at set times the governance of such figures as the Episcopus Puerorum, the Lord of Misrule, the Abbot of Unreason, l'Abbé des Fous or l'Abbé de Liess. In America, plantation owners often allowed their slaves unusual liberties on festive occasions.

Uncontrolled disorder, unlike controlled disorder, is terrifying; and the conception of dangerous inversions was vivid in the minds of Americans of the nineteenth century. The disorder of the French Revolution had included the Terror. The implications of the feminist movement were bad enough, but much more frightening was the prospect of domination by blacks. Slave insurrections—real and imaginary—were a standard bogeyman in the antebellum South: images of arson, castration, rape, and murder filled essays and addresses and invested southern minds as they must have that of Clemens's father when he helped send to prison abolitionists who had tried to assist slaves to "head for 'the polar star.'"[11]

During the 1840s and 1850s the very word *abolitionist* carried, for southerners, an air of the subversive, of the socially immoral; pejorative implications clung to it when Clemens related it to Orion. When Clemens was young, he displayed a mingling of affection and contempt for his older brother, but later, as Dixon Wecter says, his contempt "hardened into an amalgam of generosity and sadism."[12] He wrote scathingly of Orion in his letters to William Dean Howells, in his Autobiographical Dictations, and under cover of fictional characters. He usually described Orion as absurdly mutable, as inconstant as Dryden's Zimri; but he once asserted, apparently not in praise, that Orion "was an abolitionist from his boyhood to his death." (This was simply untrue: throughout the prewar years Orion held moderate views, so-called, and was not without racial biases.)[13]

In the fragmentary, unpublished sketch called "Autobiography of a Damned Fool" (dated 1875 by A. B. Paine), Clemens vented his distaste for Orion, on whom he modeled the protagonist. He remarked that the hero, upon becoming an abolitionist, "thinks it his duty to marry a wench. This is carrying abolitionism too far. Is notified to draw the line or will be tarred." Wecter calls this "obvious caricature"; but even as caricature the passage indicates that in 1875 Clemens thought that one of the most scandalously wrongheaded things that a white man could do or think of doing was to marry a black woman, whether on principle or not. Miscegenation was a mistake, but for a white to marry a black would be an inversion of the first magnitude.

Abolitionism as such posed an overt threat to turn antebellum southern society topsy-turvy, and during the years of Reconstruction the spectre of black dominion renewed old fears of social inversion. An atmosphere of paranoia lent vitality to the Ku Klux Klan, the Knights of the White Camellia, and other vigilante groups; and even the more cultivated and psychologically stable members of society were not immune to this aberration.

Although the miseries experienced by Clemens following his bankruptcy related directly to his personal life and only indirectly to society, they did influence his vision of the world in all of its aspects. As has been repeatedly noted, he was haunted both early and late by ideas of reversals, using in his works maskings, unmaskings, and almost innumerable doubles accompanied by the inversions that doubles make possible. Among well-known instances are the rise to wealth of that duplicitous boy Huck Finn in *Tom Sawyer*, the moral transcendence of the slave Jim in *Huckleberry Finn*, the exchange effected in *The Prince and the Pauper*, and the hourglass reversals of Thomas à Becket Driscoll and Valet de Chambre in *Pudd'nhead Wilson*.

White-black exchanges and abolitionist alarms enter into several of Clemens's less-known pieces. The article "A Scrap of Curious History" (1894) concerns an abolitionist conspiracy and the death of a constable. From 1896 until he abandoned it in 1900 Clemens contemplated or worked sporadically on "Tom Sawyer's Conspiracy," a story never entirely completed, in which Huck or Tom or another white person disguises himself as an escaped slave. Tom issues burlesque abolitionist posters, and the comically frightened villagers suppose "the abolitionists about to burn the town and run off the niggers."[14]

Clemens's late writings are strewn with stories and fragments of stories heavy with his own feelings of guilt, loss, powerlessness, and anxiety. Tortured protagonists suffer the reversal of Fortune's wheel and subjection to malign powers. A man who has enjoyed all that the heart may wish for (or dreams that he has enjoyed all that the heart may wish for) is suddenly brought to ruin (or dreams that he is brought to ruin). (Clemens's readings on dreams included William James, *The Principles of Psychology*, Sir John Adams, *Herbartian Psychology*, and George Christoph Lichtenberg's writings.) Over and over a protagonist asks himself, as had philosophers and men of letters for centuries, Is the phenomenal real? Is life a dream? Are dreams in truth reality and what we take to be reality an illusion?

All of these writings lend by their mood, if by nothing more, support to the supposition that Clemens entertained with some seriousness the idea of a frightening social reversal, a white-black reversal being the one at once most solidly based in history and the most dramatic. If Clemens had in fact purified himself of all racist sentiment, his twin notebook entries on Negro supremacy might have represented the germ for a story in which the roles of the races are justly overturned, the author's straightforward intent being to bring home to whites the problems faced by blacks in America, somewhat as Thomas Berger's *Regiment of Women* (1973) reverses the roles of the sexes. Such a story would have resembled in its polemic purpose the anthology of materials on lynching, a practice which Clemens abominated, that he actually did consider compiling but set aside—accepting the advice of Frank Bliss, his publisher—as dangerous to the sales in the South of his other works.[15]

The opposite of a novel representing a just reversal by which wicked whites are punished would be one in which innocent whites are tyrannized over by evil blacks. In actuality Clemens wrote neither of these stories but one which partakes of each. Only symbolically and by extension does it suggest a possible national reversal in white-black power relations. "Which Was It?" exhibits chiefly his own peripeteia and private anguish, is a tormented rumination on his life.

Arthur G. Pettit proposes that Clemens is not only projecting the common fear of the overturn of society by ex-slaves who would outbreed, outnumber, and outvote whites but is "calling for punishment for white sins."[16] In fact Clemens is not in this tale a frank social moralist. The story exhibits cross-lights. It stresses the bitter injustices that whites have inflicted on an originally generous-spirited black, but it also stresses the loving relationship between superior whites and inferior blacks; and its most considered attention is reserved for the weak, conscience-ridden George Harrison, who bears the brunt of the ex-slave Jasper's accumulated venom. Harrison's particular sin so far as Negroes are concerned is that he is the nephew of a slave-owner who both sired and abused Jasper. The story makes plain that if Clemens was not the racist pure and simple of his early years, neither was he cleansed of all racist emotions.

White-black relations had long fascinated Clemens. He treats, for example, the idea of whites disguised as blacks and of blacks passing for white—each a form of the inversion topos—in "Tom Sawyer's Conspiracy" (about 1897–1900) as well as in *Pudd'nhead Wilson* (1894), and most pointedly in "Which Was It?" To an extent the late tales, written when his creative energies were running low, were mere literary vocalizing by a man who had the habit of writing; but they were also exercises in self-exploration, confessions of cowardice and guilt, and appeals for forgiveness. In all of these tales, meant for himself as much as for the public, Clemens seems not to have cared greatly whether he made a properly shaped verbal construct or not. He had moved from being an industriously publishing writer-businessman to being an admired wit and Olympian sage, irresistible to reporters, a hero to the nation.

In "Which Was It?" Clemens dramatizes the theme of reversal by setting the story realistically in antebellum Hannibal ("Indiantown") and by creating a more or less believable hero, or antihero. The story is not nearly so hallucinatory as are his other dream tales. He fleshes out the agony of a reversal in fortune and a reversal in the hero's estimate of himself by having his protagonist praised by his fellow villagers for courage and probity after he has demonstrated to himself his cowardice and dishonesty, and, late in the story, by having him subjected in secret to physical and psychological degradation by an avenging mulatto.

Although Clemens diminishes man in other ways, he omits here any novelistic device analogous to looking through the wrong end of a telescope. Man's virtue is depreciated, but he is not scrutinized as though by some cosmically enormous Gulliver, man being "less than the billionth fraction of a microbe."[17] Clemens begins, however, in his usual frame-story way. A happily married man, George Harrison, nods off for a few moments. When he awakens fifteen years appear to have passed, and his life is in tragic disorder. His wife and daughters died in a fire at the time of his nap, a son remains; his aged, honorable father, fallen on bad times, has borrowed from Squire Fairfax, and, turned dishonorable because of mental problems that no one is aware of, pays his debt with counterfeit bills.

A series of melodramatic complications follows. Lies, misunderstandings, overheard plots, misplaced papers, insane imaginings, and a fortune inherited by Harrison from a wicked uncle make a jumble of the action. The manuscript breaks off before the hero awakes, presumably to find his wife and daughters alive and the torments he has suffered to be the figments of a dream.

Out of the confusion emerges the central story of a weak man's fall, suffering, and psychic disintegration; but there are many divagations, divertimenti, and enlargements. George Harrison's is only the paradigmatic case: the honor of every man and woman is said to be relative, not absolute. George falls, committing unintentionally a murder, when in order to preserve the appearance of family honor he tries to steal back the counterfeit bills that his father has given the Squire. (Perhaps for narrative purposes only, Clemens seems to equate the appearance of honor with honor itself.)

Shams abound. The book is turgid with reversals. The perceived surfaces of life are an illusion: behind the bland facade of public integrity lies ugly turpitude. Major and minor characters suffer from secret greed and secret sin. Public honor is secret dishonor; courage is cowardice; a wife must lend her husband masculine firmness and rationality; village quietude overlies subterranean turmoil. The fallen hero is tortured by the praise he receives for his courage and rectitude. Almost as an afterthought, as one of the excessively complicating elements in plotting, Clemens works in that special topos, the white-black inversion, a synecdochic representation of the social upheaval he had predicted in his notebooks. Because the mulatto Jasper knows the scandalous secrets of Harrison and of a white mother and son (the Gunnings) he is their master. Circumstances permit him to create a variant, concealed from all but his chief victims, on the ancient, protean topos, the world turned upside down.

Harrison's life is first turned upside down by the loss of his wife and daughters, next by the dishonorable actions that reveal to him the superficiality of his probity. For an ex-slave to force him to perform humiliatingly servile actions in secret is simply an additional turn of the screw, a peripeteia that occupies only 20 of the 250 pages that Clemens wrote before abandoning the manuscript. The generalized allegorical value of Harrison's plight is, nevertheless, spelled out: the abused mulatto learns to hate and curse the white race, rejoices that in fifteen years "he had spared no member of it a pain or a shame when he could safely inflict it," and says of his animus against Harrison, "Dey's a long bill agin de lowdown ornery white race, en you's a-gwyneter *settle* it." That Jasper is the representative black and Harrison the representative white tends to be obscured, however, by the extended treatment given to more general reversals in Harrison's life.

This is definitely not the story that a white supremacist would have told. So far as Jasper is involved, it is clearly retributive. By the code of an eye for an eye, the white man gets what whites in general have earned. It is also possible that, so far as Clemens is concerned, it is expiatory, with Clemens taking upon himself the guilt attributed to his race in addition to a personal guilt from which he just possibly may have suffered. (Pettit thinks that Clemens may have suffered guilt because of a sexual misdeed during his boyhood.)[18] Whether the tale is autobiographical in this way or not is speculative. What is clear is that it exploits the fears of an imagined social revolution and reflects deep ambivalences in Clemens's mind. The author, engaged in a kind of psychomachia, attempts to achieve psychic equilibrium, to work out symbolically his exorbitant sense of loss, of betraying, and of being betrayed. The story is awash in desolation and self-pity.

Consideration of selected characters in "Which Was It?" provides a relatively direct way to see the extent to which the story reflects Clemens's mental life. Clemens suffered from something like a prolonged identity crisis; and he had, in addition, the habit of projecting, of endowing characters in his fictions with his own feelings and interests. His people speculate, make bad decisions, are temperish, vacillating, and childish. When autobiographical heroes come calamitously to grief, he frequently arranges matters so that the protagonists can, like him, confess responsibility, suffer, and be absolved.

He scatters himself among a number of the characters, female as well as male, in "Which Was It?" but identifies principally with George Harrison (see, for example, pages 232, 264–67). Through Harrison he mouths his own fears, his view of life as "a treachery and a sham," and his welcoming of death. Harrison's psychic writhings are representations of his own torments. In that respect, particularly, the story is ardently solipsistic, painfully autobiographical, an apologia.

Characters other than Harrison also partake of Clemens's nature, speak with his voice, use his vocabulary, enjoy his knowledge of books, and ruminate on the problems that during his latter years he put into such texts as *What Is Man?* Like him, they pride themselves on their knowledge of human nature, devise complicated manipulative schemes (mixedly shrewd and naive), and in other ways bear testimony to the Tom Sawyer element in Clemens's nature.

Few of the characters here or in any of Clemens's fictions may properly be called realistic. In his old age, especially, Clemens tends to allude to life or abstract from it, not to draw after it. In this story he opens the ragbag of memory and scatters hidden allusions to his family: to Jane Clemens (his mother) and to anecdotes about her; to Livy; to his children; to his brother Orion's wife, Mollie; and most of all (if we except allusions to Clemens himself) to Orion.

Clemens's derisory view of Orion, embodied in a schematized portrayal of "Hamfat" Bailey, who tries everything, may readily be considered excessive. Orion was, it is true, the recipient over the years of Clemens's annoyed charity, and he was incurably woolly. He did, nevertheless, have admirable qualities; and Clemens recognized this: he was amiable, forbearing, honest by intention, conscientious, and relentlessly eager to do good. It seems possible that Clemens's contempt for him may have been occasioned by his virtues as well as by his defects, for Clemens himself was not largely endowed with most of Orion's good qualities but was supplied to redundance with his bad. Possibly Clemens recognized in himself Orion's vacillations, naiveté, cloudy philosophizing, and dreaminess. Perhaps his attacks on Orion were manifestations of self-hatred. Hamfat undergoes changes to accommodate him to the exigencies of the plot: he becomes Samuel Clemens (pages 279–81, 379 ff., 384) and a combination of Tom Sawyer and Beriah Sellers (page 346), which is again to identify him with Samuel Clemens.

In general male and female characters are supposed, in the standard Victorian way, to be complementary. Men are in theory strong, rational, decided, and practical. Although Clemens did not care for Coventry Patmore's *Angel in the House,* his young and attractive women have the qualities that readers of Patmore approved of: modeled on Clemens's idealized conception of Livy in her youth, they love, soothe, and heal, are ill-equipped to face harsh realities.

Older women may be relatively manlike, especially those who have suffered hard knocks; they are capable of restraining foolish, volatile husbands. Mrs. Charlotte Gunning, prominent in the subplot that includes Jasper, is a mixed character, more than anything else a Samuel Clemens in skirts: scheming, manipulating, succumbing to avarice, fascinated by confidence games, proud of her understanding of the weaknesses of mankind, partly regretting her misdeeds. She enjoys one anecdotal relationship with Jane Clemens, recounting the sentimental story of Sandy, the little slave boy, that Clemens attributes to his mother in his autobiography.[19]

Blacks in the novel are all stereotypes. The ill-treatment accorded to Jasper is so exceptional as to seem anomalous. Clemens might have drawn upon the Jim of the central part of *Huckleberry Finn* or upon the Bras Coupé of George Cable's *The Grandissimes* (1880) as a model for Jasper, the avenging Negro; instead, Jasper remains a dim, instrumental figure. In his early, trusting, good-natured, family-loving aspect, Jasper is simply a "good nigger." When tried beyond all measure, he becomes neither romantically satanic nor a hero of his people. Instead, he becomes a scheming hybrid, like the half-breeds in western thrillers; and he knits his brow in order to think.

Slaves at a little white girl's birthday party "have a good time, it's their nature" (page 181). House servants belonging to the Harrisons, to the aristocratic Fairfaxes, and to the Gunnings are happy, simple creatures. As a child, Helen Fairfax was taught at home but was not lonely: "There were a dozen black domestics, the dearest and loveliest company in the world for a white child" (page 185). When the motherless Helen is of marriageable age, she and "old Liza" love each other in a way that antebellum plantation novelists or postbellum sentimentalists would have found sweetly appropriate. Martha, the Harrisons' somewhat aged slave woman, is a similar stock figure (page 261). Clemens was not above including a literarily irresponsible and historically impossible scene, one altogether contradictory of upper-class southern mores, using farcical dialogue, comic sex-play, banjo-picking, and the singing of "Camptown Races" by Jasper—all in the kitchen of the Harrison home before breakfast, with Martha adding to Jasper's "the rich voice that is the birthright of her race" (pages 419 ff.). This is the stuff of an off-Broadway musical drama of the 1920s.

The deficiencies of "Which Was It?" are perhaps as interesting as are its achievements. As has been indicated, it possesses the unhappy earmarks of most of Clemens's late writings. Plotting is mechanical, dependent on stagey devices. Characterization is superficial and inconsistently elaborated: stock figures move stiffly; the author did not care enough about them to ensure plausibility. Dialogue is awkward, often stichomythic or catechistic. The powerful Tom Sawyer component in Clemens's makeup intrudes itself (as it regularly had in the past) in the reliance on cheap effects and in the slipshod intrigue. A superfluity of misplaced ingenuity is devoted to impostures, deceits, stratagems, and artifices. The writer appropriates from his earlier texts maxims, phrasings, anecdotes, characters, and incidents. Repetition and self-plagiarism did not disturb him: anything that had succeeded once would succeed again.

Although students of dialect have expressed reservations about the exactness that Clemens claimed for the dialects employed in *Huckleberry Finn,* he did work and rework the language in that book. In "Which Was It?" the dialects attempted (German-English, Irish-English, regional black English, and varieties of regional white English) are done crudely and impatiently; eye-dialect predominates. Clemens does, nevertheless, pay through Mrs. Gunning what may be his most fervent tribute to the vernacular, calling it "the most eloquent of all speech, the quaint and odd and unconventional centre-driving language of the poor—that marvelous phrasing which is above all art, beyond the reach of all art, and goes straight to the heart—and sometimes breaks it!" (page 33). Familiar forms of comedy, in some instances plagiarized from earlier works, are inserted almost compulsively. Farce clogs the action and subverts the serious emotions. There are minstrel-show passages, puerile game elements, language play (fake Chinese), and, out of the comic arsenal that he drew on before he refined his imagery, the crudely scatological, as in referring to a purgative and a "bowel full of cats." The infusion of discordant low comedy fails to heighten, by contrast, the generally melancholy, misanthropic tone of the story. The defects and the incongruities are, however, typical of Clemens even in his writings of the 1880s; here, toward the end of his life, they are only exaggerated.

In this, as in other late manuscripts, Clemens burdens the story with amateurish philosophizing. He mulled over the nature of man and God in tale after tale, drawing on his reading in large, quasi-scholarly, popular books by W. E. H. Lecky and by Andrew D. White. Like a teething dog, he worried indefatigably the question as to whether all of man's actions are selfish in origin (see, for example, pages 302 ff., 379, 383 ff.); and he concluded that freedom of will and action are out of the question. Heredity and training are all-determining (pages 273, 279 ff., 294, 305 ff., 398–99, 419). Man is, nevertheless, given the Moral Sense; and this sense ensures his depravity: it enables him, unlike the other animals, to distinguish right from wrong and to elect to do wrong (pages 278, 375, 377–78). Each man will do wrong, will fall, if sufficiently tempted; the honor of each has its limits (pages 192–94, 219, 225, 337). Nature and fate (alternative terms for God?) are, overall, cruel and malicious (pages 271–76). Although Clemens did not use the phrase and was probably not so firm in his belief as were Milton and Hawthorne, he was at least passingly fascinated by "the Paradox of the Fortunate Fall." It is not necessarily bad that a man fall: by falling he may come to understand his limitations (pages 195, 279, 282–84). A fortunate fall could be, it seems, a supplementary way for Clemens to excuse himself for his "crimes."

The tendency of Clemens's loose collocation of arguments and assertions is, of course, to exonerate man. More particularly, it exculpates Samuel Clemens for neurotic speculating and for what Olivia Clemens, that good bourgeoise, took to be a loss of honor until she had persuaded him, following his bankruptcy, to repay his creditors, which he did, *almost* in full. Sinning man is, then, absolved in terms of secular causation and of theological causation. Man does what he does because his actions are determined by heredity or training; or he does what he does because God gave him the Moral Sense that permits him to sin. As for Clemens himself, supplementary means of absolution were usually available: scapegoats could be found; or, one must fall in order to learn how not to fall. Finally—and presumably life and fiction have their correspondences in this—what we take to be tragedy may be imaginary, unreal, a dream.

The frame-story structure is left incomplete in "Which Was It?"; in musical terms, we do not return to the tonic, but in terms of morals and action the ending, if he had reached one, would almost surely have been perfunctory, almost irrelevant. The torments and fears of the antihero are the deeply felt aspects of the tale. Psychic and material terrors are not, however, the only features that capture our attention. The reader who is

interested in Clemens and in his image as a national hero fixes inquisitively
on elements familiar from Clemens's letters, notebooks, autobiographical
writings, sketches, earlier stories, and from what we know of his reading.
Among characteristic authorial touches are a disdain for the "common
herd," admiration for aristocratic virtues, a sense of the charm of death,
and, of course, a condescending view of women and blacks.

Possibly Clemens could have published "Which Was It?" without pro-
ducing an ingenious resolution for the mechanically Byzantine entangle-
ments of the plot: he could even have dismissed the problem by having
George Harrison awaken from his dream, restored to the sunlit simulacrum
of the real world that he inhabited as the story opened, the world that
antebellum southern gentlemen in novels were supposed to live in, the
world that Clemens, with his feelings of guilt and his suicidal impulses,
liked to think he had once inhabited. Alternatively, he could have ended his
story with an imperfect, good-enough resolution that permitted loose ends
to dangle; readers were accustomed to the glossings-over of popular fiction.

Howells approved of Clemens's meandering, conversational early writings—they were like life. Clemens himself was enchanted by the planned
disorder of his Autobiographical Dictations. As he wrote to Howells from
Florence in 1904, "You will be astonished and charmed to see how like *talk*
it is . . . what a darling & worshipful absence of the signs of starch, &
flatiron, & fuss & labor & the other artificialities."[20] On the other hand,
Clemens had ridiculed inadequacies in plotting in James Fenimore Cooper
and others; that was a kind of cheating. The ending he had in mind, as the
appendix entitled "Trial of the Squire" makes plain, was, moreover, a
favorite of his, one that he would have hated to give up, a melodramatic
courtroom finale in which some Tom Sawyer surrogate leaps to his feet and,
to the amazement and tumultuous applause of the spectators, shouts out
two or three clarifying words.

Instead of finishing the story, Clemens set it aside. The emotional issues
in it were apparently too intricately intimate to be within his powers to
resolve. The relevance to Clemens's own life was, moreover, so overridingly
important to him that he managed to do very little with social themes,
including that of a society turned upside down. Nor were his emotional
ambivalences usefully deployed. He was inadequate as an objective psy-
chologist or analytical sociologist; and he had little concern for America's
economic inequities and its flawed cultural ethos. His portrayal of the

institution of slavery leaves the subject in a state of irresolution appropriate to his own division of mind concerning power relationships between blacks and whites. Irresolution of another kind may have increased the difficulty he experienced in completing the manuscript by having Harrison awaken from his dream: unlike the somnambulistic atmosphere of his cosmological stories, the mood here is psychologically contorted but recognizably quotidian—the cosmogonic trappings are stripped away.

"Which Was It?," incomplete though it is, carelessly written though it is, constitutes when taken with the Autobiographical Dictations and other late texts a remarkable Fiction of the Self. Clemens may have recognized that either of the two dreadful coups de theatre readily available to round it off would have disposed of mystifications but would also have falsified the emotional content of the book and of his life. Either ending—an awakening from the dream or the courtroom scene, singly or in combination—would have testified that his own losses and griefs were inauthentic. An optimistic dismissal of tragedy and of psychic terror could, then, have been unacceptable: the dream is dreamed in Hannibal, and Hannibal was to Clemens his own world, one he preferred to consider palpable and true. Hannibal also has an air of truth for the reader. The familiar scene helps to make "Which Was It?," of all the anguished stories of Clemens's final decade, the most emotionally convincing and, perhaps inevitably, the most encyclopedically revealing of the Representative American's fears and anxieties, of the shape of his life, and of the content and texture of his mind.

MYTHS,

PARADOXES,

AND THE

BOURGEOIS

HERO

▲ ▲ ▲ ▲ ▲ ▲ ▲ ▲ ▲

Myths and symbols develop lives of their own. They have helped to form perceptions of Mark Twain, much as symbols and myths helped to form Twain's conception of America. They contributed to an American sensibility and *mentalité* that gave direction to his abundant creative energies. Resulting images of Twain have held our attention and belief, remained elastic and accommodative. Attitudes toward Samuel Clemens the man and Twain the writer have tended to merge: in a reversible equation, what is true of the private man is generally assumed to be true of the platform reader and popular humorist. It is, then, partly by way of images, legends, and myths, with all of their operative distortions, that we have known Samuel Clemens and his other self, Mark Twain. Our perceptions have not been unitary, however: conflicting opinions of one kind or another have always existed; confusion and discord have flourished and continue to flourish.

Mark Twain today is still mistakenly seen as a primary hero of the "mirage of the West" (as the philosophes spoke of a new order), the type of a virtuous America: in this favorable light, he stands as an aspect of the *Volksgeist,* a product of the generative and regenerating frontier, a figure representative of the genius of a democratic people. He is a homespun Diderot, a vernacular defender of the rights of man.

Although seen as representative, Twain is almost never viewed as commonplace. He becomes the Romantically hypertrophied uncommon natural man, a Rousseauian personification of the general will, a toweringly moral representative of an early, Providentially designed America. He is often pitted against a fragmented, genteel, corrupt society. Clemens himself accepted and disseminated several strands in this legend. For example, while in Vienna in 1898, he made this summarizing notebook entry: "Are you an American? / No. I am not *an* American. I am *the* American." On the other hand, he insisted, though usually dramatically, through personae, that he was not so much the representative man as the omniscient outsider, the lonely shaper of a new and better culture.

William Dean Howells placed his authoritative cachet on the most favorable aspects of the Mark Twain legend; Twain was, he affirmed, the Lincoln of our literature. Clara Clemens and A. B. Paine—those early, prominent, dedicated guardians—prevented the publication of material that might do injury to the image. Together, they helped establish the likeness of a westerner purified of boorishness, a compassionate, reconstructed southerner, a brilliantly flattering *speculum Novi Mundi.* Subsequent partisans— DeVoto, Ferguson, Wecter, Wagenknecht—took up the cause. DeVoto, reacting against disturbing challenges by Van Wyck Brooks and a handful of leftist *penseurs,* prescribed a consciously nationalistic version of the image, sure that he was engaged in a war against world communism, world fascism, and ill-informed, insipid critics. He was the defender of Mark Twain as the essence of America.

Twain symbolized for DeVoto the spirit of unspoiled democracy captured at a moment of continental majesty. This conception moved him to attempt to establish Twain as the greatest American writer, a larger than life Natty Bumppo, a Pathfinder blazing trails for others to follow. In general, critics have accepted this image and enlarged upon it: they usually portray a robustly humorous hero of the New World, a social thinker of importance, the greatest of American writers.

Clemens was born fifty-nine years after the birth of the American nation and flourished during an era of national mythmaking. America invented for the rolls of the national fiction heroic characters who were suitably representative of a Golden Age, permitting an amplitude of extension in their significations. Clemens grew up, to be sure, in Hannibal after the actual frontier had moved on, and he made his initial reputation in a Far West which had nothing to do with a frontier which denoted a line or a neutral zone between civilization and savagery. He was not, like Leatherstocking, a hero of moral spaces, nor was he the hero of Emerson's reconciliation of opposites, of Margaret Fuller's paragon whose eyes read the heavens, while his feet step firmly on the ground. Nor was he a yeoman farmer. And yet, in filling a national need, he has remained a part of the mythic past, in one way or another, continues to stand as a natural man, a New Adam in a New Garden.

For Twain personally, the Far West was an escape from the Civil War. It was a place for boyish adventure, saloon and newsroom friendships, and images—like old, flickering newsreels—of a metaphoric frontier. The literal West of his experience was an area to be exploited, a kind of modern America in the raw. His was the West of settlers and speculators who marched inexorably toward the setting sun, from one spoiled Garden to the next, eliminating the Indians, slashing the forests, mining, stretching their tentacles into the Pacific.

In *Esquisse d'un tableau historique* Condorcet stood Hesiod's scheme of a descent from the Golden Age on its chronological head and increased the number of periods in history from five to ten. In Condorcet, the best age, the most perfectly civilized, comes last. America, according to its interpreters, presented several ages synchronically, spread along a geographical line from the East toward the West, from civilized to primitive; and one could read the movement from East to West as either a progression or a regression. During the major part of Clemens's career, despite his caustic satires on military and missionary exemplifications of Manifest Destiny, he generally approved of nineteenth-century America, believed in the Idea of Progress. His opinions and preferences varied often, but for most of his life he was, by intention, not accident, a backtracker, an eastern gentleman, not an exponent of primitivism. "There is no section in America that is so good to live in as splendid old New England," he wrote to his brother in 1870; and he praised the Northeast liberally in *Life on the Mississippi* (1883).

Virginia City and Jackass Hill were not at any time his Terrestrial Paradise. He found, instead, something like a *hortus conclusus* in the handsome house in Buffalo that Jervis Langdon gave to him and Livy, and there were other avatars of the Garden. All such paradisal retreats were, when possible, presided over by a refined and tender genius of the place. Coventry Patmore, whose *The Angel in the House* (1854–62) Clemens read or read in while courting Olivia, exalted married love and the wife around whose "footsteps blow/The authentic airs of Paradise." But Clemens did not have to learn from Patmore: the spiritualized Livy to be found in Clemens's overblown letters of 1868 is recognizably like a common image of the period, one which Lionel Trilling called "the Beatrice of the *Comedy,* the Paraclete in female form." Nor, later, were notions of himself as Adam and of Livy as Eve unfamiliar to Clemens. "Eve's Diary" (1905) ends with the eloquently Victorian, much-admired line, "Wheresoever she was, *there* was Eden."

To Clemens the North was often the same as the East, thus complicating his ambivalence toward the North and the South. He condemned the South for its industrial backwardness, its treatment of the Negro, its sentimental Walter Scottism, its ignorance, and its one-party politics; but he liked aspects of its speech, its politenesses, and some of its mores. He also enjoyed the comedy, pathos, and exuberant emotions that he observed among yeomen, poor whites, and blacks. Although he could summon up a feeling of nostalgia for the South, during his mature years it was mainly in his imagination that he continued to associate with the blacks and lower-class whites with whom he had mingled in his youth. His acquaintance with blacks resolved itself into a master-servant or a benefactor-beneficiary relationship, and his associations with lower-class whites were primarily of the same sort.

The East-West polarity—at least as clear-cut for Clemens as the North-South—produced ideological, social, and intimately personal tensions. Particularly during his first years in New York and New England, when he was serving an apprenticeship to gentility, he felt the oppressive weight of alleged cultural differences. He wished to conform to the East, but he also thought himself quite good enough as he was. Unlike Howells, who was more obviously awed by the East and at the same time better fitted by his nature and by his literary inclinations to adapt to the eastern model,

Clemens nursed resentment at being condescended to or derogated. When on the defensive, he could exaggerate his Missouri speech, his western manner, or claim that his writings were water for the masses, not wine supplied to the elect.

To counter charges that Clemens, because western and an autodidact, was uncultivated, his partisans have enlarged upon his sensitivity, magnified the cultural resources of Hannibal, where he grew up, and concluded that he became a man of taste and learning. In fact, although he was a constant reader and in some ways a shrewd one, his cultural deficiencies were glaring. He could not find virtues in novelists ranging from Fenimore Cooper to Henry James. He not only could not read *The Bostonians* but announced that he would rather be damned to John Bunyan's heaven than to do so. Jane Austen was anathema to him.

Susy and Clara Clemens had strong musical interests; nevertheless, Clemens seems to have been, until late in life, almost unaware of baroque, classic, or contemporaneous music. His taste embraced a very restricted gamut; favorites were popular songs, ballads, Negro spirituals, and the music of military bands. During his several periods of residence in France— he lived abroad for approximately seventeen years—he seems to have acquired no knowledge of the remarkable late-nineteenth-century masters who gave new directions to art and poetry. One looks in vain for a sign of interest in Manet, Monet, Renoir, Cézanne, Baudelaire, Rimbaud, Verlaine, or Mallarmé. To be so blinkered, to have such cultural limitations, was, to be sure, very American.

The distortions of reality that blot the literature on Clemens have embedded themselves in the national mind. The accepted images and the accompanying analogizing are not, however, always flagrantly wrong; and they may be judged to have had their psychological usefulness to individuals and to a nation in need of totemic ancestors. Clemens's virtues and talents were not unimportant, though they were not those of the spurious portrayals— simplified and cleaned up as if for children's television, displayed in all the glowing falsity of living color.

Samuel Clemens suffered from severe psychological conflicts: his pathogenic psychological structures were, as is testified to by his life and writings, powerfully narcissistic.[1] He demonstrated an exceptional need of sympathetic support, of assistance in shoring up his notion of himself and of his capacities. In psychological terms, he was unable to establish ego dominance as opposed to dominance by some aspect of the archaic (infantile), grandiose self. He often gave the appearance of being audacious or commanding but he never attained anything like secure psychic adulthood, never achieved a mature, integrated personality, never became independent.

Signs of psychic arrestment and disorder are manifest in his vanity, oscillation between megalomania and paranoia, hypochondria, short-lived rages, moments of ebullience, periods of emotional depletion, exaggerated expressions of guilt, vulnerability to indifference or disapproval, and fascination by ideas of twinship. He invested with an excess of libidinal energy such extensions of the self as Livy, Susy, and Henry Rogers; he held life and the external world in contempt and expressed the conviction that he was singled out for torment by an omnipotent persecutor. His masochistic speculating was Dostoievskian in its almost uncontrollable nature. Perhaps equally indicative of arrestment or regression was his pursuit of little girls, even though the sexualizing of this pedophilic development displayed itself in ways that were so far as we know acceptable to the polite public and to his own self-esteem.

To speak of the real Mark Twain is to mention often unattractive, sometimes paradoxical descriptive details. He was childish, malicious, excessively ambitious, self-indulgent, destructive, vulgar, sentimental, exploitative, rationalist, skeptical, atheistic, mechanistic, antiaristocratic, and elitist. He fantasized the possession of enormous power and of wealth beyond measure. He suffered from bitterness, terror, guilt, and despair. He was more eastern than western, more urban than rural, more bourgeois than yeoman.

Toward the end of his life, he surrounded himself with a coterie of worshiping inferiors. He satirized industrial capitalism, damned money as an evil, and condemned corruption, whether in business or in the Congress; but he was a friend to business, consorted with capitalists and senators, and made full use of the Langdon coal money that came to Livy. He yearned, though rarely, for the simple life in a pastoral world; contrarily, he was a thorough materialist, devoted to luxurious living, inclined to seek out the rich and the prominent and to rise above them by virtue of his wit and charismatic public presence. He conceived of the God in whom he did not believe as all-powerful and malign but was enraptured by ingenious contemporary inventions and preached the gospel of progress. His timorousness in the face of public opinion could be marked: his late "dangerous truths" on the importance and pleasure of sexuality were not stated for publication; and his own strong erotic urges appear to have been offset by a terror of mature sexuality. He was obsessed with purity, anxious about masturbation and impotence.

His qualms about publishing his writings on sexuality are matched by his semiconcealment of his views on religion, which were almost certainly not stanchly orthodox even during the period of his courtship and became thoroughly heterodox during his last years. He reformed his early racist attitudes so decidedly that he did not need to hide his opinions on "the Negro Question," for they became what in the eastern society of his time was considered enlightened. Although he began soon after he arrived in the East to satirize displays of ignorant racism, he never fully recovered from thinking of Negroes as in some fundamental ways different and inferior. As for "the Woman Question," his progress was not dissimilar. He liked and admired women, provided they were surrogate mothers or were gentle-women and pretty or ingenues and saucy; but he never developed an appreciation of gender equality, and throughout most of his life, for all the customary, evasive reasons, he opposed having women play full political roles. In tracts, in his autobiographical writings, and in the observations and jokes that he set down in his notebooks, he aggressed outrageously against them.

It is a major irony that Americans should take a man like Clemens to be benignly humorous, optimistic, meliorist, and democratic, that the public at large should choose him—above Cooper, Emerson, Thoreau, or anyone else—as our primary literary icon of a wholesome America. Brooks was partly correct: Clemens could almost as well be thought the Nervous, Sick, Alienated, and Exploitatively Individualistic American as Laughing, Healthy, Communitarian, and marked by Civic Virtue. He was never a robustly sane Mountain Man, all comedy, courage, whipcord and rawhide; he was rather an anguished version of late-nineteenth-century Western Man, perpetually self-doubting, forever unsure of his own identity.

Excepting a few of his ideas about religion (which were very much those of a village atheist), man (whom he viewed as would a cynic who has sipped perfunctorily at the waters of the Enlightenment), and sexuality (a subject which absorbed him but was nevertheless pretty much terra incognita), Clemens's mind was abundantly furnished with the commonplaces of his era. He had little to say that was politically or socially or philosophically novel, no advanced positions to stake out on women, blacks, economics, or democracy. One of the reasons for his popularity was and is the bourgeois normality of his openly expressed assumptions, the ordinariness of his heterodoxies and of his more covert anxieties.

Clemens differed most importantly from those around him in his mastery of a range of writing skills, the energy of his language, his ear for the literary adaptation of common speech, and the richness of his fantasy life. By means of talent and technique, he could sometimes give literary expression to his affective problems.

His tensions were all too familiar to other nineteenth-century Americans. He dreamed their self-aggrandizing dreams. He oscillated between optimism and pessimism, cynicism and sentimentality. For him youth is to be perpetuated; age may be redeemed only by death. Evil inheres in money (which is to be sought after) and in the past (though nostalgia was for him a frequent emotion). He deplored aristocracy, religion, and tradition but was fascinated by each. Bits and pieces of life are to be explored and enjoyed even though the promises of existence are fraudulent and some variety of determinism operates.

At frequent intervals, Clemens's restlessness became acute; he was in one or another kind of flight from society, from responsibility, and from reality. When he could not escape into simpler, sunnier worlds, real or imagined, he could have suicidal inclinations and wish for death. He repudiated nearly all of his old friends. His distrust of life permitted him to congratulate acquaintances on the deaths of husbands, wives, or children and to observe that his daughter Susy had died at the right time. He fled physically from one place to another. He was narcissistically and Romantically escapist in his insistence on duality.

In considering forces and talismanic devices that protected Clemens against anxieties and stresses, the importance of Livy to her husband would be difficult to exaggerate. Whether we see her in the role of surrogate mother (a parent imago) or in the role of alter ego (as some aspect of the grandiose self), she was the principal long-term stabilizing influence on Clemens. She gratified his need for empathic association, served as a reassuringly secure and potent other self, and set libido free for the creative work that Clemens otherwise tended to dislike. Livy was not equipped by nature or by training to be the editor-critic that he insisted she become; but it could be argued, much as Clemens himself repeatedly did, that it was only through her encouragement and the controls she exercised that the demands and urges of Clemens's infantile self were appropriately channeled. There were, of course, lesser bulwarks against irrationality, depletion, and despair: his authentic successes—as on the platform and in writing—were usually a solace, as were friends and reviewers who corrected, appreciated, and praised him.

In view of the characteristics attributed to Clemens as an American eidolon, it would seem to be strange that he should have elected to spend out of America approximately half of the years between the date of his marriage in 1870 and the death of his wife in 1904. The reasons that he gave were practical: to protect copyright, to reduce household expenses, for Livy's health, for seclusion in order to write, to gather materials for proposed books, but it seems likely that trips to Europe were another kind of fuguing, a psychic shield. He fled the stresses occasioned by his speculating; he may also have fled stresses occasioned by his being a westerner in the East, condescended to by those who thought it unfastidious to like Clemens or his works. (Even Howells's ordinarily high, unstinting praise carried with it the implication that Clemens was a kind of lusus naturae.)

Europe offered a favorable psychic climate. The elite of England, Germany, and Austria—supposedly models for the American East—valued with few obvious reserves the amusing speaker and writer from the New World. To be lionized in cultures that American ladies and gentlemen sought when they wished to acquire polish supplied ego-gratification to Clemens. In theory he could have retreated from the East to the American West, but in actuality this was impossible, and not just because he could not have moved Livy to Hannibal, Virginia City, or San Francisco.

In truth, Clemens became by choice an easterner who internalized most of the tastes and values that he sometimes went through the motions of rebelling against. He could confound that fraction of the American genteel that continued to be supercilious by becoming, like Franklin, the admired American in Europe, or he could rise above them by joining exclusive clubs and by living among moneyed acquaintances in New York or by surrounding himself with sycophants in his mansion in Connecticut. He became a not uncommon kind of American artist, the transcendent outsider. He did not fully associate himself with the popular writings on which his reputation rests: they were not intimately parts of him; they were objects for the market. His later works, incompletely realized as they are, reveal the intensity of his feelings of both anomie and of transcendence.

So far as his personal culture goes, Clemens seems to have learned surprisingly little from the Europe that opened itself to him: he observed it as might a transient journalist of the New Adamic stamp, imposed his personality upon it, and mined it for material. When the English feted him, he used their admiration as a defense against American sneers. If he was offended by American bad manners, disorder, and political corruption, he contrasted the politeness, order, and effective civil service of Germany. If tormented by ideas of sexual impurity, he made the English aristocracy and the French nation his pharmakoi. When he abhorred flux and haste, he praised Europe. When he was approbative of purity, democracy, and progress, he referred to the United States as a model.

The more malleable of the Americans whom Henry James translated to Europe are shocked by their encounters with a strange culture into increased sensitivity and a heightened awareness of the self. Unlike these fictional, open Americans, Clemens had little inclination to relate vulgarity and evil. James's characters manage to enlarge their natures by becoming less provincially American without becoming either vapidly or viciously European. Clemens was not Europeanized for either good or bad. Often restless in America, he was never at home on the Continent. His particular variety of flight and transcendence left him, in a melancholy way, his own man.

During his later years, Clemens repeatedly referred to his capacities as a truth teller, competent to expose the lies and hypocrisies of the world but compelled to withhold his excoriating though possibly redemptive messages from publication because society was not ready for his disclosures— he and his family would suffer if he dared to expose the absurdities and evils which the world blandly accepts. Hubris of this sort came to something like a verbal climax when he made what he called his last appearance on the *paid* platform: he spoke like a departing ruler or a dying culture hero addressing a host of woebegone followers: "I wish to consider that you represent the nation, and that in saying good-bye to you I am saying good-bye to the nation."[2]

A few critics have thought that a number of the writings that Clemens left unpublished at his death (many of which have now been put in print) are of great social importance, but this belief is hallucinatory. By and large, the tales and sketches, mainly unfinished, that he left unpublished are mechanically programmatic; they illustrate shallow propositions, contain few effective images. The dialogue is frequently wooden, sometimes argumentatively stichomythic, and the plotting is mechanically melodramatic.

Clemens's reputation would seem destined to rest in the future as it now does on the books of his middle years. *Huckleberry Finn,* by far his best work, has been credited with numinous qualities, evocations of the primitive, a saving humor, a libertarian ethos, mythic depths, and an inspiring vision of man. Conventionally, the properties seen in the writings are attributed to the writer. Some of the writings do merit serious attention, and the man and his writings are indeed related; nevertheless, important corrections are likely to be made in the standard views.

All critical studies tend to be reductionist, and this volume does not pretend to be a full, sufficient basis for judging the man or his writings. I have focused on closely defined topics and themes. My exploration of selected neuroses does not constitute a full-scale inner life of Samuel Clemens: he is more than, though not contradictory to, the sum of isolated neuroses. His personality did not show itself as disturbingly pathological at all times and in all areas. He did not always mismanage his life.

Appraisals of the writings based on the assumption that they reflect with precision the nature of a mythic hero or of a prophetic wise man may not be validated. Clemens's place in the literary pantheon has not been settled. Improved understanding of the life, a new psychology of the author, and a new sociology of the texts may be expected to influence the criticism that is yet to come.

If the heroically representative saint of an imagined culture has not yet faded into daguerreotype dimness, the historical Samuel Clemens of his eastern and European years who is now emerging is more the Romantic solitary than the Neoclassic communitarian; more the bourgeois man of affairs, driven by neurotically vulgar ambitions for status and money, than the pilot, miner, reporter, and convivially equalitarian friend of vagabond-ish companions; more the product of the culture and of his own desires, aspirations, and psychological needs and disabilities than the regrettably warped victim of friends, relatives-by-marriage, and editors.

In his works that have been best liked, Clemens celebrated standard eastern moralities and ideologies. The Romantic cult of art hardly touched him—his materialist devotion was to the universal capitalist solvent: money. He held no exalted, unwavering vision of man's progress through religion, advances in science, or what J. A. Froude called "progressive intelligence," that is, evolution through man's own enlightened thinking. His shaky reliance was, rather, on a progress that might be achieved through technological innovations and entrepreneurial manipulations. He frequently undervalued the social subversions of his comedy and over-valued such sentimental works as *Joan of Arc* and his late, unimpressively grandiose, philosophical compositions. (He spoke more than once during his career of wishing to escape from "Mark Twain.") Toward the end of his life little that he wrote directly served what Freud called the pleasure principle.

The legendary Mark Twain belongs to the mythic substrate of America. To recognize this is to begin to understand the biases and the gusting emotions of hagiographic biographers and critics. The idealized, complex, highly adaptive image of Mark Twain has exacted an almost unqualified devotion, more so than have those of such less regularly empathetic figures as Davy Crockett, George Washington, and Benjamin Franklin. In Mark Twain we have erected an image of ourselves and then venerated it. We have admired ourselves as western adventurer, cracker-barrel philosopher, epigrammatist, humorist; as critic of established churches, hypocritical gentility, and the corrupting power of money. The hero of this myth of origins, this myth of national character, is, of course, a great hairy mammoth that never existed except as a projected image.

Freud understood, as nearly everyone now does, that the historian colors his record: "We must take into account what he unintentionally puts back into the past from the present or from some intermediate time, thus falsifying his picture of it." Freud noted, also conventionally, that the memories of a nation are analogous to recollections of childhood. Myths and legends may be protectively revised to take on the usefulness of screen memories.[3] But projected figures are not infinitely negotiable; normative forces operate. Clemens, it begins to appear, was more badly cast for his monumental role than are most heroes. Although it is difficult to topple monuments, he is unlikely to remain fixed eternally among the foremost in the company of our demigods.

The Mark Twain to come will be less suitable than the Mark Twain that is now being displaced for inflating America's self-esteem: only in political addresses is America the site of a shining idyll. He may, nevertheless, continue to stand among those figures who are more representative than, in the usual sense, heroic. Such tormented writers as Poe, Hawthorne, and Melville were inextricably American; and Samuel Clemens, bourgeois materialist and moral masochist, may well be destined to remain a mirror. We can continue to see ourselves in him: we spring from a like environment; we have our virtues and our defects; his ideologies are our ideologies—if we are infatuated with him, that is narcissism; if we despise him, that is self-hatred. What we shall no longer be comfortable in believing is that he was uniquely, wholesomely heroic, the marvellous child of American Nature in its untamed grandeur and, on that account, the author of a nearly flawless novel.

NOTES

▲ ▲ ▲ ▲ ▲ ▲ ▲ ▲

CHAPTER 1. THE CRITICAL BATTLEGROUND

1 *The Ordeal of Mark Twain* (New York: E. P. Dutton, 1920), 15; and *Days of the Phoenix* (New York: E. P. Dutton, 1957), 174.
2 See *The New America* (London: Cape, 1922), 34.
3 *America's Coming-of-Age* (New York: Huebsch, 1915), 9–10, 176, 179–80.
4 *The Literary History of the United States,* ed. Robert E. Spiller et al. (New York: Macmillan Co., 1948), 2:917.
5 *The Cycle of American Literature* (New York: Macmillan Co., 1955), 150–51.
6 James R. Vitelli, ed., in Brooks, *The Ordeal of Mark Twain* (New York: E. P. Dutton, 1970), xiii.
7 See William Wasserstrom, *The Legacy of Van Wyck Brooks* (Carbondale: Southern

230 NOTES TO PAGES 10-18

Illinois Univ. Press, 1971), 13, 68; and Wilson, "Mr. Brooks's Second Phase," *New Republic* 193 (Sept. 30, 1949): 452.

8 "The Americanism of Van Wyck Brooks," *Partisan Review* 6 (1939): 81.

9 *The Armed Vision* (New York: Alfred A. Knopf, 1948), 111.

10 *The Uneasy Chair: A Biography of Bernard DeVoto* (Garden City, N.Y.: Doubleday and Co., 1974), dedication.

11 *The Uneasy Chair,* 186; and Robert E. Spiller, ed., *The Van Wyck Brooks-Lewis Mumford Letters* (New York: E. P. Dutton, 1970), 286.

12 In the opening chapter of *The Literary Fallacy* (Boston: Little, Brown, 1944), DeVoto explains that he tried to avoid making Brooks the main target of that book but found he could not. DeVoto's published statements in praise of Brooks as the best of a bad lot may, however, have been tinged with insincerity. In a letter of April 29, 1944, he advised Winfield Townley Scott that Scott was correct in thinking that he, DeVoto, had overrated Brooks's books: "His mind seems to me to be effeminate, soft, and diabetic—with a sugar content altogether intolerable. For purposes of analysis I had to take him far more seriously than in reality I do." DeVoto explained that he wanted to make Lewis Mumford his focus in *The Literary Fallacy,* but Mumford's books were so bad that he could not. See *The Letters of Bernard DeVoto,* ed. Wallace Stegner (Garden City, N.Y.: Doubleday and Co., 1975), 130.

13 DeVoto's change in attitude toward Twain is most fully revealed in *Mark Twain at Work* (Cambridge: Harvard Univ. Press, 1942), but it is apparent, too, in his introduction to *The Portable Mark Twain* (New York: Viking, 1946). He delighted in what he took to be Brooks's reversal. In connection with his best summary characterization of Brooks's early thought, he remarks with satisfaction that Brooks first tacitly recanted and then specifically disavowed that thought. See *The Literary Fallacy,* 28 ff. At approximately the time that he was writing this, DeVoto commented adversely on *The Ordeal* in a letter of June 10, 1942, and added, "I think that Brooks now thinks just about as I do in regard to that book." DeVoto's late conversion is indicated in letters. See *The Letters of Bernard DeVoto,* 87, 197.

14 See *The Uneasy Chair,* 34; and "We Brighter People," *Harvard Graduates' Magazine* 39 (1931): 323–37. In his letter DeVoto echoes a quotation from J. B. Yeats, the artist father of W. B. Yeats, that Brooks included not in *The Ordeal* but in *America's Coming-of-Age.* The quotation (about fiddles tuning up all over America) impressed DeVoto as peculiarly foolish, and he referred to it several times in later writings.

15 *The Letters of Bernard DeVoto,* 68, 25.

16 For examples of Brooks's statements, see *Emerson and Others* (New York: E. P. Dutton, 1927), 234, 238, 240. For the Mumford observations, see *The Van Wyck Brooks-Lewis Mumford Letters,* 84, and *The Uneasy Chair,* 114, 140, 404, 412.

17 In *The Uneasy Chair,* 251–59, and in *The Letters of Bernard DeVoto,* 120–36, Wallace Stegner gives a view of DeVoto's lectures at Indiana University, the

book made from the lectures (*The Literary Fallacy*), and the essay by Lewis. Cousins published DeVoto's chapter in the *Saturday Review of Literature* 26 (April 8, 1944): 5–8, and Lewis's rejoinder in the next issue, 26 (April 15, 1944): 9–12. The largely inconsequential letters that followed began to appear in the issue for April 29.

18 *From the Shadow of the Mountain* (New York: E. P. Dutton, 1961), 196.

19 *The Uneasy Chair,* 144, 188–89, 257–79. Stegner says, page 115, that years earlier, within months of the publication of *Mark Twain's America*, DeVoto started planning a new edition that would moderate his attack on Brooks but that the new edition did not come until 1951, and when it did it incorporated no changes. In view of DeVoto's many repetitions of his charges against Brooks, it is hard to believe that he was very serious about relenting.

20 *Mark Twain's America* (Boston: Little, Brown, 1932), 41, n. 3.

21 Bellamy, *Mark Twain as a Literary Artist* (Norman: Univ. of Oklahoma Press, 1950), 30; Spiller, *Literary History of the United States* 2:1140; James R. Vitelli, *Van Wyck Brooks* (New York: Twayne Publishers, 1969), 89; Wasserstrom, *The Legacy of Van Wyck Brooks*, 25, 43; Hyman, *The Armed Vision*, 114–16.

22 *The Van Wyck Brooks-Lewis Mumford Letters,* 85, 87.

23 *Days of the Phoenix,* 172–74. By "literary history" Brooks had to mean *The Times of Melville and Whitman* (New York: E. P. Dutton, 1947). His only other statement of any length on Twain appeared (too late for him to be referring to it) in his biography of William Dean Howells: *Howells, His Life and World* (New York: E. P. Dutton, 1959), 78–90. In this short chapter, favorable in tone, he concentrates on the relationship between Howells and Twain.

24 *From the Shadow of the Mountain,* 85–88.

25 I am indebted to William Wasserstrom for sending me a paper by one of his students, whose name appears to have been lost, that identifies what the student takes to be the more important differences in the two editions of *The Ordeal*. I have used the parallel passages cited in coming to my own tentative conclusions.

26 See *Days of the Phoenix,* 172–74; and *From the Shadow of the Mountain,* 55. For the friendly dissent, see Lewis Leary, ed., *A Casebook on Mark Twain's Wound* (New York: Thomas Y. Crowell Co., 1962), 10–11; and *The Van Wyck Brooks-Lewis Mumford Letters,* 218–19.

27 Cowley, ed., in Brooks, *The Ordeal of Mark Twain* (New York: Meridian Books, 1955), 9.

28 "Mark Twain: An Unsentimental Journey," *The New Yorker* 36 (April 9, 1960): 167–78.

29 *The Ordeal,* 15. In the revised edition, Brooks rewrites this passage and omits the name of James: "A great writer of the past is known by the delight and stimulus which he gives to mature spirits in the present, and time, it seems to me, tends to bear out the familiar assertion that Mark Twain's appeal is largely an appeal to rudimentary minds." *The Ordeal of Mark Twain,* 2d ed. (New York: E. P. Dutton, 1933), 28. Had someone challenged Brooks to point out where James said any such thing? I find nothing like this in James, who was either noncom-

mittal, sympathetic, or complimentary in what he wrote about Clemens. He went so far as to remark that he found sublimity in *Life on the Mississippi*. Yet there may be some basis for Brooks's attribution. Justin Kaplan (who is sure that he did not read the 1920 edition of *The Ordeal*) could not in 1981 remember his source for an opinion attributed to James that he published in 1966: "James regarded Clemens' work as that of a buffoon and vulgarian." See Leon Edel, *Henry James: The Untried Years, 1843–1870* (New York: J. B. Lippincott, 1972), 36–39; Kaplan, *Mr. Clemens and Mark Twain* (New York: Simon and Schuster, 1966), 139; and a letter from Kaplan to Guy A. Cardwell, Nov. 1, 1981.

30 *The Uneasy Chair*, 288. For a characteristic statement by DeVoto contrasting what he thought of as his inductive method with the deductive method of Brooks, see *The Letters of Bernard DeVoto*, 62–63.

31 See Hugh Lloyd-Jones, "Gladstone on Homer," *Times Literary Supplement*, Jan. 3, 1975; and Antonia Fraser,"The Life of Charlotte Brontë," *Times Literary Supplement*, Jan. 24, 1975; and *A Casebook*, 32.

CHAPTER 2. AN ADAM FROM THE WESTERN GARDEN

1 An enormous literature treats the idea of nature and such related ideas as those of the earthly paradise and of the City of God. I have made use of a number of sources but list here only the volumes on which I have most depended: Durand Echeverria, *Mirage in the West: A History of the French Image of American Society to 1815* (Princeton: Princeton Univ. Press, 1957); Edwin Fussell, *Frontier: American Literature and the American West* (Princeton: Princeton Univ. Press, 1965); John Dixon Hunt, *The Figure in the Landscape: Poetry, Painting, and Gardening during the Eighteenth Century* (Baltimore: The Johns Hopkins Univ. Press, 1976); R. W. B. Lewis, *The American Adam: Innocence, Tragedy, and Tradition in the Nineteenth Century* (Chicago: Univ. of Chicago Press, 1955); Leo Marx, *The Machine in the Garden: Technology and the Pastoral Ideal in America* (New York: Oxford Univ. Press, 1964); Edmundo O'Gorman, *The Invention of America* (Bloomington: Indiana Univ. Press, 1961); Max F. S. Schulz, *Paradise Preserved: Recreations of Eden in Eighteenth- and Nineteenth-Century England* (Cambridge: Cambridge Univ. Press, 1985); and Henry Nash Smith, *Virgin Land: The American West as Symbol and Myth* (Cambridge: Harvard Univ. Press, 1950).

2 Robin M. Williams, Jr., *American Society: A Sociological Interpretation*, 2d ed. (1951; rev. ed., New York: Alfred A. Knopf, 1961), 8.

3 See *Mark Twain: The Critical Heritage*, ed. Frederick Anderson (New York: Barnes and Noble, 1971), 34–35, 51; *Mark Twain: A Biography* (New York: Harper and Bros., 1912), 3:1579; and John S. Tuckey, ed., *Mark Twain's Fables of Man* (Berkeley: Univ. of California Press, 1972), 20.

4 *Mark Twain-Howells Letters: The Correspondence of Samuel L. Clemens and Wil-*

liam D. Howells (Cambridge: Harvard Univ. Press, 1960), 1:xiv. For evidence on bowdlerizing, see Guy A. Cardwell, "The Bowdlerizing of Mark Twain," *ESQ* 21 (1975): 179–93.

5 See *The Complete Works of Ralph Waldo Emerson* (Boston: Houghton Mifflin Co., 1903), 5:273, and William Dean Howells, *Literary Friends and Acquaintance: A Personal Retrospect of American Authorship,* ed. David F. Hyatt and Edwin H. Cady (1st ed. 1900; Bloomington: Indiana Univ. Press, 1968), 57, 49, 28, 164.

6 See *Literary Friends and Acquaintance,* 164; and William Cooper Howells, *Recollections of Life in Ohio, from 1813 to 1840,* introd. William Dean Howells (Cincinnati: Robert Clarke Co., 1895), iii, vii, 144–45. William Cooper Howells, at the urging of his son, worked intermittently for ten or twelve years on these memoirs. When he left them unfinished at his death in 1894, Howells was sufficiently interested to revise them for publication, writing in his introduction that he valued them for "the perspective they afforded of the times and conditions long past away." He praised his father's often idealized memories as dealing with simple things: "Such as he depicts the early life of Eastern Ohio, the early life of America was every-where during the whole pioneer period."

7 See the Nevada City, Calif., *Nevada Democrat,* July 24, 1862; cited from Paul Fatout, *Mark Twain in Virginia City* (Bloomington: Indiana Univ. Press, 1964), 5–6.

8 See Mark Twain, *Early Tales & Sketches,* vol. 1, *1851–1864,* ed. Edgar Marquess Branch and Robert H. Hirst (Berkeley: Univ. of California Press, 1979), 1:33.

9 Olov W. Fryckstedt, *In Quest of America: A Study of Howells' Early Development as a Novelist* (Cambridge: Harvard Univ. Press, 1958), 15, 18, 24, 34–35, 39, 42, 210, et passim. Fryckstedt traces nuances and shifts in Howells's attitudes toward the West, the East, and Europe.

10 Henry Nash Smith, a powerful critic of what he took to be the fossilized "dominant culture," cites Howells and adds, not, as we have seen, altogether correctly, that the *Atlantic* "represented the apex of civilization and refinement, whereas the Far West stood for 'barbarism.'" See *Mark Twain: The Development of a Writer* (Cambridge: Harvard Univ. Press, 1962), 92–93.

11 *My Mark Twain: Reminiscences and Criticisms,* ed. Marilyn A. Baldwin (New York, 1910; edited rpt. Baton Rouge: Louisiana State Univ. Press, 1967), 84. "My Mark Twain," Howells's major work on his recently dead friend, was first published as "My Memories of Mark Twain" in *Harper's Monthly Magazine,* July–Sept. 1910.

12 *Life in Letters of William Dean Howells,* ed. Mildred Howells (Garden City: Doubleday, Doran and Co., 1928), 1:221. The piece by Clemens that Howells liked was probably "Facts Concerning the Carnival of Crime in Connecticut," and the Holmes poem was "How the Old Horse Won the Bet."

13 For statements by Twain and by others on his reading, I depend primarily on the following sources: Olin H. Moore, "Mark Twain and Don Quixote," *PMLA* 37 (June 1922): 324–46; Alan Gribben, *Mark Twain's Library: A Reconstruction* (Boston: G. K. Hall, 1980), 1:xvii–xx; 371–72; and *My Mark Twain.*

14 *Mark Twain-Howells Letters* 2:533.

15 *Mark Twain's Notebooks & Journals,* ed. Frederick Anderson et al. (Berkeley: Univ. of California Press, 1979), 3:343.

16 *Mark Twain's Library.* See also *Frontmatter, Book News from G. K. Hall and Co.* 2, no. 2 (February 1980). Gribben examined more than seven hundred volumes that have survived from Clemens's personal library, which included more than twenty-five hundred titles. He looked, too, at books which Clemens borrowed from friends and libraries. His descriptive notes include Clemens's comments and marginalia and comments by others on Clemens's reading. Some of the books listed by Gribben belonged to Clemens's wife or daughters.

CHAPTER 3. AFFINES AND BUSINESS

1 *Mark Twain: The Man and His Work* (rev. ed., Norman: Univ. of Oklahoma Press, 1961), 156, n. 10.

2 See, for example, Edmund R. Leach, "The Structural Implications of Matrilineal Cross-Cousin Marriage," *Journal of the Royal Anthropological Institute of Great Britain and Ireland* 81 (1951): 23–55, esp. 40–46; Edmund R. Leach, *Political Systems of Highland Burma* (London: G. Bell and Son, 1954), 74, 78, 84, 153, 169, 257; and Luc de Heusch, "The Debt of the Maternal Uncle: Contribution to the Study of Complex Structures of Kinship," *Man,* n.s. 9 (Nov. 4, 1974): 609–719.

3 *The Standard Edition of the Complete Psychological Works of Sigmund Freud,* ed. James Strachey et al. (London: Hogarth Press and the Institute of Psycho-Analysis, 1953–74), 7:150. Matter taken from Freud in the paragraphs immediately below is from 13:13–17. When Freud turns from common observation and anthropology to the findings of psychoanalysis to produce reasons for tensions between son-in-law and mother-in-law, his propositions lose, so far as I can tell, all relevance with respect to Clemens.

4 *Mark Twain's Autobiography,* ed. A. B. Paine (New York: Harper and Bros., 1924), 2:190.

5 *The Love Letters of Mark Twain,* ed. Dixon Wecter (New York: Harper and Bros., 1949), 270.

6 *Crowding Memories* (Boston: Houghton Mifflin Co., 1920), 152.

7 The letter of February 27, 1869, to Livy, then his fiancée, appears in *Love Letters,* 67–72. The pseudo-letter first appeared edited by Bernard DeVoto in *Harper's Magazine* 192 (Feb. 1946): 106–09.

8 See letters of September 3, 1869, January 13, 1870, and January 14, 1870, *Love Letters,* 106–08, 134–37, 137–39.

9 S. C. Webster, *Mark Twain, Business Man* (Boston: Little, Brown, 1946), 102.

10 *Memories of a Hostess,* ed. M. A. DeW. Howe (Boston: Little, Brown, 1946), 102.

11 Letter of May 17, 1869, *Love Letters,* 95–96.

12 Letter of about December 1, 1868, *Love Letters,* 36.

13 Letter of December 29, 1868, *Love Letters,* 36. Jervis Langdon would seem to have been an easy man to like. A sympathetic account of his life (1809–70) is given by Thomas K. Beecher, his pastor, in a memorial address. Beecher says that Langdon was modest, persevering, industrious, honorable, and philanthropic. He started as a clerk in a country store, changed occupations several times, and became rich (after making and losing several small fortunes) during the last decade of his life. It was only for that last decade that the Langdons moved from "a modest little house on Union Street" to the handsome mansion that they occupied when Clemens courted Livy. See the privately printed pamphlet, *Jervis Langdon, Died on Saturday the Sixth of August, 1870.*

14 Letter of December 1, 1868, *Mark Twain to Mrs. Fairbanks,* ed. Dixon Wecter (San Marino, Calif.: Huntington Library, 1949), 52–53.

15 *Love Letters,* 65–67. Seventeen letters from Clemens to Mrs. Langdon ranging in time from November 19, 1869, to December 27, 1889, are held by the Mark Twain Memorial, Hartford, Conn.

16 *My Father Mark Twain* (New York: Harper and Bros., 1931), 72, 87.

17 Justin Kaplan, *Mr. Clemens and Mark Twain* (New York: Simon and Schuster, 1966), 305.

18 *Mark Twain to Mrs. Fairbanks,* 137.

19 *Mark Twain-Howells Letters: The Correspondence of Samuel L. Clemens and William D. Howells,* ed. Henry Nash Smith and William M. Gibson (Cambridge: Harvard Univ. Press, 1960), 2:574.

20 Dewey Ganzel, *Mark Twain Abroad: The Cruise of the Quaker City* (Chicago: Univ. of Chicago Press, 1968), 21–22, 304; *Mark Twain's Notebooks & Journals,* ed. Frederick Anderson et al. (Berkeley: Univ. of California Press, 1975), 1:331 (hereafter cited as *Notebooks*).

21 *Traveling with the Innocents Abroad,* ed. Daniel M. McKeithan (Norman: Univ. of Oklahoma Press, 1958), 23–25.

22 Robert D. Jerome and Herbert A. Wisbey, Jr., *Mark Twain in Elmira* (Elmira, N. Y.: Mark Twain Society, Inc., 1977), 4, 52, 203–05.

23 *Notebooks* 3:457; Kaplan, *Mr. Clemens and Mark Twain,* 302; *Mark Twain's Letters to His Publishers,* ed. Hamlin Hill (Berkeley: Univ. of California Press, 1967), 360–61.

24 See Kaplan, *Mr. Clemens and Mark Twain,* 302; and *Notebooks* 3:457, 459, 514–16. Fifteen letters from Clemens to Charles J. Langdon are held by the Mark Twain Memorial, Hartford, Conn. They range in time from June 17, 1879, to December 12, 1908.

25 *Mark Twain's Letters to His Publishers,* 357–61; *Love Letters,* 270; *Mr. Clemens and Mark Twain,* 320; and *Mark Twain's Correspondence with Henry Huttleston Rogers, 1893–1909,* ed. Lewis Leary (Berkeley: Univ. of California Press, 1969), 158–59.

26 *Mark Twain's Correspondence with Henry Huttleston Rogers,* 342.

27 *Mark Twain-Howells Letters* 1:236–37, 238–39. The late Frederick A. Anderson

in a letter of March 16, 1978, to Guy A. Cardwell wrote that the cancellation in this letter is so difficult to decipher that Clemens must have meant for it to be unreadable.

28 *Love Letters,* 68–69. This passage has been cut by the editor, but its puzzling nature almost surely derives from unknown aspects of the context, not from the omissions. Other letters to Livy make plain that Clemens and Livy were friendly with the Slees.

29 *Mark Twain's Autobiography* 2:135–36; and *Mr. Clemens and Mark Twain,* 96–97.

30 *Love Letters,* 108–09.

31 See letter of September 3, 1869, *Love Letters,* 108–09; Louis J. Budd, *Mark Twain: Social Philosopher* (Bloomington: Univ. of Indiana Press, 1962), 41–42; and *Notebooks* 2:302–33.

32 *Harper's Magazine* 192 (Feb. 1946): 196–99.

33 *Mark Twain's Notebook,* ed. A. B. Paine (New York: Harper and Bros., 1935), 235.

34 *Report from Paradise,* ed. Dixon Wecter (New York: Harper and Bros., 1952), 87–94.

35 *What Is Man? and Other Philosophical Writings,* ed. Paul Baender (Berkeley: Univ. of California Press, 1973), 65–70; n., 538–40. In a letter of May 17, 1978, to Guy A. Cardwell, Baender writes that Andrew Langdon's being a nephew of Jervis Langdon is confirmed by his obituary notice in the Buffalo *Express* and by a genealogy that Andrew himself prepared for the Buffalo Historical Society. His father was John LeDroit Langdon (b. 1806). Clemens mentioned Andrew Langdon vaguely in 1906, calling him "a relative of the Langdon family." See *Mark Twain's Autobiography* 2:104.

36 *What Is Man? and Other Philosophical Writings,* 539. A possibly relevant entry is to be found in Clemens's notebooks. On November 12, 1881, Clemens thought of Louise Messina (otherwise unidentified) for the first time in three years. On November 14 he received a letter of November 12 from Andrew Langdon addressed from Chicago. The letter asked indirectly for a contribution of money for Louise Messina. So far as the entry goes, Clemens's interest centered on the coincidence involved. See *Notebooks* 2:402.

37 *Mr. Clemens and Mark Twain,* 94; n., 394. Kaplan believes that the letter of February 27 was "the first of several such comments, increasingly bitter" about the family coal business." As we have seen, however, the "Letter from the Recording Angel" has no bearing, nor do texts that Kaplan cites in a letter to me of November 1, 1981. (See "Open Letter to Commodore Vanderbilt," *Packard's Monthly,* March 1869, with a rejoinder in the April issue; "Revised Catechism," New York *Tribune,* September 27, 1871; and "King Leopold's Soliloquy," which has been reprinted many times.) Kaplan generously concedes that his citations may not support the case he attempted to make in *Mr. Clemens and Mark Twain.* What his references and others like them in fact demonstrate is that Clemens sometimes condemned heartless and corrupt practices that gave business a bad name.

38 Edmund R. Leach, "Anthropological Aspects of Languages: Animal Categories and Verbal Abuse," in *New Directions in the Study of Language,* ed. Eric H. Linneberg (Cambridge: Massachusetts Institute of Technology, 1964), 37–38.
39 Hamlin Hill, *Mark Twain: God's Fool* (New York: Harper and Row, 1973), 90.
40 *My Father Mark Twain,* 290. Information on Clemens's estate appears in the *Twainian* (July-August 1965): 1–4.
41 *Mark Twain's Autobiography* 2:42.

CHAPTER 4. ART AND MONEY

1 James A. Henrietta, "Families and Farms: *Mentalité* in Pre-Industrial America," *The William and Mary Quarterly,* 3d series, 35 (Jan. 1978): 3, 9.
2 Chap. 14 of vol. 2 ("De l'industrie littéraire").
3 A. B. Paine, *Mark Twain: A Biography* (New York: Harper and Bros., 1912), 2:519; and *My Mark Twain: Reminiscences and Criticisms* (New York: Harper and Bros., 1910), 80.
4 *Mark Twain: A Biography* 1:519.
5 *The Ordeal of Mark Twain* (New York: E. P. Dutton, 1920), 43, et passim.
6 *Mark Twain's America* (Boston: Little, Brown, 1932), 117–21, 192–98, 229–31; and Wallace Stegner, *The Uneasy Chair: A Biography of Bernard DeVoto* (Garden City, N.Y.: Doubleday and Co., 1974), 91, 128, 145–46, 237, 339.
7 See *Mark Twain, Business Man* (Boston: Little, Brown, 1946); *Mark Twain in Eruption: Hitherto Unpublished Pages about Men and Events,* ed. Bernard DeVoto (New York: Harper and Bros., 1940), 165–95; and Hamlin Hill, ed., *Mark Twain's Letters to His Publishers, 1867–1894* (Berkeley: Univ. of California Press, 1967), 2–8.
8 *Mr. Clemens and Mark Twain* (New York: Simon and Schuster, 1966), 94–97; and *Mark Twain's Letters to His Publishers,* 2–3.
9 *Mark Twain: God's Fool* (New York: Harper and Bros., 1973), xix–xx, xxii. Additional evidence may be found in *Mark Twain's Correspondence with Henry Huttleston Rogers, 1893–1900,* ed. Lewis Leary (Berkeley: Univ. of California Press, 1969); and in *Mark Twain's Notebooks & Journals, (1883–1891),* ed. Frederick Anderson et al. (Berkeley: Univ. of California Press, 1979), vol. 3, esp. pp. 1–3, 62, 175–77, 225–26, and 297–99. (Hereafter cited as *Notebooks.*)
10 Edward Wagenknecht, *Mark Twain: The Man and His Work,* 3d ed. (Norman: Univ. of Oklahoma Press, 1960), 142–43.
11 *Mr. Clemens and Mark Twain,* 61.
12 *Mark Twain to Mrs. Fairbanks,* ed. Dixon Wecter (San Marino, Calif.: Huntington Library, 1949), 203–04. The letters to Mrs. Fairbanks supply additional evidence of this kind, as does *The Love Letters of Mark Twain,* ed. Dixon Wecter (New York: Harper and Bros., 1949).
13 *Mark Twain: A Biography* 1:287, 339.
14 See letter of February 13, 1869, in *Love Letters,* 65. Clemens defended himself in this letter and in a letter of February 5 to his family, page 64, against the

supposition that he was marrying for money. He wrote similarly on "St. Valentine's, 1869," that is, on February 14, to Joseph Twichell. See *Mark Twain to Mrs. Fairbanks,* 74, 101, 102. For Paine's remarks, see *Mark Twain: A Biography* 2:728.

15 See Edith Colgate Salisbury, *Susy and Mark Twain: Family Dialogues* (New York: Harper and Row, 1965), 23; Everett Emerson, *The Authentic Mark Twain: A Literary Biography of Samuel L. Clemens* (Philadelphia: Univ. of Pennsylvania Press, 1984), 192; *Mark Twain: A Biography* 2:929–31; and *Mark Twain's Correspondence with Henry Huttleston Rogers,* 335, 365, et passim.

16 Letter of January 1, 1879, in *Susy and Mark Twain,* 95.

17 *Love Letters,* 164–69; and *Mark Twain: A Biography* 2:730. Justin Kaplan notes that "by 1881 Mark Twain's scale of living was so high that just running the house and providing champagne, canvasbacks, fillets of beef, and ice-cream cherubs for his procession of visitors cost about as much as he earned from royalties and investments." *Mr. Clemens and Mark Twain,* 235.

18 Letter of February 17, 1878, in *Mark Twain's Letters,* ed. A. B. Paine (New York: Harper and Bros., 1917), 1:319.

19 Ibid.

20 *Mark Twain's Correspondence with Henry Huddleston Rogers,* 181–82.

21 See *Mark Twain: A Biography* 2:996; and *Mark Twain's Correspondence with Henry Huttleston Rogers,* 126.

22 See *Mark Twain's Letters to His Publishers,* 6–7, 364. Various figures are given for the total amount that Clemens paid to creditors; the total given above is taken from *Mark Twain's Correspondence with Henry Huttleston Rogers,* 242, n. 1.

23 See *Mark Twain: A Biography* 2:903–15; and *Mark Twain's Correspondence with Henry Huttleston Rogers,* 31–43, et passim.

24 See *Mark Twain: A Biography* 2:907–08; *Love Letters,* 256, 264, 265; *Mr. Clemens and Mark Twain,* 304; and Clara Clemens, *My Father Mark Twain* (New York: Harper and Bros., 1931), 108–09.

25 *Mark Twain: A Biography* 2:186–87.

26 Letter of July 31, 1894, in *Love Letters,* 308–09. See also *Love Letters,* 298; *Mark Twain: A Biography* 2:983–85; *Mr. Clemens and Mark Twain,* 330; and *Mark Twain's Correspondence with Henry Huttleston Rogers,* 25. On occasions unrelated to the bankruptcy, Livy sometimes commented on her husband's being considered hard in business affairs: "Do be careful in your dealings with people with the magazines and all that you do not drive too close a trade with them. Be generous my darling, even if we are as poor as church mice. Don't let anyone have the chance to say that you look too closely after your own interest." "Family Letters of the 1890's," ed. Chester L. Davis, *Twainian* 36 (Nov.-Dec. 1977): 1–4.

27 *Mark Twain's Correspondence with Henry Huttleston Rogers,* 153–59.

28 Paine cut drastically the statement to the *Times,* but it appears in damaging entirety in the collection of Clemens's letters to Rogers. Louis Budd adds additional information, as about Clemens's tirelessness in giving self-exculpatory interviews. See *Mark Twain: A Biography* 2:1006–07; *Mark Twain's Corre-*

spondence with Henry Huttleston Rogers, 181; Budd, *Our Mark Twain: The Making of His Public Personality* (Philadelphia: Univ. of Pennsylvania Press, 1983), 125–26; and *Mr. Clemens and Mark Twain,* 330.

29 For some of Clemens's expressions of guilt followed by fury, see *My Father Mark Twain,* 179; and *Love Letters,* 317, 320–28.

30 *Mark Twain's Correspondence with Henry Huttleston Rogers,* 244; Dennis Welland, *Mark Twain in England* (London: Chatto and Windus, 1978), 15; *Mark Twain: God's Fool,* 33; *Mr. Clemens and Mark Twain,* 329.

31 *Mark Twain: A Biography* 2:1044; *Mark Twain's Correspondence with Henry Huttleston Rogers,* 244, 282–90, 293; *Mr. Clemens and Mark Twain,* 348–49; *Our Mark Twain,* 130–33.

32 *My Mark Twain,* 55.

33 Henry Nash Smith, ed., *Mark Twain of the Enterprise* (Berkeley: Univ. of California Press, 1957), 23. For details immediately below, see *Mark Twain's Letters* 2:92; *Mark Twain: A Biography* 3:1371–72; *Love Letters,* 276, 319; and *Susy and Mark Twain,* 339.

34 See, for example, *The Psychoanalysis of Fire,* ed. Ernest Bornemann (New York: Urizen Books, 1976), 254, 259, 320–22, 236; and *Notebooks* 3:520, 521, 525, et passim.

35 *My Father Mark Twain,* 34; *Mark Twain: A Biography* 2:725; *Mark Twain of the Enterprise,* 16, 47, 203; and Stephen Fender, "'The Prodigal in a Far Country Chawing of Husks': Mark Twain's Search for a Style in the West," *The Modern Language Review* 71 (Oct. 1976): 739.

36 *Mr. Clemens and Mark Twain,* 18. Kaplan may exaggerate in saying that all his life Clemens liked to fantasize about small men with giant strength; but the raftsmen passage in *Life on the Mississippi* contains an example, and even more apropos is a notebook entry: "Write a story for boys about a *small* man with (unsuspected) gigantic strength—always surprising people with it." *Notebooks* 2:377.

37 *Mark Twain's Fables of Man,* ed. John S. Tuckey (Berkeley: Univ. of California Press, 1972), 18–29, 315–85.

38 Letter of May 1, 1977, from Dr. Gerard Fountain to Guy A. Cardwell. I am indebted to Dr. Fountain for reading parts of this chapter that touch on gambling as a neurosis. I am similarly indebted to Dr. Paul Graves Myerson.

39 *The Psychoanalytic Theory of Neurosis* (New York: W. W. Norton and Co., 1945), 372–73. Much the same things said by Fenichel are also said by Alfred H. Stanton under the heading "Personality Disorders," in *The Harvard Guide to Modern Psychiatry,* ed. Armand M. Nicholi, Jr. (Cambridge: Harvard Univ. Press, 1978), 291–92. Stanton adds that the gambling is usually accompanied by inhibition of normal sexual responses.

40 *The Psychology of Gambling* (New York: International Universities Press, 1958), 70–71, 79–82, et passim.

41 Clemens probably first met Hawley on March 6, 1869. The story of Hawley and his association with Clemens may be revived from a number of sources. See *Love*

Letters, 81; *Mark Twain-Howells Letters: The Correspondence of Samuel L. Clemens and William D. Howells* (Cambridge: Harvard Univ. Press, 1960), 1:133, 277–78, 2:501, 502, 597–98, 864–65; *Mark Twain to Mrs. Fairbanks*, 73–74; and the indices to his published notebooks. Information about Hawley and the exhibition may be found in Joseph and Frances Gies, *The Ingenious Yankee* (New York: Thomas Y. Crowell, 1976), 6–10, and in numerous reports, including, especially, U.S. Centennial Commission, *Reports of the President, Secretary, and Executive Committee, together with the Journal of the Final Session of the Commission* (Philadelphia: J. B. Lippincott, 1879).

42 *Mark Twain to Mrs. Fairbanks*, 199, 202; and *Love Letters*, 249–50.

43 Letter of June 12, 1870, in *Mark Twain, Business Man*, 114–15. One critic observes that Clemens interested himself in machines much as a poet does in poems: the machines are devices for creating order from chaos. Clemens is supposed to have preferred that the Paige typesetter not be finished; thus he would not be forced out of the world of mechanics into that of capitalists. The first notion seems to be a restatement of what Clemens himself said about inventions and poetry (see below). The second parallels in a distorted way the idea that the pathological gambler wishes to lose. See Tom Burnam, "Mark Twain and the Paige Typesetter: A Background for Despair," *Western Humanities Rev.* 6 (1951–52): 29–30.

44 *Mark Twain: A Biography* 2:910.

45 *Mark Twain in Eruption*, 9. Other references to inventions are similarly enthusiastic. For example, a brief paean of 1888 praises inventors as having made England great; and Clemens gave sometimes testy answers to charges that mechanical typesetters would throw printers out of work. See *Notebooks* 3:191–92, 197, 399–400, 437.

46 *Mark Twain, Business Man*, 137, 218–20; *Mark Twain: A Biography* 2:752–54; *Mark Twain-Howells Letters* 1:438–40.

47 Information about Clemens's losses appears in many sources, including *Mark Twain: A Biography* 1:434; and *Mark Twain: God's Fool*, 32–33, 44, 60.

48 *Mark Twain: A Biography* 2:725–30, 1056–58; 3:1150–52; *Mark Twain: God's Fool*, 259. Some of Clemens's many investments were not outright gambles. For a list of his holdings at the beginning of 1883, see *Notebooks* 2:491.

49 See *Mark Twain: A Biography* 2:725, 903; *Love Letters*, 119–21, 361; *Mark Twain to Mrs. Fairbanks*, 114.

50 Although Paine sets the end of January 1898 as a final date for paying off creditors, Rogers did not settle all undisputed obligations until some time in March, and on March 17 Clemens wrote that on March 15 he had first heard of the "big fish" (American rights to an invention by Jan Szczepanik) that he landed two days later. *Mark Twain: A Biography* 2:1056; *Mark Twain's Correspondence with Henry Huttleston Rogers*, 320–27.

51 *Mark Twain to Mrs. Fairbanks*, 236; *Notebooks* 3:601–02; *Love Letters*, 270; *Mark Twain's Correspondence with Henry Huttleston Rogers*, 20; *Mark Twain: A Biography* 2:966.

52 By March 14, 1899, Rogers had built Clemens's capital up to $51,995. For this

and additional information, see *Mark Twain's Correspondence with Henry Hut-tleston Rogers,* 327–46; 392, n. 2.

53 *Mark Twain: A Biography* 2:728.

54 Ibid.

55 Georg Simmel, *The Philosophy of Money,* trans. Tom Bottomore and David Frisby from 2d German ed. of 1907; 1st ed. 1900 (London: Routledge and Kegan Paul, 1978), 322. Simmel—who has been criticized as being old-fashioned and too little grounded in economics—can be illuminating, nevertheless, on the philosophical aspects of money; and I follow him at several points.

56 *Notebooks* 2:62, 479.

57 *Mr. Clemens and Mark Twain,* 110, 124–29.

58 *Mark Twain: A Biography* 2:996; epigraph for chap. 13, *Pudd'nhead Wilson; Notebooks* 3:71, 433. The maxim appears in the notebooks and, slightly altered, in *Following the Equator,* chap. 56.

59 Bernard DeVoto arrived at an optimistic but— when superficially considered—not totally dissimilar conclusion. DeVoto believed that at the end of Clemens's life he came back from "the narrow edge between sanity and madness" after trying unsuccessfully in hundreds of manuscript pages to find a philosophical or narrative formula for ridding himself of feelings of guilt for the catastrophes that had beset him and his family. In *The Mysterious Stranger* he decided that nothing exists but "a homeless thought"; thus his own "smaller agony" and personal guilt were also a dream. And so, according to DeVoto, he "brought his talent into fruition and made it whole again." The weaknesses in DeVoto's extended argument are too many and too complex for examination here; I would observe only that Clemens could not bring *The Mysterious Stranger* to completion. DeVoto's interpretation seems to arise from a wish to appropriate for Clemens a version of the happy ending devised for Shakespeare by the critics who have treated his last plays as evidences of hard-won calm after tragic storm. *The Mysterious Stranger* is thus, like the latter part of Beethoven's Sixth Symphony, indicative of clearing skies—a flute's scale and shepherd's hymn. For lack of biographical and textual evidence, DeVoto's argument trails off into such verbiage as "surcease of sorrow," "travail," "autumnal pity and compassion," "the silver echo of mortality," and "the thread of pain." *Mark Twain at Work* (Cambridge: Harvard Univ. Press, 1942), 117–30.

60 *Mark Twain's Letters* 2:640–41.

61 *Mark Twain's Fables of Man,* 129–30, 131–32.

CHAPTER 5. OLIVIA, GENDER, AND TASTE

1 See Brooks, *The Ordeal of Mark Twain* (New York: E. P. Dutton, 1920); and DeVoto, *Mark Twain's America* (Boston: Little, Brown, 1932).

2 "The Case for Mark Twain's Wife," *University of Toronto Quarterly* 9 (October 1939): 9–21.

3 *Mark Twain: The Fate of Humor* (Princeton: Princeton Univ. Press, 1966), 65–67.

4 The defense of Twain against charges of submitting to injurious censorship is given its fullest form in an essay by James M. Cox. Cox erects an elaborate structure of interpretation that is, I think, quite at odds with Clemens's life and writings. Stuart M. Tave in *The Amiable Humorist* (Chicago: Univ. of Chicago Press, 1960) described a type of humor that developed in England during the eighteenth and early nineteenth centuries. Taking a leaf from Tave, Cox argues that Clemens's assumption of the role of suppliant was not "a sell-out" but part of his marvellous amiability. He was playing a part, humoring his audience. In actuality, the southwestern comedy that was the basis for Twain's humor was markedly not amiable; and Twain gloried in verbal aggressions, diatribes, invective, and abuse. See "Humor and America: The Southwestern Bear Hunt, Mrs. Stowe, and Mark Twain," *Sewanee Rev.* 83 (Oct.-Dec. 1975): 573–601, esp. 597–98.

5 "Bret Harte and Mark Twain in the Seventies," *Atlantic Monthly* 130 (September 1922): 348.

6 *Mark Twain's Notebooks & Journals,* ed. Frederick Anderson et al. (Berkeley: Univ. of California Press, 1975), 2:96; and Mark Twain, "Chapters from My Autobiography," *North American Rev.* 185 (August 2, 1907): 689–90. Extended evidence that Olivia was the parent with authority may be had from Clemens's "A Record of the Small Foolishnesses of Bay and Susie Clemens," the Clifton Waller Barrett Collection, Alderman Library of the University of Virginia; and Caroline Thomas Harnsberger, *Mark Twain: Family Man* (New York: Citadel Press, 1960), 61. For Clemens's complaint, made in a letter to Richard Watson Gilder, see Albert Bigelow Paine, *Mark Twain: A Biography* (New York: Harper and Bros., 1912), 3:1221.

7 *Mark Twain's Notebook* (New York: Harper and Bros., 1935), 67–68.

8 See Dixon Wecter, ed., *Mark Twain to Mrs. Fairbanks* (San Marino, Calif.: Huntington Library, 1949), iii, xxi, xxv–xxvi; *Mark Twain & Huck Finn* (Berkeley: Univ. of California Press, 1960), 29–39; and *Mr. Clemens and Mark Twain* (New York: Simon and Schuster, 1966), 44–45.

9 *Mark Twain Abroad: The Cruise of the Quaker City* (Chicago: Univ. of Chicago Press, 1968), 17, 18, 88–89, 92, 272–74. Ganzel offers conflicting opinions on the capacities of Mrs. Fairbanks. He writes (page 18) that she possessed considerable grace, imagination, taste, perception, and discrimination. Later (pages 88–89 and 272–74) he says there is no evidence that she was an accomplished writer and that when Clemens thanked her for her help he was simply flattering her. Ganzel also writes that although Paine's position on Mrs. Fairbanks's influence was ludicrously wrong, it has been accepted by virtually every biographer. I cannot find that this is correct. I rely, however, on Ganzel for many details about the cruise.

10 *My Mark Twain: Reminiscences and Criticism* (New York: Harper and Bros., 1910), 170; from "Mark Twain: An Inquiry," first published in the *North American Review,* February 1901. *Mark Twain's America* and *Mark Twain at Work* (Cambridge: Harvard Univ. Press, 1942), passim. *Mark Twain: The Man*

and His Work (New Haven: Yale Univ. Press, 1935), 51. *Mark Twain: Man and Legend* (Indianapolis and New York: Bobbs-Merrill Co., 1943), 121. *The Washoe Giant in San Francisco* (San Francisco: George Fields, 1938), 13. *The Literary Apprenticeship of Mark Twain* (Urbana: Univ. of Illinois Press, 1950), 26, 27, 62, 153, 186. *Mark Twain: A Collection of Critical Essays* (Englewood Cliffs: Prentice-Hall, 1963), 3.

11 "'The Prodigal in a Far Country Chawing of Husks': Mark Twain's Search for a Style in the West," *The Modern Language Review* 71 (Oct. 1976): 737–56.

12 Henry Nash Smith, *Mark Twain: The Development of a Writer* (Cambridge: Harvard Univ. Press, 1962), 13.

13 *Mark Twain: The Development of a Writer,* 13; and *Mark Twain: A Biography* 1:310.

14 *Mark Twain to Mrs. Fairbanks,* xxiii–xxiv, n. 2.

15 *Mark Twain to Mrs. Fairbanks,* 110; and *Mark Twain's Letters to His Publishers,* ed. Hamlin Hill (Berkeley: Univ. of California Press, 1967), 28. (Angle brackets indicate deletions.)

16 *Mark Twain to Mrs. Fairbanks,* xxii.

17 *Mark Twain's Letters,* ed. A. B. Paine (New York: Harper and Bros., 1917), 2:526–28.

18 See John S. Tuckey, ed., *Mark Twain's Fables of Man* (Berkeley: Univ. of California Press, 1972), 2–3.

19 *Mark Twain to Mrs. Fairbanks,* 21–22. References immediately below are to pages 28–29 and 33–34.

20 *The Love Letters of Mark Twain,* ed. Dixon Wecter (New York: Harper and Bros., 1949), 37.

21 Letter of March 11, 1871, *Mark Twain's Letters to His Publishers,* 57.

22 See *Mark Twain-Howells Letters: The Correspondence of Samuel L. Clemens and William D. Howells,* ed. Henry Nash Smith and William M. Gibson (Cambridge: Harvard Univ. Press, 1960), 1:49, 107–08; and Guy A. Cardwell, *Twins of Genius* (East Lansing: Michigan State College Press, 1953), 25.

23 *Memories of a Southern Woman of Letters* (New York: Macmillan Co., 1932), 85, 173–74.

24 See *Mark Twain: The Development of a Writer,* 104; and letters of January 14 and April 25, 1864, in *Mark Twain of the Enterprise,* ed. Henry Nash Smith (Berkeley: Univ. of California Press, 1957), 139, 182.

25 Branch, in *The Literary Apprenticeship of Mark Twain,* 191–93, refers to five articles, but I have found only three. Letters to the *Alta,* May 19, 1867, and to the New York *Sunday Mercury,* April 7, 1867, simply contain, among other things, summary reports on the controversy that Clemens provoked in St. Louis by his three newspaper articles. According to Annie Moffett Webster's memory of "a humorous literary duel between her Uncle Sam and a woman who signed herself 'Cousin Jenny,'" Clemens said privately that his task would have been easier if Cousin Jenny had not had all the arguments on her side. See S. C. Webster, *Mark Twain, Business Man* (Boston: Little, Brown and Co., 1946), 48.

26 *Love Letters,* 180.

27 *Europe and Elsewhere,* ed. A. B. Paine (New York: Harper and Bros., 1923), 24–30; and *Notebooks* 3:637.

28 *Mark Twain's Notebook,* 256.

29 *Mark Twain Speaking,* ed. Paul Fatout (Iowa City: Univ. of Iowa Press, 1976), 374–76.

30 The literature on this subject is extensive. For contemporary articles one may consult such sources as *The Westminster Review, Macmillan's Magazine, Dublin University Magazine,* and *Fraser's Magazine.* The fiction of the period is, of course, full of it, as may be seen in Jane Austen, the Brontës, Meredith's *Diana of the Crossways,* and, most especially, sentimental novels. For a brief review of English feminism and its sources, see John Killham, *Tennyson and "The Princess": Reflections of an Age* (London: Athlone Press of the Univ. of London, 1958).

31 *Lectures on Rhetoric and Belles Lettres* (Dublin, 1783), 1:13, 15–16.

32 See *Mark Twain to Mrs. Fairbanks,* xxiii; *Love Letters,* 304; and *Sam Clemens of Hannibal* (Boston: Houghton Mifflin Co., 1952), 176.

33 *Mark Twain & Huck Finn,* 31–32.

34 See Mildred Howells, *Life in Letters of William Dean Howells* (New York: Doubleday, Doran and Co., 1928), 1:12; and Edwin H. Cady, *The Road to Realism: The Early Years, 1837–1885, of William Dean Howells* (Syracuse: Syracuse Univ. Press, 1955), 75, 99.

35 Clara Clemens, *My Father Mark Twain* (New York: Harper and Bros., 1931), 67–68; and Edith Colgate Salsbury, *Susy and Mark Twain: Family Dialogues* (New York: Harper and Row, 1965), 313.

36 *My Mark Twain,* 41. For some of the facts about the *Tom Sawyer* matter, see *Mark Twain-Howells Letters* 1:90–113 et passim.

37 *Mark Twain: The Development of a Writer,* 99–100.

38 Reported by Frank Marshall White in *Outlook* 96 (Dec. 24, 1910): 961–67. See also Archibald Henderson, *Mark Twain* (New York: Frederick A. Stokes, 1910), 183.

39 Tony Tanner brings together for his own purposes a number of representative selections that indicate the seriousness with which Clemens attempted sublimity. See *The Reign of Wonder: Naivety and Reality in American Literature* (Cambridge: Cambridge Univ. Press, 1965), 104–26. See, too, for example, Clemens's letter of March 13, 1882, *Mark Twain to Mrs. Fairbanks,* 250.

40 Letter of March 13, 1882, *Mark Twain to Mrs. Fairbanks,* 250. Mrs. Partington, frequently bewildered by her nephew Ike, is a comic small-town character in a number of books by Benjamin P. Shillaber.

41 *Which Was the Dream?,* ed. John S. Tuckey (Berkeley: Univ. of California Press, 1967), 12, 28.

42 See *Mark Twain-Howells Letters* 2:689, 693, n. 2. See also *Mark Twain's Mysterious Stranger Manuscripts,* ed. William M. Gibson (Berkeley: Univ. of California Press, 1969), 16, or, for a more complete but less accurate text, *Mark Twain's Notebook,* 256.

43 See *The Elementary Forms of the Religious Life,* 2d ed., trans. Joseph Ward Swain; introd. Robert Nisbet (London: George Allen and Unwin, 1976); and Maurice Godelier, *Perspectives in Marxist Anthropology,* trans. Robert Brain (Cambridge: Cambridge Univ. Press, 1977).

44 *The Standard Edition of the Complete Psychological Works of Sigmund Freud,* ed. James Strachey et al. (London: Hogarth Press and the Institute of Psycho-Analysis, 1953–74), 13:18.

45 See especially *Mr. Clemens and Mark Twain* and *Mark Twain: God's Fool;* but even relatively idolatrous books cite incidents and letters that reveal strained relationships between daughters and parents. See, for example, Mary Lawton, *A Lifetime with Mark Twain: The Memories of His Faithful and Devoted Servant* (New York: Harcourt, Brace and Co., 1925); *My Father Mark Twain; Mark Twain Family Man;* and *Susy and Mark Twain.*

CHAPTER 6. SEXUALITY AND THE CLEMENSES

1 "Mark Twain and Sexuality," *PMLA* 71 (Sept. 1956): 596–616.

2 Moral masochism and a sense of guilt were so frequently manifested by Clemens and have been noted so often that it comes as a surprise when his expressions of feelings of guilt are considered by scholars to be in any way novel or without significance. For example, Arthur Scott comments on a poem that Clemens wrote on August 18, 1892, in memory of his daughter Susy: "Most original and most curious is the sense of guilt. . . ." See *On the Poetry of Mark Twain with Selections from His Verse* (Urbana: Univ. of Illinois Press, 1966), 31.

3 See A. B. Paine, *Mark Twain: A Biography* (New York: Harper and Bros., 1912), 1: 24–25; Dixon Wecter, *Sam Clemens of Hannibal* (Boston: Houghton Mifflin Co., 1952), 53; and Lewis Leary, ed., *Mark Twain's Correspondence with Henry Huttleston Rogers, 1893–1909* (Berkeley: Univ. of California Press, 1969), 144, n. 1.

4 *Mark Twain at Work* (Cambridge: Harvard Univ. Press, 1942), 102.

5 *The Standard Edition of the Complete Psychological Works of Sigmund Freud,* ed. James Strachey et al. (London: Hogarth Press and the Institute of Psycho-Analysis, 1953–66), 12:316; 19:141–45.

6 Michael G. Cooke, *Acts of Inclusion: Studies Bearing on an Elementary Theory of Romanticism* (New Haven: Yale Univ. Press, 1979), 165.

7 Letter of November 28, 1868, to Livy; and letter of January 23, 1869, to Twichell. *The Love Letters of Mark Twain,* ed. Dixon Wecter (New York: Harper and Bros., 1949), 26, 57.

8 Letter of March 1, 1869, *Love Letters,* 76.

9 *Love Letters,* 18–20.

10 Letter of January 6, 1869, *Love Letters,* 44.

11 This conception of the home has wide, much-discussed relationships. The cultivated Roman sought peace on his Sabine farm, the English poet of the seventeenth century debated the merits of the active and the contemplative life,

and English architects of the nineteenth century redesigned the country house to make it comfortable for visitors from London. See, for one discussion among many, Jenni Calder, *Women and Marriage in Victorian Fiction* (New York: Oxford Univ. Press, 1976).

12 A typical expression from Livy would be her postscript to a letter of January 20, 1902, from Clemens to Clara: "I adore you." *Love Letters,* 332.

13 *The Harvard Guide to Modern Psychiatry,* ed. Armand M. Nicholi, Jr. (Cambridge: Harvard Univ. Press, 1978), 219–20.

14 "Autograph Manuscript of Olivia Susan Clemens' Biography of Her Father," Clifton Waller Barrett Collection, Alderman Library, University of Virginia, page 1. Quoted widely.

15 E. C. Salsbury, *Susy and Mark Twain: Family Dialogues* (New York: Harper and Row, 1965), 326–27, 331–32, et passim.

16 *Susy and Mark Twain,* 372–73.

17 Caroline Thomas Harnsbarger, *Mark Twain: Family Man* (New York: Citadel Press, 1960), 140–42.

18 *Susy and Mark Twain,* 318–20, 322–23.

19 For relevant information about Clara, see Hamlin Hill, *Mark Twain: God's Fool* (New York: Harper and Bros., 1973), 48, 68, 85, 96–97, 105–06, 121–22, 146, 184–85, 203, et passim; and *Mark Twain: Family Man,* 142–43, 226–27, 233, 240, 269.

20 *Mark Twain-Howells Letters: The Correspondence of Samuel L. Clemens and William D. Howells,* ed. Henry Nash Smith and William M. Gibson (Cambridge: Harvard Univ. Press, 1960), 2:634, n. 2.

21 For references to Jean's circumstances, here and below, see *Mark Twain: God's Fool,* xxvi–xxvii, 120–21, 143, 144, 151– 52, 154–55, 167–79, 185–86, et passim; and *Mark Twain: Family Man,* 69, 252–53.

22 See, for example, Sigmund Freud, "Some Psychical Consequences of the Anatomical Distinction between the Sexes," *Standard Edition* 19:248–58.

23 *Mark Twain: God's Fool,* xxvii.

24 Clara Clemens, *My Father Mark Twain* (New York: Harper and Bros., 1931), 91–94.

25 *Mark Twain: Family Man,* 207.

26 *Mark Twain: God's Fool,* 44–45, 170–71. Clemens's attitude toward premarital sex may have been conditioned by memories of his sister Pamela, who is said by Rachel M. Varble to have been pregnant at the time of her marriage to William A. Moffett, which took place while both were on a visit in Kentucky. See *Jane Clemens: The Story of Mark Twain's Mother* (New York: Doubleday and Co., 1964), 201.

27 Letter begun on September 21, 1906, in *Mark Twain's Letters to Mary,* ed. Lewis Leary (New York: Columbia Univ. Press, 1961), 62–63.

28 For Miss Lyon's recollection, a long excerpt from Clara's letter, and Howells's response to Clemens, see *Mark Twain: God's Fool,* 146, and *Mark Twain-Howells Letters* 2:816–17.

29 *Love Letters,* 4.

30 Gordon S. Haight, "Male Chastity in the Nineteenth Century," *Contemporary Review* 219 (Nov. 1971): 252, 259. State and federal statutes intended to deter obscenity, which had come to mean sexual explicitness in art and in writing, were passed in the late 1830s and early 1840s. Anthony Comstock's crusades of the 1870s made obscenity a national issue. See W. Cody Wilson and Michael J. Goldstein, eds., "Pornography: Attitudes, Use, and Effects," *The Journal of Social Issues* 29 (1973): 8.

31 *The Psychoanalysis of Fire,* trans. Alan C. M. Ross (Boston: Beacon Press, 1964), 30.

32 See Richard Sennet, "The Desire to Know," *The New Yorker,* July 16, 1979, 101.

33 Mark Kinkead-Weekes, *Samuel Richardson, Dramatic Novelist* (London: Methuen and Co., 1973), 493–94.

34 For this and similar observations, see letters of December 11 and 12, 1873, and of January 2, 1874, *Love Letters,* 185–86.

35 See *Mark Twain: God's Fool,* 230–31 et passim for an account of Miss Lyon and of the treatment accorded her by the Clemenses.

36 Mark Twain, *Mark Twain's Travels with Mr. Brown,* ed. Franklin Walker and G. Ezra Dane (New York: Alfred A. Knopf, 1940), 41.

37 Notebooks, 32 I, 5, Mark Twain Papers. For excerpts and interpretations see *Mark Twain's Notebook,* ed. A. B. Paine (New York: Harper and Bros. 1935), 348–52; Justin Kaplan, *Mr. Clemens and Mark Twain* (New York: Simon and Schuster, 1966), 341–42; Arthur G. Pettit, *Mark Twain & the South* (Lexington: Univ. Press of Kentucky, 1974), 139, 141, 149, 151–53; and Susan K. Harris, *Mark Twain's Escape from Time* (Columbia: Univ. of Missouri Press, 1982), 138–39, n. 2.

38 *What Is Man? and Other Philosophical Writings,* ed. Paul Baender (Berkeley: Univ. of California Press for Iowa Center for Textual Studies, 1973), 407, 416–17; *Letters from the Earth,* ed. Bernard DeVoto (New York: Harper and Row, 1962), 17–18, 20; and *Mark Twain: A Biography* 3:1531–33. The "Letters" were written in 1909, first published in 1962.

39 *Standard Edition* 12:144, 174–76; 21:185, 193, n. 194; et passim.

40 Edward Wagenknecht, *Mark Twain: The Man and His Work* (New Haven, 1935; rev. ed., Norman: Univ. of Oklahoma Press, 1961), 148.

41 Van Wyck Brooks mentions this passage in *The Times of Melville and Whitman* (New York: E. P. Dutton, 1947), 289, identifying it as an instance of prudery. Maxwell Geismar, in *Mark Twain: American Prophet* (Boston: Houghton Mifflin, 1970), 61–62, mistakenly defends it as an instance of irony. Neither critic knew the antecedent passage in the notebooks.

42 *Mark Twain's Notebooks & Journals (1877–1883),* ed. Frederick Anderson et al. (Berkeley: Univ. of California Press, 1975), 2:319 (hereafter cited as *Notebooks*). "The Tribune" is a room in the Uffizi Gallery, Florence. For Clark's more relevant comments, see *The Painting of Modern Life: The Art of Manet and His Followers* (Princeton: Princeton Univ. Press, 1984), 93–136.

43 For some of the above details I depend on Charles Hope, "Renaissance Beauties," *New York Review of Books,* May 23, 1987, 35–37.

44 I cite these verses from the second edition (limited to nineteen copies) of the pamphlet printed in April 1937 for the Hammer and Chisel Club. My copy was furnished to me by the late Frederick Anderson, then editor of the Mark Twain Papers, enclosed in a letter of March 16, 1978. The verses, comments on the verses, and a letter by Clemens that accompanied them may be conveniently found in *The Mammoth Cod and Address to the Stomach Club,* intro. by Gershon Legman (Milwaukee: Maledicta Press, 1976), 15–27. Anderson places the lines as written after 1900, intended in all probability for a small group making a pleasure excursion on Henry H. Rogers's yacht. Legman places the poem as probably written in 1902 for such an excursion.

45 See *The Mammoth Cod and Address to the Stomach Club,* 22–25. Like "The Mammoth Cod," this sketch has been both privately printed and circulated in typescript. Paine mentions that Clemens addressed the Stomach Club in 1879. The editors of the second volume of the *Notebooks* write that when in Paris in 1879 Clemens "found a congenial group in the artists and literary men of the Stomach Club," and Clemens mentions the club several times. See *Biography* 2:643; and *Notebooks* 2:288, 318, 345, 350.

46 *What Is Man?,* 448–49; and *Letters from the Earth,* 49–51.

47 The passages in the King James Version of the Bible that Clemens may have had in mind with respect to pissing have nothing to do with any prohibition. See 1 Sam. 25:22, 34; 1 Kings 14:10, 16:11, 21:21; and 2 Kings 9:8. Merely the use of the word *piss* in the Bible seems to have affected him powerfully. In 1879 he set down a reminder of the time he read "that dreadful verse" (2 Kings 18:27) during family worship. See *Notebooks* 2:302–03. The only reference in the King James Version of the Bible to masturbation (or, more properly, coitus interruptus) that is mentioned by the usual concordances occurs in Genesis 38:9.

CHAPTER 7. IMPOTENCE AND PEDOPHILIA

1 That students of Mark Twain not immediately concerned with questions of sexuality are beginning to make comments that bear on problems such as that of probable impotence is a relatively recent development. For example, Stephen Fender, who studied the influence of the West on Clemens's prose style, observes that the story of the western years confirms previous understandings about the writer's personality: he was sexually repressed, had ambiguous feelings about his family, and liked to play unrealistic roles. (The "previous understandings" are not so well established as Fender implies.) See " 'The Prodigal in a Far Country Chawing of Husks': Mark Twain's Search for a Style in the West," *The Modern Language Review* 71 (Oct. 1976): 753.

2 *Mark Twain to Mrs. Fairbanks,* ed. Dixon Wecter (San Marino, Calif.: Huntington Library, 1949), xxvii; letter of September 18, 1881, 245.

3 *The Love Letters of Mark Twain,* ed. Dixon Wecter (New York: Harper and Bros., 1949), 319. The letter is to Susan Crane. A different kind of comment that has its own kind of interest but may not be used as evidence is an observation by James M. Cox on style. Cox believes that in late writings Clemens's voice takes on "strained tones of impotence and effeminacy." See "The Approved Mark Twain: The Beginning of the End," *Southern Review* 4 (Spring 1968): 548. Nor can we make much of a notebook entry for March (?), 1885: Clemens wrote (in German), "Before fifty: 'We're getting old.' After fifty: 'We've become old.'" See *Mark Twain's Notebooks & Journals,* ed. Frederick Anderson et al. (Berkeley: Univ. of California Press, 1975), 3:102 (hereafter cited as *Notebooks*). See also *Notebooks* 2:440–41 for two entries of possible relevance made in January 1882, one about a man who says, "Alas, I have no ⟨stones⟩ nuts"; and the other about a man whose character was said to be unique, but by the time the word reached him, it has become *eunuch*. Immediately before the first of these notes, Clemens remarks severely, "There are men who require in ⟨a⟩ the future wife two qualities, only—money & sex."

4 *What Is Man? and Other Philosophical Writings,* ed. Paul Baender (Berkeley: Univ. of California Press for Iowa Center for Textual Studies, 1973), 435–41; see also 409; or see *Letters from the Earth,* 37–42. In a note (*What Is Man?,* 439–40) Clemens recounts an example of stories of a common type about insatiable women, this one of "a buxom royal princess" of the Sandwich Islands. That the subject of the unsatisfiable woman had, for whatever reasons, its fascination for him is also indicated by a story in "1601," where other stories disparage the sexual powers of the human male.

5 *The Mammoth Cod and Address to the Stomach Club,* intro. by Gershon Legman (Milwaukee: Maledicta Press, 1976), 4, 5, 7, 10–11, 23.

6 Legman offers much the same speculative readings in his *Rationale of the Dirty Joke: An Analysis of Sexual Humor,* second series (New York: Breaking Point, Inc., 1975), 588, 591, and 755–58.

7 Clemens wrote "1601. Conversation, As It Was By the Social Fireside, in the Time of the Tudors" about 1876 in his study at Quarry Farm "one summer day" while "reading up" for *The Prince and the Pauper.* As printed by Erskine Scott Wood in 1882, the anecdote in question runs: "Now was Sr Walter minded of a tale hee once did hear ye ingenious Margrette of Navarre relate, about a maid, which beeing like to suffer rape by an olde archbishoppe, did smartly contrive a device to save her maydehedde, &said to him, , First, my lord,I prithee, take out thy holy tool & piss before me.' wch doing, lo hys member felle, &wolde not rise again." (Faulty spacing is as in the printed text, but raised letters are not reproduced here.) For a copy of Wood's edition, see the Clifton Waller Barrett Collection, Alderman Library, University of Virginia.

8 The story is incorporated in passages of the Autobiographical Dictation that adversely criticize Theodore Roosevelt. It facetiously offers a fictitious, analogical personal experience. A turkey hen tries over a period of several weeks to hatch out a porcelain egg. The gobbler then takes over, sits on the egg for two entire

summers, and at last hatches out of it a doll's tea set of fourteen pieces, "and all perfect except that the teapot had no spout, on account of the material running out." There is no more reason to suppose that the teapot without a spout refers to an impotent Clemens than to think that the fourteen pieces of the set are an accurate description of his fractured personality. See *Mark Twain in Eruption: Hitherto Unpublished Pages about Men and Events,* ed. Bernard DeVoto (New York: Harper and Bros., 1940), 23–24.

9 First published in the *Cosmopolitan* for August 1898 and first collected in 1900 in a revision of *How to Tell a Story and Other Essays.*

10 One version of these stanzas was published in *The Mammoth Cod and Address to the Stomach Club.* See pages 4 and 10–11. Gershon Legman, the editor, says that he received his copy of the poem from George Frederick Gundelfinger, an eccentric Yale alumnus, more than thirty years before he published it in 1976. A second version, with stanzas reversed and several differences in wording, is preserved at Yale. For information about the text at Yale I am indebted to a letter of March 8, 1978, from Donald Gallup, then curator, Collection of American Literature. The verses are part of the Freer gift of the Willard Morse Collection that went to the Beinecke Rare Book and Manuscript Library of the Yale University Library. Each of the two four-line stanzas is written on a slip of paper now inlaid to 8½ × 11-inch size. These stanzas, one of which I quote below, are published by Alan Gribben in his introduction to *Mark Twain's Rubáiyát* (Austin and Santa Barbara: Jenkins Publishing Co., 1983), 21.

11 Hamlin Hill, *Mark Twain: God's Fool* (New York: Harper and Bros., 1973), 128; and *Mark Twain's Letters to Mary,* ed. Lewis Leary (New York: Columbia Univ. Press, 1961), 101.

12 *Mark Twain: God's Fool,* 268.

13 *Enchantment: A Little Girl's Friendship with Mark Twain* (Norman: Univ. of Oklahoma Press, 1961).

14 *Mark Twain in the Movies: A Meditation with Pictures* (New York: Viking Press, 1977). The snapshots published by Seelye were preserved among the papers of Isabel V. Lyon.

15 *Mark Twain: God's Fool,* 268.

16 *My Father Mark Twain* (New York: Harper and Bros., 1931), 274. Clara is correct in supposing that beginning quite early Clemens had a special fondness for "children." In a notebook entry for July 1866 he wrote, "Young girls innocent & natural—*I* love 'em same as others love infants." The language here is strikingly suggestive of what I argue below to be two of the cultural explanations for common attitudes toward children—they are related to nature and to purity. The entry does not indicate that Clemens suffered from a psychoneurotic condition in 1866. By 1908, however, the situation was very different. In that year he wrote ninety-four letters to little girls, nearly half of his total correspondence. "Almost always they were long, chatty, childlike letters, frequently composed over a number of days. All pleaded for visits." See *Notebooks* 1:120; and *Mark Twain: God's Fool,* 195.

17 A. B. Paine, *Mark Twain: A Biography* (New York: Harper and Bros., 1912), 3:1440. Paine's position became the uncritical orthodoxy. In *Mark Twain: Man and Legend* (Indianapolis: Bobbs-Merrill Co., 1943), 313, John DeLancey Ferguson writes, "In his increasing loneliness he found the greatest happiness in the company of children, little girls for choice." Edward Wagenknecht explains, "But after his own girls had grown up or died, he turned to other little girls for solace, as if through them he wished to recapture the past." See *Mark Twain: The Man and His Work* (New Haven, 1935; rev. ed., Norman: Univ. of Oklahoma Press, 1961), 127.

18 *Mark Twain and the Happy Island* (Chicago: A. C. McClurg, 1913), 76; and *Mark Twain: God's Fool*, 203–04.

19 *Mark Twain: God's Fool*, 195.

20 Ibid., 128.

21 *Mark Twain in the Movies*, 101–02.

22 These propositions would appear to be both basic to psychoanalysis and commonsensical. Lord Raglan, who was not an analyst, made similar statements in *Jocasta's Crime: An Anthropological Study* (London: Methuen and Co., Ltd., 1933), 30.

23 "Three Theories of the Theory of Sexuality," *The Standard Edition of the Complete Psychological Works of Sigmund Freud*, ed. James Strachey et al. (London: Hogarth Press and the Institute of Psycho-Analysis, 1953–66), 7:148. Observations on pedophilia may be found in *The International Encyclopedia of Psychiatry, Psychology, and Neurology* 8:443; *The Harvard Guide to Modern Psychiatry*, ed. Armand M. Nicholi, Jr. (Cambridge: Harvard Univ. Press, 1978); Michael J. Goldstein, "Exposure to Erotic Stimuli and Sexual Deviance," *The Journal of Social Issues* 29, no. 3 (1973): 197–219; and P. H. Gebhard et al., *Sex Offenders: An Analysis of Types* (New York: Harper and Row, 1965).

24 *Sex Offenders*, 81.

25 Berl Kutchinsky, "The Effect of Easy Availability of Pornography on the Incidence of Sex Crimes: The Danish Experience," *The Journal of Social Issues* 29, no. 3 (1973): 163–81.

26 Valdemar Hartman, "Some Observations of Group Psychotherapy with Paedophiles," *Canadian Journal of Corrections* 4 (Oct. 1961): 492–99.

27 "Exposure to Erotic Stimuli and Sexual Deviance," 212, 217.

28 *Harvard Guide*, 461.

29 *Enchantment*, 45, 58, 189.

30 See *Holiday House: A Series of Tales*, 1st ed. 1839 (New York: Robert Carter and Bros., 1879), iii–vi.

31 See a memorial sketch dated February 1, 1906, in *Mark Twain's Autobiography*, ed. A. B. Paine (New York: Harper and Bros., 1924), 2:26. Clemens wrote something similar stressing girlishness to Mary Rogers on August 14, 1906. He also writes that by accident he had portrayed Mary as the Eve of his "Eve's Diary," an idealizing sketch that is often supposed to have been a portrait of Livy. It seems less than complimentary to Livy, at any rate, for Clemens to let

Mary understand that *she* was his ideal woman. See *Mark Twain's Letters to Mary,* 42.

32 Letter of March 24, 1874, *Mark Twain to Mrs. Fairbanks,* 186. The letter cited immediately below appears on pages 193–97. Dixon Wecter, the editor, called this "one of the most felicitous letters ever received by a debutante."

33 *Mark Twain: God's Fool,* 127. Clemens was distressed when Gertrude turned sixteen but still ventured to send her a kiss, though it came "within an ace of being improper! Now, back you go to 14! then there's no impropriety."

34 Jean H. Hagstrum, "Eros and Psyche: Some Versions of Romantic Love and Delicacy," *Critical Inquiry* 3 (Spring 1977): 521–42; and Hagstrum, "Blake and British Art: The Gifts of Grace and Terror," in *Images of Romanticism: Verbal and Visual Affinities,* ed. Karl Kroeber and William Walling (New Haven: Yale Univ. Press, 1978), 61–80, esp. 78–79. See also Webber, *Milton and His Epic Tradition* (Seattle: Univ. of Washington Press, 1979), 67, 69, 136.

35 Lorenz Eisner, "Cages, Prisons, and Captives in Eighteenth-Century Art," in *Images of Romanticism,* 15–19. That youthful innocence and vulnerability to sexual assault go hand in hand is a constant theme in such novels as Smollett's *Ferdinand Count Fathom* (1753).

36 Stephen Marcus, *The Other Victorians: A Study of Sexuality and Pornography in Mid-Nineteenth Century England* (New York: Basic Books, 1966), 15.

37 See, for example, *Mark Twain in the Movies* and Leslie Fiedler, "Come Back to the Raft Ag'in, Huck Honey," *Partisan Review* 15 (June 1948): 664–71.

38 See Russell Trainer, *The Lolita Complex* (New York: Citadel Press, 1966).

39 *Mark Twain: God's Fool,* 173–74. Hill cites a letter of November 4, 1947, from Carlotta Welles Briggs to Dixon Wecter. Hill further reports (pages 259–60) that Helen's preference for young men "affected Clemens with unseemly jealousy" and that Paine sequestered notes that Clemens wrote to her. Paine passes this matter over lightly. See *Biography* 3:1558.

40 See *Enchantment,* 69–70; and a letter of August 25–28, 1906, in *Mark Twain's Letters to Mary,* 48.

41 *Mark Twain and the Happy Island,* 110, 134.

42 *The Autobiography of Mark Twain: Including Chapters Now Published for the First Time,* ed. Charles Neider (New York: Harper and Bros., 1959), 368–70.

43 *Enchantment,* 14.

44 *Enchantment,* 67.

45 Letter of November 13, 1909, in *Mark Twain and the Happy Island,* 134–35. Much is made of the hugging and kissing in *Mark Twain in the Movies.*

46 See *Mark Twain's Satires & Burlesques,* ed. Franklin R. Rogers (Berkeley: Univ. of California Press, 1967), 185–200.

47 *Mark Twain and the Happy Island,* 144.

48 This possibility rests on a vague allegation in a letter of January 2, 1912, from Julian Street to A. B. Paine, now in the Henry E. Huntington Library, copy in the Mark Twain Papers at Berkeley. The letter quotes Albert Lee, an employee of Robert Collier (of *Collier's Magazine* and an intimate of Clemens's), as claiming to know something very terrible that had happened shortly before Clemens's

death. If true, drugs or alcohol could have had something to do with the matter, for Clemens seems to have used both to kill pain or to put himself to sleep. See *Mark Twain: God's Fool*, 261.

49 *Mark Twain in the Movies*, 101–03. For the relevant passages, see *Notebooks* 2:132, 134.

50 *Mark Twain and the Happy Island*, 172–73. Miss Illington (1881–1934) played leading roles in light comedies and in mystery plays. Miss Burke (1886–1970) married Florenz Ziegfeld, Jr., in 1914. She starred in light roles in the theater and was a success, too, in motion pictures.

51 I rely here on Karen Horney, who explores modern Western neuroticisms as in part the product of forces normal in our culture. See *The Neurotic Personality of Our Time* (New York: W. W. Norton and Co., 1937).

CHAPTER 8. TENDENTIOUS JOKES

1 *Mark Twain's Notebooks & Journals*, ed. Frederick Anderson et al. (Berkeley: Univ. of California Press, 1975), 1:7. The editors comment that the later notebooks "present an almost oppressive repetition of tag lines for anecdotes and expurgated dirty jokes which must have become excessively familiar to the companions to whom they were told." Simple citations below to any of the three volumes now published will be given within parentheses in the text, e.g., (2:136); references other than simple citations will use the shortened title, "*Notebooks*." The editors present Clemens's cancellations within angle brackets, indicate doubtful or marginally legible words by brackets, and replace illegible letters with dashes within brackets. In several instances I have simplified the full text for ease in reading.

2 See *Notebooks* 1:321, 331, and, possibly, 330. *Fornication* belonged for Clemens to a different linguistic category, and he boldly spelled it out, as on pages 336 and 344.

3 See *Jokes and Their Relation to the Unconscious*, trans. James Strachey (London: Routledge and Kegan Paul, 1960), 142–43. I shall not review, as many have, theories of comedy from Aristotle forward or suggest that Freud has said the last word on jokes. Remote as a number of distinguished anthropologists might consider themselves to be from Freud, the joking relationships (*parentés à plaisanteries*) with which they concern themselves, as one theory has it, are analogous to Freud's ideas in an important way: they involve antagonism (as well as friendliness) and constitute an outlet for relieving tension and obviating conflict. Continuingly useful in explicating this subject are articles by A. R. Radcliffe-Brown, especially "On Joking Relationships," *Africa* 13 (July 1940): 195–210; and "A Further Note on Joking Relationships," *Africa* 19 (April 1949): 122–40.

4 *Patriotic Gore: Studies in the Literature of the American Civil War* (New York: Oxford Univ. Press, 1962), 507–19.

5 Mary Douglas argues that *all* jokes subvert an accepted order and that the

beating of Thersites, apparently in defense of the dominant order, is in the light of the context not an exception to the rule: the leaders of the Greeks are the endangered element, facing possible mob action. See *Implicit Meanings: Essays in Anthropology* (London: Routledge and Kegan Paul, 1975), 99.

6 A. H. Maslow and Béla Mittelmann, *Principles of Abnormal Psychology: The Diagnosis of Psychic Illness* (1941; rev. ed., New York: Harper and Bros., 1951), 331–33.

7 *Notebooks* 3:302. Clemens inserts a query to himself above the line, wondering whether to revise "son's" to read "husband's." Later he reminds himself of this anecdote again, 3:369.

8 *Notebooks* 2:57, n. 30; 2:59. In a letter of January 30, 1879, Clemens wrote to Howells of *A Tramp Abroad* that he had "rung in that fragrant account of the Limberger cheese & the coffin-box full of guns" but wanted Howells's advice as to whether he should leave it out. For an account of the withholding from publication and publication of this anecdote, see *Mark Twain-Howells Letters,* ed. Henry Nash Smith and William M. Gibson (Cambridge: Harvard Univ. Press, 1960), 1:248, 251, n. 2; and 2:701, 702, n. 5.

9 *Notebooks* 3:24. "The ceiling is a crust of cut diamonds; the walls are single emeralds carved in arabesques; the floor a polished ruby. When he goes thither to sth, a Roman Emp precedes him with a torch, a Grand Lama of Thibet lifts up the, whilst a Pope of Rome asks a blessing—& when he goes to sthl. a Roman Emp carries the candle, Pope Alex VI lifts up the — for him & when he gets thro he — — — — with an Irishman."

10 *Notebooks* 2:541. In much the same category as this reportage is the story of "A Gourd Float." During a flood a little black girl falls off the roof of a cabin into the water, but her mother shows no anxiety: "Nebber mind, nebber mind. She's got a gou'd on." See *Notebooks* 2:573.

11 *Notebooks* 2:68. In December 1866 Clemens made notes for a similar story telling how Captain Edgar Wakeman, with whom he sailed from San Francisco en route to New York, administered croton oil to an obnoxious Jew. See *Notebooks* 1:260, 263–64, 266–67.

12 See *Notebooks* 3:303. Clemens either did not object to or fostered publications of "1601," beginning, apparently, in August 1880. More than fifty editions are known to exist. For additional information about "1601," see A. B. Paine, *Mark Twain: A Biography* (New York: Harper and Bros., 1912), 2:579; *The Auto-biography of Mark Twain,* ed. Charles Neider (New York: Harper and Bros., 1959), 268–71; *Mark Twain in Eruption: Hitherto Unpublished Pages about Men and Events,* ed. Bernard DeVoto (New York: Harper and Bros., 1940), 203–11; and *Mark Twain-Howells Letters: The Correspondence of Samuel L. Clemens and William D. Howells* (Cambridge: Harvard University Press, 1960), 1:147–48.

13 Just as Clemens found French to be trivial and German to be unlearnable and grotesquely comic, so did he measure any speech as a variant from the norm, the norm being standard nineteenth-century American English. When he considered writing a critique "in modern style" of a play by Shakespeare, he expected to make it amusing by reducing it "to quaint old English." See *Notebooks* 3:78.

14 *Notebooks* 3:233. The editors indicate that Clemens was generous in representing the humor of his acquaintance Robert J. Burdette, a newspaper wit, in *Mark Twain's Library of Humor*.

15 *Notebooks* 3:370. It is unusual for Clemens to spell out *shit*.

16 *Notebooks* 3:113; noted again, 371.

17 *Notebooks* 1:137; 2:279. A note (not included in the notebooks) for use in writing *Huckleberry Finn* mentions a "poor white family & cabin at woodyard in Walnut Bend. Capt. Ed. Montgomery." See Bernard DeVoto, *Mark Twain at Work* (Cambridge: Harvard University Press, 1942), 64. The name Utterback appears in Clemens's recollections of Hannibal. A male Utterback turns up in *Notebooks* 2:381, though not in the index; and a Mrs. Utterback, a "faith doctor" who lived five miles from Hannibal and once cured Clemens's mother of toothache, is mentioned in *Mark Twain's Autobiography*, ed. A. B. Paine (New York: Harper and Bros., 1924), 108. Captain Montgomery is James E. Montgomery, captain of the *City of Memphis* when Clemens piloted that boat in 1860. See *Notebooks* 2:536, n. 30; and *Life on the Mississippi*, chaps. 29, 49.

18 January 28, 1866, San Francisco *Golden Era*; cited from *The Washoe Giant in San Francisco*, ed. Franklin Walker (San Francisco: George Fields, 1938), 104–05.

19 "Come Back to the Raft Ag'in, Huck Honey!," in *The Collected Essays of Leslie Fiedler* (New York: Stein and Day, 1971), 1:143. First published in the *Partisan Review* 15 (June 1948): 664–71.

20 *Notebooks* 2:310, n. 40. In a letter of February 23, 1879 (original in the Mark Twain Memorial, Hartford, Conn.), addressed to Livy's mother, Clemens mentions placing his nephew, Samuel Moffett, to room, board, and study German with Clara Spaulding's almost divine German baroness.

21 The notebooks indicate that during his later years Clemens worked much harder on German than he did on French. He probably knew more French than German, yet to speak or understand French could be baffling for him. (See *Notebooks* 1:551–52; 2:119, 126, 170, and, although the joke may not be on himself, 308.) He gave a humorous address burlesquing the French language on December 8, 1881. For notes that he drew on for this speech, see 2:410.

22 *Notebooks* 2:58. The editors are lenient, calling this "sly wordplay," and they point out that the "last reference in the note is to the assonance of 'hölle' and 'hohle'—hell and hole."

23 *Notebooks* 2:70. Spacing above "Draw the line at ——" suggests that Clemens may have had two homophonic jokes in mind.

24 *Notebooks* 3:155. Clemens's first note on the Slavic nudes, made on August 29 (misdated August 28), reads: "All day the ladies bathed naked in full view of the ship. They don't consider it any harm, I suppose. At Odessa all ages & sexes bathed together." See *Notebooks* 1:411.

25 *Notebooks* 2:222, 224, 259, 319, 323.

26 At the end of October 1885 Clemens indicated his intention of obtaining a copy of *Les Amours du chevalier de Faublas* (1787–90), an erotic novel by Jean-Baptiste Louvet de Couvrai. See *Notebooks* 3:207.

27 *Notebooks* 2:316–28. Clemens's abysmally low opinion of French sexual morals

was formed before he first visited France, possibly from his reading or from what he believed about the French in New Orleans. For example, shortly before he sailed from New York on board the *Quaker City* for Europe and the Holy Land (June 8, 1867), he wrote, "French virtue in woman: Only one lover and don't steal." *Notebooks* 1:323.

28 For illustrative animadversions against the English, see *Notebooks* 2:321; 3:400–02, 409, 414–15, 538, 540, 542, 618.

29 See, for example, *Notebooks* 3:525–27.

30 *Notebooks* 2:482–83. The editors supply facts about the case.

CHAPTER 9. RACISM AND *HUCKLEBERRY FINN*

1 Emeric de Vattel, *Droit des gens, ou Principes de la loi naturelle appliqué à la conduite et aux affaires des nations et des souverains* (Neuchâtel, 1758).

2 Clemens's major references to Indians are traced out by James C. McNutt, "Mark Twain and the American Indians: Earthly Realism and Heavenly Idealism," *American Indian Quarterly* 4 (Aug. 1978): 223–42.

3 See A. Irving Hallowell, "The Backwash of the Frontier: The Impact of the Indian on American Culture," in *The Frontier in Perspective*, ed. Walker D. Wyman and Clifton B. Kroeber (1957; repr. Madison: Univ. of Wisconsin Press, 1965), 233.

4 Mark Twain, *Mark Twain's Travels with Mr. Brown*, ed. Franklin Walker and G. Ezra Dane (New York: Alfred A. Knopf, 1940), 164–66.

5 Ibid., 20–21, 35–36.

6 This and the two immediately following assertions of racism are mentioned, together with a few others, in Jack P. Wysong, "Samuel Clemens' Attitude towards the Negro as Demonstrated in 'Puddn'head Wilson' and 'A Connecticut Yankee at King Arthur's Court,'" *Xavier University Studies* 7 (July 1968): 41–43. Booth discusses the issue in *The Company We Keep: An Ethics of Fiction* (Berkeley: Univ. of California Press, 1988), 3–4, 423, 457–78.

7 *Mark Twain: A Biography* (New York: Harper and Brothers, 1912), 1:400.

8 Sholom J. Kahn, *Mark Twain's Mysterious Stranger: A Study of the Manuscript Texts* (Columbia: Univ. of Missouri Press, 1978), 163.

9 Jay Martin, "The Genie in the Bottle: Huckleberry Finn in Mark Twain's Life," in *One Hundred Years of "Huckleberry Finn": The Boy, His Book, and American Culture*, ed. Robert Sattelmeyer and J. Donald Crowley (Columbia: Univ. of Missouri Press, 1985), 60. Martin's interpretation is supported (with the help of an unwarranted textual change) by the clear misreading of an incident that took place in 1884.

10 *Mark Twain: Man and Legend* (Indianapolis: Bobbs-Merrill Co., 1943), esp. 21, 42, 227–28, 254.

11 *Mark Twain: The Man and His Work* (1st ed. Yale Univ. Press, 1935; Norman: Univ. of Oklahoma Press, 1961). See esp. 29, 128, 220–23.

12 *Sam Clemens of Hannibal* (Boston: Houghton Mifflin Co., 1952). For Wecter's remarks on Clemens and Negroes, see esp. 72–73, 99–100.

13 *Mark Twain's Hannibal, Huck & Tom,* ed. Walter Blair (Berkeley: Univ. of California Press, 1969), 28–40.

14 Juan Comas, *Racial Myths* (Paris: Unesco, 1951), 8.

15 *The American Notebooks,* ed. Claude M. Simpson (Columbus: Ohio State Univ. Press, 1972), 151.

16 Much of the evidence for Clemens's racism that I cite appears in Arthur G. Pettit, "Mark Twain and the Negro, 1867–1869," *Journal of Negro History* 56 (April 1971): 88–96; and in Arthur G. Pettit, *Mark Twain & the South* (Lexington: University Press of Kentucky, 1974). Pettit devotes a chapter to the question of miscegenation, pages 141–55.

17 *Mark Twain's Notebooks & Journals, 1855–1873,* ed. Frederick Anderson et al. (Berkeley: Univ. of California Press, 1975), 1:286, 362, 362–63. Clemens's desire to restrict the vote went beyond wishing to exclude uneducated Negroes, of course. In September 1878 he wrote, "If we never allowd a foreigner to vote or hold office our integrity would be irreproachable. Our foreigners have taught us rascality & now it is our *habit*." See *Notebooks* 2:180–81. Additional examples of racist attitudes from Clemens's early years could be supplied. For example, in P. T. Barnum's museum in New York, he found peanut stands everywhere, "and an impudent negro sweeping up the hulls." Speaking of the horse-cars, he complained mildly that white New Yorkers do not give seats to young ladies; but he became savage in noting that Negroes remain "stuck up comfortably" while lovely young white ladies are standing: "then I wanted a contraband for breakfast." See *Mark Twain's Travels with Mr. Brown,* 71, 117, 227.

18 *Notebooks* 2:501, 557, 547.

19 April 30, 1882. See *Notebooks* 2:582.

20 Pettit, *Mark Twain & the South,* 129–30.

21 Mark Twain, *Mark Twain's Letters to the Rogers Family* (The Millicent Library Collection), ed. Earl J. Dias (New Bedford, Mass.: Reynolds-DeWalt Printing, Inc., 1970), 26.

22 *Mark Twain & the South,* 134.

23 *Mark Twain-Howells Letters: The Correspondence of Samuel L. Clemens and William D. Howells,* ed. Henry Nash Smith and William M. Gibson (Cambridge: Harvard Univ. Press, 1960), 1:194–99, 202. This entire letter of August 25, 1877, exemplifies the way in which Clemens and Howells (and presumably other members of the eastern establishment) could at once sentimentalize blacks and patronize them. Howells was so moved that in his reply of September 17, he begged for permission to publish the letter. Before this incident, as Arthur G. Pettit points out, Clemens thought Lewis was crude and boorish; and in the late story "Refuge of the Derelicts" he becomes a physical giant and a mental pygmy. See *Mark Twain & the South,* 95–97.

24 *Notebooks* 3:57; and *Mark Twain-Howells Letters* 2:509–10.

25 For my comments on eugenics, I rely on Daniel J. Kevles, *In the Name of*

Eugenics: Genetics and the Uses of Human Heredity (New York: Alfred A. Knopf, 1985), esp. 9, 47.

26 Edwin McDowell, "Mark Twain, a Letter on Debt to the Blacks," in *Huck Finn among the Critics: A Centennial Selection,* ed. M. Thomas Inge (Frederick, Md.: Univ. Publications of America, 1985), 411–12. First published in the *New York Times,* March 14, 1985, 1, 16.

27 *Mark Twain & Huck Finn* (Berkeley: Univ. of California Press, 1960), 323. Blair, like others, calls attention to Clemens's admiration for Frederick Douglass and to his financing college educations for two Negroes to support the contention that Clemens was not a racist. My disagreement with Blair (and with any number of other defenders of Clemens) has to do with the extent to which Clemens had "overcome childhood prejudices." I take it to be obvious that when openly institutionalized forms of subjection are legally abolished, they tend to perpetuate their effects less openly or, if necessary, covertly and illegally. When self-consciously enlightened individuals disapprove of legally institutionalized devices to maintain racial hierarchy, they may, nonetheless, preserve internalized attitudes. Color prejudice, in particular, dies hard.

28 Blair, *Mark Twain & Huck Finn,* 358. Beverly R. David points out, I think accurately, that the illustrations represent Jim as a man in the early chapters and as a tall boy late in the novel. Clemens required Kemble to put clothes on both Huck and Jim, avoid the sexual, the ugly, and the brutal, and in general make the characters "pleasant folk to look at." (Sketches of Jim are concentrated in the early and late chapters; and it may be of interest to note that Kemble used a boy as his model for all characters.) See "The Pictorial *Huck Finn*: Mark Twain and His Illustrator, E. W. Kemble,"in *Huck Finn among the Critics,* 270–76. First published in *American Quarterly* 26 (Oct. 1974): 331–51.

29 *Mark Twain's Autobiography,* ed. Albert Bigelow Paine (New York: Harper and Bros., 1924), 1:100–01.

30 To trace so far as we know it the origins of this passage, see *Notebooks* 2:509–10; Bernard De Voto, *Mark Twain at Work* (Cambridge: Harvard Univ. Press, 1942), 67; and *Mark Twain-Howells Letters* 2:465–66.

31 That Clemens propounds a morality superior to the morality of genteel America is the widely accepted thesis of Henry Nash Smith's *The Development of a Writer* (Cambridge: Harvard Univ. Press, 1962).

32 An example of this pragmatism would be a notebook entry for January 1885 in which Clemens expresses a desire to mingle pathos with his ordinary humorous fare in a way that would "fetch" his audiences, moving them to tears as well as to laughter:

"Read A True Story just as I heard it.

"If it goes—then Jim's little scarlet fever daughter & similar things." *Notebooks* 3:89.

33 "Mark Twain," in William Dean Howells, *My Mark Twain,* ed. Marilyn A. Baldwin (Baton Rouge: Louisiana State Univ. Press, 1967), 114. This essay appeared in the *Century Magazine* for September 1882, but Howells made comparable statements both earlier and later.

CHAPTER 10. A WORLD TURNED UPSIDE DOWN

1 *Mark Twain's Notebooks & Journals,* ed. Robert Pack Browning et al. (Berkeley: Univ. of California Press, 1979), 3:88 (hereafter cited as *Notebooks*). (Quotations from the notebooks are sometimes simplified for ease in reading.) Arthur G. Pettit supposes, with some probability, that this notebook entry reflects discussions that Clemens said he had with Cable on "a deep subject." See *Mark Twain & the South* (Lexington: Univ. Press of Kentucky, 1974), 132.

2 *Notebooks* 3:358–59. This entry is headed "Prophecy," but the editors think that the title may have been added by A. B. Paine. Turning a black woman out of doors naked would not have been so offensive to Clemens, it seems, as similar treatment accorded to a white woman by blacks. At any rate, he canceled (and the editors show within angle brackets) the "stripped naked" in his synopsis, probably as too powerful an image, and put the white women into night clothes.

3 For the text, and for information about it, see John S. Tuckey, ed., *Which Was the Dream? and Other Symbolic Writings of the Later Years* (Berkeley: Univ. of California Press, 1968), 20–22, 177–78, 568, 571, and 179–429. (Further simple references to *Which Was the Dream?* are given in this text within parentheses.)

4 John Higham and Paul K. Conkin, eds., *New Directions in American Intellectual History* (Baltimore: Johns Hopkins Univ. Press, 1979), 121–22.

5 A. B. Paine, *Mark Twain: A Biography* (New York: Harper and Bros., 1912), 2:1021.

6 Justin Kaplan, *Mr. Clemens and Mark Twain* (New York: Simon and Schuster, 1966), 336.

7 Ibid., 336–37.

8 John S. Tuckey, ed., *Mark Twain's Fables of Man* (Berkeley: Univ. of California Press, 1972), 3.

9 See Paul Baender, ed., *What Is Man?: and Other Philosophical Writings* (Berkeley: Univ. of California Press, 1973), 8–10.

10 Ibid., 251; and Tuckey, ed., *Fables of Man,* 20–21, 26–27.

11 Dixon Wecter, *Sam Clemens of Hannibal* (Boston: Houghton Mifflin Co., 1952), 72–73.

12 Wecter, *Sam Clemens of Hannibal,* 226. For the quotation from "Autobiography of a Damned Fool," see 233.

13 Ibid., 232–33.

14 For discussions of the article and story and for the story itself, see Walter Blair, ed., *Mark Twain's Hannibal, Huck & Tom* (Berkeley: Univ. of California Press, 1969), 152–62; 163–242. For an indication that Clemens simply liked a burlesque conspiratorial atmosphere, see his letter of October 3, 1902, to Howells in which he says that he is working on a tale "not unlike Tom's fabrication" in the later chapters of *Adventures of Huckleberry Finn.* See *Mark Twain-Howells Letters: The Correspondence of Samuel L. Clemens and William D. Howells,* ed. Henry Nash Smith and William M. Gibson (Cambridge: Harvard Univ. Press, 1960), 2:746–47, n. 2.

15 For brief discussions of Clemens's aborted writings on lynching, see Pettit, *Mark Twain & the South*, 135–36; and Kaplan, *Mr. Clemens and Mark Twain*, 364–65.

16 Pettit, *Mark Twain & the South*, 178.

17 See "What Is Man?" fragments in *What Is Man?*, 486.

18 *Mark Twain & the South*, 165–75. Pettit sees in the late writings an inability to distinguish between fantasy and reality and a monomania concerning unclean actions or thoughts, possibly rooted in some forbidden sexual experience for which young Sam let an innocent black boy take harsh punishment. Since Pettit wrote, more has become known about the exceptional interest in prepubescent girls that Clemens displayed in his old age; that interest could be as likely a source for his anxieties about unclean thoughts and actions as a hypothecated sexual action during his childhood. See Hamlin Hill, *Mark Twain: God's Fool* (New York: Harper and Row, 1973), xxvi, 127–28, 187–88, 195–96, 203–04, 260–61.

19 *Mark Twain's Autobiography*, ed. A. B. Paine (New York: Harper and Bros., 1924), 1:101–02.

20 *Mark Twain-Howells Letters* 2:778.

CHAPTER 11. MYTHS, PARADOXES, AND THE BOURGEOIS HERO

1 For a general survey of narcissism, see Heinz Kohut, *The Analysis of the Self: A Systematic Approach to the Psychoanalytic Treatment of Narcissistic Personality Disorders*, The Monograph Series of the Psychoanalytic Study of the Child, No. 4 (New York: International Universities Press, 1971).

2 Speech of April 19, 1906, for the Robert Fulton Monument. See *Mark Twain Speaking*, ed. Paul Fatout (Iowa City: Univ. of Iowa Press, 1976), 517.

3 See "The Development of the Libido," *The Standard Edition of the Complete Psychological Works of Sigmund Freud*, ed. James Strachey et al. (London: Hogarth Press and the Institute of Psycho-Analysis, 1953–74), 16:326; and *The Psychopathology of Everyday Life*, in *Standard Edition* 6:47–48.

INDEX

▲ ▲ ▲ ▲ ▲ ▲ ▲ ▲ ▲ ▲

This index is selective, not exhaustive. After certain entries this selectivity is especially indicated by the phrase "mentioned *passim*." The cited writings of Samuel L. Clemens follow other entries on Clemens and are listed under the heading "SLC Works." Writings by Bernard DeVoto and by Van Wyck Brooks are treated similarly. Throughout the index, references to Clemens are abbreviated to SLC.

Abolitionism, 206

Adam, the new, 28, 29, 34

Advertiser. See Boston, Massachusetts, *Advertiser*

Aldrich, Lilian (Mrs. Thomas Bailey): opinions on Clemenses, 36, 50

Allen, Grant, 3

Alta California. See San Francisco *Alta California*

America: definitions of, 4, 9–10

America: idea of. *See* SLC as metaphor

America: images of, 218, and mentioned *passim*

Androgynes, 151

Art: commercialism in, 68; high and low, 67

Athenaeum, 4

Atlantic Monthly, 30, 37, 40

Bachelard, Gaston: on the meaning of money, 81

Baender, Paul: edits "Letter from the Recording Angel," 62

Bakhtin, Mikhail, 25, 162

Barthes, Roland, 26

Bellamy, Gladys C., 19

Bergler, Edmund: on gambling, 84

Blair, Hugh, 113

Blair, Walter, 17; on Jim in *Adventures of Huckleberry Finn*, 195–96

Bliss, Elisha, Jr.: proposes a book to SLC, 72

Bliss, Francis E.: opposes scheme for public to pay debts of SLC, 80

Booth, Wayne: on racism in *Adventures of Huckleberry Finn*, 185

Boston, Massachusetts, *Advertiser*, 9

Bourne, Randolph, 10, 12

Brooks, Van Wyck, 2–4, 5; criticized by Bernard DeVoto, 16–17; revisions of *The Ordeal of Mark Twain*, 19–22; on SLC's attitude toward money, 69; and mentioned *passim*

Brooks, Van Wyck, works:
America's Coming of Age, 11
Days of the Phoenix, 10, 20
Flowering of New England, 14
Letters and Leadership, 15
Ordeal of Mark Twain, 3, 9, 26, 47, and mentioned *passim*
Pilgrimage of Henry James, 14
Times of Melville and Whitman, 20–23, 26
Wine of the Puritans, 10, 11, 15